Pan Breakthrough Book

D1337600

Pan Breakthrough Books open the door to successful self-education. The series provides essential knowledge using the most modern self-study techniques.

Expert authors have produced clear explanatory texts on business subjects to meet the particular needs of people at work and of those studying for relevant examinations.

A highly effective learning pattern, enabling readers to measure progress step-by-step, has been devised for Breakthrough Books by the National Extension College, Britain's leading specialists in home study.

Roger Carter, who lectures in business studies at Buckinghamshire College of Higher Education, combines teaching and textbook writing with work as a company director. He has acquired extensive and varied business experience, with the BBC, in the National Health Service and as administrative officer in the Overseas Civil Service in the Solomon Islands.

Roger Carter's publications include Quantitative Methods for Business Students *(1980) and* Business Administration: A Textbook for the Computer Age *(1982).*

Pan Breakthrough Books

Other books in the series

Pan Breakthrough Books

The Business of Data Processing

Roger Carter

A Pan Original
Pan Books, London and Sydney

First published 1984 by Pan Books Ltd,
Cavaye Place, London SW10 9PG
© Roger Carter 1984
ISBN 0 330 28204 2
Printed in Great Britain by
Richard Clay (The Chaucer Press) Ltd,
Bungay, Suffolk

If you wish to study the subject-matter of this book in more
depth, write to the National Extension College, 18 Brooklands
Avenue, Cambridge CB2 2HN, for a free copy of the
Breakthrough Business Courses leaflet. This gives details of
the extra exercises and professional postal tuition which are
available.

Contents

Acknowledgements

My thanks to:

Allan Packer for advice on the technical aspects of this book; Tim Burton of the NEC for advice on the self-assessment aspects; Mastercare Ltd of High Wycombe for permission to use the case study material in Chapter 5.

The Pinecrafts case study in the Appendix and figures 20 and 32 are taken from my book *Business Administration: A Textbook for the Computer Age*, published by Heinemann.

Preface

Why read this book?

This is not like the other data processing books you may have looked at. It does not assume that you already know something about the subject, nor does it assume that you are receiving classroom tuition. Instead, it takes great care to talk you through the subject, it makes liberal use of examples to enable you to relate your learning to the real world, and it includes lots of short exercises to allow you to test, apply, and consolidate your understanding.

Perhaps you run your own small business and you want to know how a small business computer system might help – then read this book, and note that Chapter 7 is written especially for you. Perhaps you work in an office or a data processing department of a larger company and you want to know more about the subject to enhance your job satisfaction and your promotion prospects – then buy this book. Or perhaps you are a college student studying data processing as part of a business course and you want an easy-to-understand textbook – this book is for you too.

The design of the book

Each chapter begins with a brief outline of the topics covered. This gives you a mental map of the territory you are about to cover. Your journey through the chapter is broken down into a few major sections, each of which is divided into short subsections. Each subsection covers a specific learning point, and will generally be followed by a *self-check* question or an *activity* to enable you to check and apply your learning.

You will need to spend only a few minutes on a self-check question, answering it by referring to the material in the text. An activity will often take rather more time, for it will require you to apply what you have learned to a real-life situation, such as your workplace, or to do a little research in your local library. These self-check questions and activities form an essential part of the course, and hints or outline answers will normally be given to help you in answering them. Learning is an active process; you will tend to retain the material that you handle as you work through the questions and activities, and you will tend to forget the material that you do not use.

Each major section in a chapter is followed by *review* questions. These give you the opportunity to look over and consolidate a large chunk of learning. Whereas self-check questions and activities can be answered by jotting down a few brief sentences or sketches, review questions are more formal exercises, and your answers to them, if written up properly, could form your course notes.

Keep your answers to questions and activities in sequence in a folder. You will need to refer back to some of them in subsequent exercises.

Readership

The book is suitable for anyone wishing to learn about data processing in business, whether they are studying at home or attending a college-based course of lectures. It meets the needs of students working towards the following awards:

BTEC National Award Option Module 'Information Processing 1'
BTEC National Award in Computer Studies Modules 'Introduction to Computing' and 'Information in Organisations'
BTEC Post-Experience Award in Computing

It also meets the needs of students taking data processing as part of a course of studies leading to a professional qualification.

The assignment programme

For the benefit of students attending a course of college lectures the book includes a programme of assignments covering the BTEC National Award Information Processing 1 Module learning objectives and some of the BTEC National Award in Computer Studies objectives. This assignment programme is based on a case study of Pinecrafts, a small furniture firm (see the Appendix at the end of the book). This was a winning entry for the 1980 Case Study of the Year Competition. Two supporting video programmes are available (see the Appendix).

The assignments are located at the ends of Chapters 2, 4, 6, and 8, with an additional assignment for the 'Information in Organisations' module located after the case study in the Appendix.

A final word

To quote from the beginning of Chapter 1, 'Paperwork may be boring, but data processing assuredly is not. Exciting new developments are taking place that will change the face of business and affect all of our lives.' Perhaps your only contact with the computer to date has been through space invaders, puck monsters, and other fascinating games. I hope that, as you read this book, you will find the computer's application to the real world of business even more fascinating.

Roger Carter

1 | Data in business

Introduction

Mike's business

Mike used to work in the sales office of a large manufacturer. He spent most of his day working with forms – entering customers' names and addresses, part numbers and quantities, and other details, as well as calculating totals, posting forms, and filing and retrieving forms. He was doing then what computers do today: recording, calculating, filing, retrieving, and communicating lots of numbers and names. In other words, he was *processing data*.

Of course, there were many other people in the company doing similar work. There were buyers in the purchasing office, clerks in the accounts office, and clerks in the wages office, all entering names and numbers on forms and working out totals, all filing, retrieving, and communicating forms. In fact, more people were employed in offices working with forms than worked in the factory making things.

One day Mike got fed up with processing data, and decided to take up decorating instead. He reckoned that papering walls and painting wood was much more interesting than filling in forms. And sure enough, it was more interesting. He worked hard, built up his reputation, and within a few years he was employing a number of people. He was running a successful business.

There was one snag, however. In order to run his business he had to keep books of account, he had to produce quotations and invoices for customers, he had to send orders to suppliers, he had to make out job sheets and work out wages. He found that he needed to check that customers paid on time, that materials arrived on time, and that his employees kept to their work

schedules. He needed to make monthly checks on his receipts
and expenses to ensure that his cash position and his profits
remained healthy. In fact, a large part of his job involved doing
the same sort of thing as he did when he worked in the sales
office: processing data.

Self-check

Underline the items of 'data' that appear in the following
piece of text:

> On 16 July 1984 Mike purchased five tins of paint from J. Smith
> Ltd, at a price of £2 per tin.

(Don't read the answer until you have had a go at answering the question – cover it with a card. Always observe this
rule when answers are given to exercises!)

ANSWER

You should have underlined the date, Mike, J. Smith Ltd, 'five
tins of paint', and '£2 per tin'. It is these names and numbers that
will appear on the invoice that Mike receives from J. Smith Ltd.

Self-check

What is data processing? Jot down on a piece of paper a
simple definition.

ANSWER

The task of recording, storing, calculating, and communicating
all the data used in running a business.

Don't worry if your answer differs slightly – there are a
number of possible and equally valid definitions.

Where is Mike going?

One raw material used by every business, large or small, is
paper. Paperwork, the traditional means by which data is recorded, stored, analysed, and communicated, abounds. Most
workers spend their lives in offices, surrounded by it. Some like

to believe that a bureaucratic government, or bureaucratic company management, bound by red tape and intent on printing endless reams of forms, is to blame, but this is too simple a view. Data is as important to business as the raw materials that enter the factory gates. A business that is starved of it, or which cannot process it efficiently, will soon fail.

Paperwork may be boring, but data processing assuredly is not. Exciting new developments are taking place that will change the face of business and affect all of our lives. The pen is being replaced by the keyboard, paper by the screen. The computer is taking over the boring office tasks, leaving people like Mike free to get on with the much more interesting job of making money.

To take advantage of these developments Mike needs to do some homework. He must find out:

- why he needs data in his business;
- what data he needs;
- how that data might be collected, stored, and used so that his needs are met in the most cost-effective way.

In this chapter and the next we are going to accompany Mike as he finds out exactly why he needs data to run his business (there are quite a lot of reasons), and what data he needs. Then in Chapters 3 to 5 we are going to explore with him what is involved in processing data, and from there we move on to a consideration of how he should go about computerising his business and how data processing should be organised in it.

Like Mike, you might run a small business. You might work in an office or in the data processing department of a larger business. You might be a college student on a business course. Whatever your background, there is probably one thing you share with Mike: you know very little about silicon chips or computer programming or managing big business. This book is written with Mike in mind. If you can identify with him, you're in business!

Your mental map of this chapter

In this chapter, then, you will be finding out why data is needed to run a business. You will be learning about how data is generated and used in each business activity – whether in the boss's office, in the factory, in the sales office, or in the buyer's office. You will also be learning how all this data flows through the business, and you will be drawing flowcharts to represent these flows.

If you haven't already read the Preface, do so now. It explains the design of the book and the purpose of the exercises. Here's an exercise that will lead you into the first major section of the book. Remember – cover the answer with a card until you have written down your attempt at it.

Activity

Choose an event or activity that you help to run, or would like to help to run. Examples are planning a holiday or an outing, or organising a dance. Spend a few minutes making a list of the data you need to run it, and then write down against each item of data why you need it.

PART-ANSWER

As an example of the way in which you might answer this question, suppose you were involved in organising a jumble sale. Part of your answer would then be:

Data	Reason
1 Expected numbers of customers.	To decide number of helpers and size of hall required.
2 Details of possible venues: size, charges, and dates available.	To decide where and when to hold the event.
3 Availability of transport.	To decide how and when to collect jumble.
4 Characteristics of potential customers.	To decide advertising method, timing of event, pricing policy.

Don't skip this activity. Your answers will be used in later exercises!

Running a business

What is Mike doing?

Mike's decorating business appears to be very different from the manufacturing business that he left. In reality, however, it is doing essentially the same things: buying and hiring materials, labour, etc. from one market, converting these materials and that labour to goods and services, and selling those goods and services to another market.

What Mike receives into his business is called his *inputs*, what passes out of his business is called his *outputs*. Mike's business, like that of the manufacturer he used to work for, operates on his inputs to convert them to his outputs. These *operations* include transport and storage of paint, wallpaper, and other materials, stripping walls and wood, and papering and painting.

Look at figure 1. It shows this view of Mike's business in diagrammatic form. Note that the inputs, operations, and outputs are distinguished by being placed in separate boxes, and that these are linked by arrows to show the flow of work through the business.

Inputs		*Operations*		*Outputs*
Labour, equipment, materials, etc.	→	Stripping walls and wood, papering and painting	→	Papered walls and painted wood, profits

Figure 1. Mike's business

Activity

Construct a diagram like figure 1 for the event that you used in the first activity. Write down as many inputs and outputs as you can. You will need to spend about five minutes on this activity, and on each of the subsequent activities in this section.

HINT

You will have not only physical inputs (labour, materials, etc), but data inputs also. Use your answer to the first activity to assist you with these. Don't read the rest of this hint until you have had a go at answering this question.

In the case of the jumble sale, the inputs include the helpers, the hall, the transport, the jumble, and data on these and on potential customers. The operations include collecting jumble, sorting it, and selling it. The outputs include goods supplied to customers, money paid into the bank, and lots of unsold jumble!

Why does Mike need data?

Mike's business seems simple enough. He hires labour (his own and his employees'), he buys and stores paint, wallpaper, paste, brushes, and so on, and he organises his business so that the labour and materials are converted into papered walls and painted wood.

However, this is only the visible part of Mike's business, the tip of the iceberg. What we do not see is the mass of data that is flowing through the business, some of it whirling around in Mike's head, much of it being entered as names and numbers on forms and in books.

In the next few pages we are going to see why Mike needs all this data. We are going to examine the main tasks involved in running a business, and the data requirements of each.

Strategic planning

Before Mike started up in business he needed to do some market research. This might have involved talking to other tradesmen running decorating businesses to find out the type of decorating work that potential customers were likely to want, the quality standards expected, the prices they were prepared to pay, the size of the potential market in his locality, and the strength of the competition. It could have involved him in carrying out a survey of a sample of people living in his locality – knocking on doors and asking questions.

The market research data collected by Mike enabled him to decide whether running a decorating business was a viable proposition, and it enabled him to design the type of service he would offer. Should he limit himself to straight paperhanging and painting, or should he include brickwork and plastering, building extensions, etc.?

This in turn enabled him to plan the inputs he needed – what labour, if any, to hire, what equipment and vehicles to buy, and whether to rent a lock-up garage as a store. It enabled him to determine the amount of start-up capital needed. Furthermore, it enabled him to fix his objectives, i.e. to decide and set his sights on where he wanted his business to be in two or three years' time and what profit to aim for.

This process is called *strategic planning*. To summarise what has been said above, it involves:

- collecting data about the business's environment (mainly the market for its outputs and the market for its inputs);
- using this data to design the output and decide the objectives;
- then planning the inputs.

Strategic planning is not a once-only job. The plans and decisions must be continually revised, for the business's environment changes as fashions alter and technology advances. Mike needs to collect data on his markets constantly, and he needs to study his sales trends, so that he can take account of these changes by modifying the sort of service he provides. If he does not adjust his business to take account of advancing fashions and advancing technology, then he will fall behind the competition, his order book will begin to dry up, and his business will expire.

Activity

Referring again to the event you discussed in previous activities, write down what your strategy is, and state what data you used in formulating that strategy.

HINT

Your answer should state your objectives, the design of the event, and what inputs are needed to achieve your objectives and design. Refer to your answer to the first activity for the data required. Don't read the rest of this hint until you have attempted the question.

In the case of the jumble sale your objective is to raise a certain minimum sum of money by attracting a certain minimum number of customers, and to achieve this the inputs needed include booking a hall of a certain size, recruiting a certain number of helpers, collecting a certain amount of jumble. You will design the jumble sale in the sense of deciding the best date and time, the best pricing policy, whether to run a tombola, and so on.

Data for these decisions is needed on previous jumble sales (for expected number of customers and likely takings), on competing jumble sales (so that dates and times do not clash), and on potential customers (this will affect design).

Operational planning

Strategic planning concerns planning the outputs and the inputs of the business, but it does not deal with planning the operations of the business (i.e. the conversion of the inputs to the outputs). This latter form of planning is most important, for a businessman like Mike must ensure that his operations are carried out efficiently so that he achieves the profit envisaged by his strategic plans.

This is called *operational planning*. It means planning the work of the business so that customers' orders are met. This involves firstly *scheduling* the work, i.e. deciding when Mrs Smith's kitchen is to be decorated, and when Mr Jones's roof is to be fixed. Secondly it involves *loading* the work, i.e. deciding which of his men to put on Mrs Smith's job, and which on Mr Jones's.

Mike's production schedule will determine most of his purchase requirements – what materials to buy in, and when to buy them. Mrs Smith's wallpaper will have to be ordered two weeks before her job is due to start, Mr Jones's tiles will need to be on hand in time for his job.

In summary, operational planning involves:

- receiving data on jobs to be done;
- scheduling and loading the work so that these jobs are pro-

duced efficiently and on time;
* determining what materials are needed and when.

If operational planning is not done properly, production will be disorganised, hold-ups will occur, and the business will not make its hoped-for profit.

> *Activity*
>
> Referring to the event discussed in previous questions, write down your operational plans and the data you used in formulating these plans.

HINT

You should list the jobs that need to be done, when they should be done, and who should do them. State also what materials are needed and when.

In the case of the jumble sale, operational planning involves planning the collection of jumble (what helpers and transport are needed, and when), planning the advertising, and planning the event itself (the division of labour amongst the various jobs). Data is needed both on the future output of the event (what customers will want to buy), and on the inputs (the availability of transport and of helpers).

Control

Having planned his production and obtained the materials required, Mike has to ensure that his men achieve the plans. Mrs Smith's kitchen and Mr Jones's roof must be finished on time, otherwise Mike's labour costs will rise and his profits will fall, and the next job will be delayed. Also, of course, the standard of workmanship must be acceptable.

The process of ensuring that the planned output of the business is actually achieved is called *control*. It involves getting feedback data on the output of the business – in other words, carrying out regular checks on performance – and comparing this with the planned output. If the planned output is not being achieved, then adjustments must be made to the inputs – by exhorting the men to work harder, for example, or getting them to work overtime, or improving the methods of work or the equipment.

In summary, we can say that control involves:

- receiving feedback data on performance;
- comparing this with the planned output;
- deciding upon and making input adjustments in the event of under-achievement.

Activity

Referring to the event you discussed in earlier activities, write down how you will control the work.

HINT

State how you will check performance and compare with your plans, and what action you will take if your plans are not being achieved.

For the task of collecting jumble in the jumble sale example, control involves checking that an adequate amount of jumble is being collected, and arranging further leaflet drops and further transport if it is not. The other jumble sale tasks must also be controlled, of course.

Mike the manager

Strategic planning, operational planning, and control are what *management* is about. As you have learned, they each involve using data to make decisions:

- Strategic planning involves using data on the business's environment to make decisions on its long-term objectives – what it should produce, and what resources it needs.
- Operational planning involves using data on the planned output of the business to make decisions on how its operations should be programmed so that it can achieve these objectives – which jobs should be done when, where, and by whom.
- Control involves using data on the actual output of the busi-

ness to decide what must be done to achieve the operational plans – what measures to take to ensure that jobs are finished on time and to the required standard.

This, then, is the first main reason why so much of Mike's time is taken up with handling data. Without data he could not plan, organise, or control his business, and although it could continue for a while without this management activity, it would eventually come to a halt.

Self-check

Jot down a brief definition of 'management'. Explain in a sentence why data is needed for this task.

ANSWER

Management is the task of planning and controlling a business and its operations. Planning and control each involve making decisions. To make sensible decisions you need data.

Operations

Mike's business operations, remember, are the tasks needed to convert his inputs to outputs. They include much more than getting men and materials together to produce a decorated room. Orders have to be received from customers – this is an essential operation – and payment has to be collected. The men have to be paid for their work, and so the calculation and payment of wages is another essential operation. Stocks of materials have to be checked and replenished, and suppliers have to be paid, and these are further business operations.

At first glance these operations seem similar to the management tasks spoken of in the subsection above – they involve data and paperwork – but in reality they are more akin to production (paperhanging, painting, or whatever). For they have nothing to do with management decision-making, they are entirely to do with converting inputs to outputs.

Look again at figure 1. The inputs, operations, and outputs shown there are only one part of Mike's business, albeit the central part. What is portrayed in that figure are the *prime inputs* needed for the production side of Mike's business (decorating), and the *prime outputs* that result from that production. A more complete picture of the business would show non-production operations, such as the sales, purchases, and wages tasks referred to above, and the inputs and outputs of these.

Figure 2 shows Mike's business with these 'non-prime' inputs and outputs inserted. Note that they consist of data, whereas the prime inputs and outputs of a business such as Mike's are physical items such as materials and decorated rooms.

Inputs	*Operations*	*Outputs*
1 Labour, materials, etc.	1 Decorating	1 Decorated rooms, profits
2 Customer orders, payments →	2 Sales	2 Invoices, bank slips →
3 Supplier quotations, invoices	3 Purchasing	3 Purchase orders, remittances
4 Wage rates, deductions	4 Wages	4 Wages slips, paycheques

Figure 2. Mike's business

Activity

Refer to your answer to the activity on page 15, and list the prime inputs and outputs and then as many non-prime inputs and outputs as you can.

ANSWER

For the jumble sale, the prime inputs are the helpers' labour and transport, the jumble, and the hall. The prime outputs are the goods bought by customers, the money paid into the bank, and the left-over jumble. The non-prime inputs include data from previous jumble sales on the expected number and characteristics of customers, data on the availability and prices of halls, data on the availability of helpers and transport, and data on jumble collected so far. The non-prime outputs include data on the amount of jumble left over, data on the amount of money collected, and data on the number and characteristics of customers for planning future jumble sales.

Self-check

Study figure 2 and list the non-production tasks that are indicated there. One is producing invoices from customer orders. Don't worry if you are not sure what these tasks are or what they involve; we shall be dealing with them fully in the next main section of this chapter.

Mike the clerk

When Mike is carrying out these non-production operations he is not wearing his manager's hat but his clerk's hat. The work that he is doing is not managerial decision-making, it is *clerical work*. Figure 2 shows some of the clerical tasks that he must do: producing invoices from customer orders, bank slips from payments received, purchase orders from supplier quotations, remittances from supplier invoices, and paycheques from data on wage rates and deductions. All these tasks involve handling data.

Clerical work is just as essential as managerial work. If Mike stopped doing any of these tasks his business would collapse as surely as if he stopped painting and decorating. This is the second main reason why Mike must spend so much of his time handling data.

Review

Briefly explain in your own words the meanings of the following terms: data processing; management; clerical work; planning; control; operations. (Five minutes.)
(The answers are in the section you have just read.)

Business operations

In this section you will learn about the business operations referred to above (production, sales, purchasing, and wages), and about their data inputs and outputs.

Self-check

Jot down one data input and one data output for each of the above four business operations.

ANSWER

You have learned what some of these inputs and outputs are in the previous section and in figure 2. A data input for production is the work schedules, an output is feedback data on performance. Customer orders, supplier quotations, and wage rates are inputs for sales, purchases, and wages respectively; invoices, purchase orders, and wage slips are outputs.

Production

Production is the process of converting the prime inputs of a business to the prime outputs. In the case of the jumble sale, production is the task of getting all the jumble together, sorting it, and setting it up on stalls for sale. Although the jumble sale helpers are not producers in the sense of manufacturing goods, they are producers in the sense of providing a service.

A manufacturer will normally carry out production in a production department located in a factory quite separate from the 'office' side of the business. Furthermore, the production activities will require skills and equipment quite different from those required by the office activities. In the case of a commercial business, such as a bank or an insurance company, the prime inputs and outputs will be mainly data rather than physical items, and the production activities will then take place alongside the other activities in the office.

Production activities vary enormously from business to business. It is these that distinguish a bank from a car manufacturer from a supermarket. Managerial and clerical activities, on the other hand, are very much the same everywhere – which is why the same computers and the same computer programs can be used in widely differing businesses.

Production not only produces the prime outputs of the business – the goods and services supplied to customers – it also produces data used by other parts of the business. Each man must record how long he spends on each job, so that the labour content of jobs can be costed and customers charged the correct amounts. This data is also needed for the wages calculations, unless a fixed weekly wage is paid. He must also record the materials consumed on the job, so that the material costs can be worked out. If this is not done, then customers might be charged too little, in which case the business would make insufficient profit and would soon fail, or they might be charged too much, in which case the business would lose trade to its competitors and would again fail. The hours worked may be recorded on *time sheets*, or in larger businesses on *clock cards*.

In addition, data on the consumption of materials will be used to generate purchases. In a larger business than Mike's this will be done by a formal stock control system, described in the section on purchasing below.

The data generated by Production is also used by a businessman like Mike in his managerial tasks of operational planning and control. Firstly, knowledge of how long jobs took in the past enables Mike to programme more accurately future jobs. Secondly, it provides feedback data on the performance of his men and on the costs of jobs, so that he can assess whether the output targets are being achieved and take corrective action if they are not.

Figure 3 shows in diagrammatic form the generation of data by Production. It is often the case that data produced for operational purposes (in this case for charging customers, ordering from suppliers, and calculating wages, shown by the horizontal arrow in the figure) is also used for management purposes (as shown by the vertical arrow in the figure).

> Data on goods produced, and on consumption of labour and materials, to Operational Planning and Control.

> ↑

Production	→	Costings to Sales.
		Hours worked to Wages.
		Materials required to Purchasing.

Figure 3. Data generated by Production

Note that in this figure the convention adopted in figures 1 and 2 is followed: outputs are shown leaving the box marked 'Production' on the right. In the self-check question below you should show the inputs entering at the left.

|| *Self-check*

|| Try drawing a diagram like figure 3 showing the data inputs to Production.

PART-ANSWER

One data input is the operational plans (a downwards arrow at the left, indicating that this is generated by management). Another is data on each job (a horizontal arrow, indicating that this is generated by another operation, i.e. Sales – see figure 4).

Note that operational plans may be communicated to workers by *job sheets*, one for each man specifying what tasks he has to do and how long each should take. Note also that operational planning, when applied to factory production, is termed *production planning*.

Information outputs

Before moving on to the other business operations, let's pause for a moment and consider some major implications of what we have just said for data processing.

We have seen that there are two sorts of data output, represented by the horizontal and vertical arrows in figure 3 (and also in figures 4, 5, and 6):

The horizontal arrows represent data relating to transactions between one part of a business and another, or between a business and its customers or suppliers. These transactions normally involve the exchange of money, goods, or services. For example, clock cards relate to a service (the provision of labour) supplied by workers, wages slips relate to the money paid to those workers.

The data relating to an individual transaction will appear on a *document*. Invoices, purchase orders, and bank paying-in slips are all documents, each one containing data relating to an individual sale, purchase, or payment. It is these documents that generate action at the operational level in a business (i.e. the clerical and shop-floor level), causing goods to be moved, services to be supplied, and money to be paid. (I shall sometimes refer to these as 'action documents', to distinguish them from certain other types of document that are used in business.)

The vertical arrows represent data relating to all the transactions that take place over a given period of time (often a month), collected together and summarised in a *report*. Reports are produced at the operational level (by clerks or by computer) but are used at the management level for decision-making. (I shall sometimes refer to these as 'management reports'.)

For an everyday example of these two types of output, think of your bank account:

- The cheques and paying-in slips are documents relating to individual transactions (making payments and receiving payments).
- The bank statements are twice-yearly reports summarising all payments made and received in the period.

You use the latter to control your account. If the balance shown on your statement is low, then you will cut down on your purchases and so limit the payments made.

These two types of output are collectively referred to as *information*, not as data. The term *data* is normally used to describe data inputs only, not outputs. Thus data is what goes in, information is what comes out. Information is 'processed data'. We shall adopt this *data/information* convention from now on.

Note that the second type of output, the reports, is often called 'management information', to distinguish it from the information which appears on documents (which are used at the operational level).

Self-check

Look at figure 2, and list the information that appears there. Are any reports included?

ANSWER

The items in the right-hand box are information. There are no reports.

> ### Activity
>
> Obtain examples of documents and reports relating to a certain type of transaction in your firm (or a friend's firm), and study them. Try to find out and write down the use that is made of each item of information appearing in those documents and reports. You could choose sales documents and reports, for example, or stock documentation and reports, or purchases documentation and reports, or payroll.
>
> If you are a full-time student and not employed, it is most important that you attempt this activity. Obtain documents, if you can, from a parent's or a friend's firm, or look up examples in a book in the business section of your college library.

Sales

Let's move on now to the remaining operational tasks. We have already dealt with Production; Sales is next on the list.

However good the workmanship of Mike and his men, the business will collapse unless people can be persuaded to buy its output. Mike must therefore be a salesman, persuading people to buy his product. In a large business a specialist sales department will be responsible for this task.

In response to a potential customer's inquiry Mike will have to make out a *quotation* or *estimate*, setting out what is involved in the job and the price he will charge. Mike must use his production experience here to estimate how much labour and materials will be consumed on the job, and therefore what his costs will be. He must also use his knowledge of the market to tell him what is the going rate for the job. He will use this cost information and this market information to arrive at a price which is roughly in line with prices charged by other firms and which also gives him a reasonable profit.

A great deal of information is generated by Sales. In the first place the details of *orders* received by Mike will eventually be passed on to the men, perhaps in the form of instructions for each job entered on *job sheets*. Secondly, the orders will be used by Mike in his management capacity to draw up the production programme for the weeks or months ahead.

Then, when the job is finished, a small businessman like Mike must don his clerk's hat and collect the payment due from the customer. This task normally involves:

- Making out and sending an *invoice* itemising the goods and services that have been supplied, together with the prices and the total amount payable.
- Keeping a record of the amount payable in a *sales ledger*. The data in this is recorded in customer order; in some sales ledger systems, for example, there is a ledger card for each customer filed alphabetically (by customer name) or numerically (by customer code number). The invoiced amounts are recorded on the customers' cards in date sequence. This filing arrangement assists subsequent retrieval of the data (see below).
- Sending a *statement* to the customer at the end of the month listing all unpaid invoiced amounts and the total. The statement is compiled from the data in the sales ledger, and it is a request to pay. Statements are normally used only by businesses supplying trade customers on a regular basis. For Mike, who supplies private customers on an irregular basis, the invoice will probably be the request to pay, and no statement will be sent.
- Recording in the sales ledger all payments received from customers, and checking these with the invoiced amounts.
- Chasing customers who do not pay within a reasonable period (usually a month), initially by sending a reminder letter, ultimately by employing the services of a trade protection agency or a solicitor.
- Periodically entering amounts received from customers in the bank *paying-in book*, depositing the money in the bank, and entering the amounts in the income section of the *cash book* (entries in this book being made in date order).

In the income section of the cash book the sales will be analysed under various headings – in Mike's case these might include 'decorating work', 'repairs', 'building work'. By totalling the amounts entered under each heading Mike obtains management information. He can determine which parts of his market are growing and which are declining, and he can adjust his business strategy accordingly. He can also check whether his sales are on target, and this check may prompt further action.

The information generated by Sales is shown in figure 4.

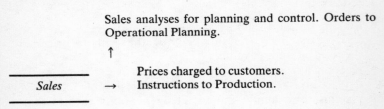

Figure 4. Information generated by Sales

Self-check

Draw a diagram like figure 4 showing the data inputs to sales.

PART-ANSWER

One of these is the customer's inquiry. Another is cost data from production. These should be represented by a horizontal arrow. A vertical downwards arrow should be included for instructions from management on adjustments in e.g. sales strategy.

Purchasing

The two major costs of a business are the purchase of materials and equipment (dealt with here), and the hire of labour (dealt with in the next subsection).

Businesses will obviously attempt to buy their inputs at the best possible price, and so will compare the offerings of a number of suppliers. This is often done by referring to their records of previous dealings with these suppliers (see below), or by sending *inquiries* to several, receiving back *quotations*, and choosing the most favourable. In a large business this process of choosing the best suppliers and placing the orders will be carried out by a purchasing department.

Businesses will also try to avoid holding unnecessarily high levels of stock (as this ties up money and storage space), and at the same time they will try to avoid running out of stock (as this causes production hold-ups and lost sales). Great care will therefore be taken in deciding the timings and sizes of orders. Fast-moving items will be ordered in greater quantities and more often than slow-moving items.

This task of deciding the timings and sizes of orders is called *stock control*, and in a large business it will normally be carried out by the production planning department, using data on both the current stock levels (from the *stock records*) and on materials expected to be consumed during the next production period (from the production plan).

The stock records may consist of a set of stock cards, one for each stock item, showing all quantities received and issued and the balance in stock. Balances which fall below the reorder level generate purchases. Stock records are held in stock item sequence (either alphabetically by name of item, or numerically by item code number), the receipts and issues of an item being recorded on the relevant stock card in date sequence. Holding the records in this way obviously assists in the retrieval of the data.

A small businessman like Mike will, of course, be his own production planner and his own buyer, and he will carry out these tasks in a fairly informal way. He will also do the mundane clerical work of filling in *purchase orders* to order his stocks (or, in Mike's case, buying direct over the counter at a builders' merchants). Larger businesses also keep *purchase records* for each line of stock bought, in which they record the alternative suppliers for each stock item, the prices charged by each, and details of orders placed and received. The data held on these records enables the business to select the best source of supply when placing future orders, as well as enabling it to pursue queries on past orders. These records will be held in stock item order (either alphabetically by item name or numerically by item code number), purchases being recorded in date order under the appropriate item name or number.

Then when the goods are delivered Mike will have to sign the supplier's *receipt note*. This is retained by the supplier as evidence that Mike has received the goods in a satisfactory condition, and that he can therefore be invoiced for them.

Self-check

Spend a few minutes listing the data inputs and information outputs of

1 stock control
2 production planning
3 purchasing

that are relevant to the task of ordering stock.

ANSWER

1 Receipts and issues are input (recorded on the stock records); stock balances are output to production planning, or stock items that fall below the reorder level are output to purchasing.
2 Stock balances are input from stock control, stock needs are input from the production plan; reorder requirements are output to purchasing.
3 Reorder requirements are input from production planning or from stock control; purchase orders are output to suppliers.

Besides ordering goods and materials, a small businessman like Mike will also have to carry out the clerical tasks involved in paying each of his suppliers. These are:

● Receiving the supplier's *invoice*, and checking with his purchase records that he actually ordered and received the goods listed, and that he is being charged the correct price. If it is not correct he will contact the supplier and ask for an adjustment. He may not consider it worth his while to carry out a formal check, particularly if the sums involved are small, and may instead quickly glance at the invoice to ensure that it is from one of his usual suppliers for goods normally ordered, and that the price charged looks about right.

- Keeping a record of the amounts due to each supplier in a *purchase ledger* (sometimes called a *bought ledger*). This will be kept in the same way as the sales ledger – by supplier name or code number, the individual entries being in date order under the relevant supplier.
- Receiving the supplier's *statement* at the end of the month listing all invoiced amounts due for payment, and reconciling this with the entries in the purchase ledger.
- Writing out a *cheque* and *remittance advice note* for the total due that month, and indicating in the purchase ledger which invoiced amounts are being paid (this prevents double payment). The remittance advice note enables the supplier to match the payment with his sales ledger entries. (As an alternative to this note the customer may return the supplier's statement with his cheque.)
- Using the purchase ledger to time his payments so that suppliers are paid by the due date but maximum advantage is taken of any credit offered by them.
- Entering the amount paid on his *cheque book stub*, and also in the expenses section of his *cash book*.

Analyses of purchases for control purposes.

↑

Purchases →   Orders, receipts, and payments
to suppliers. Costs to Production.

Figure 5. Information generated by Purchasing

In this section of the cash book the purchases will be analysed under various headings, e.g. materials, wages, telephone, vehicles. By periodically totalling the entries under each heading Mike, wearing his manager's hat, can isolate his major cost areas, and he can determine which of his costs are increasing unduly. This will concentrate his attention on the critical areas of his business and so enable him to control it more effectively. Also, knowledge of movements in his material costs will enable

Mike to make accurate quotations for future jobs.

The information generated by Purchasing is shown in figure 5.

Self-check

Draw a diagram like figure 5 showing the data inputs to purchasing.

PART-ANSWER

One is suppliers' quotations (horizontal arrow). Another is timings and quantities of orders (vertical arrow from operational planning).

Wages

As with the purchase of inputs of materials and equipment, Mike will wish to hire the most suitable labour inputs at the best price. In a large business this task of selecting labour and fixing wage rates is carried out by the personnel department.

Mike will undertake this task himself, wearing his manager's hat. He will compare applicants for the jobs he is offering by interviewing and by examining references, and he will ensure that those selected have the appropriate skills and experience. He will fix the wage rates at somewhere around the norms for the industry, bearing in mind that to pay less than the going rate will create resentment and cut down the effort that his men put into the job, and paying too much above it will increase his costs and make him less competitive in his output market.

Mike might attempt to motivate his workers by basing their rates of pay on their output, e.g. by paying them for each job the labour figure quoted in his estimate. Payment-by-results schemes such as this can work well, but they are difficult to manage and they can create friction between management and workers, Mike will probably settle for a fixed hourly rate for all hours worked up to forty per week, with a certain percentage on top of this rate for all overtime hours. He will, of course, expect his men to complete jobs within the time allowed in his estimates, and he will take corrective (control) action if the actual labour costs start to exceed the estimated costs.

Now Mike has to put on his clerk's hat to calculate and pay his men's wages.

> *Self-check*
>
> Jot down what you think the steps are in calculating and paying wages.

The process starts by adding up each week the hours worked by each man, as recorded on the time sheets (or clock cards). Mike then calculates for each man the gross pay, i.e. the amount payable for normal hours worked plus the amount payable for any overtime. Next, he works out the net pay by calculating and subtracting the income tax and national insurance payable (these sums are sent by Mike direct to the Inland Revenue).

All this data is entered against each man's name on the *payroll*. Each man receives a copy of his part of the payroll, and this enables him to check that Mike has done his sums correctly. This is called the wages slip, or *payslip*. Mike may pay the wages by cash, or by cheque, or by direct debit. Whichever method is used, Mike must enter the total wages paid each week in the expenses section of his cash book.

Like Production and Sales and Purchasing, Wages generates a great deal of useful information (figure 6). The wages figure that appears in the cash book will form a large element of the business's costs, and Mike, wearing his manager's hat, will keep a close watch on it. Also, the data that appears on the time sheets, combined with the hourly wage rates, will enable Mike to work out the labour costs of each job – another useful piece of information.

Totals for control purposes.

↑

| *Wages* | → | Amounts to employees and taxman. |
| | | Costs to Production. |

Figure 6. Information generated by Wages

Self-check

Draw a diagram like figure 6 showing the data inputs to wages.

PART-ANSWER

One input will be the tax rates from the Inland Revenue (horizontal arrow). Another will be the wage rates fixed by management (vertical arrow).

Review

1 List the information needed by management to carry out the tasks of

(a) strategic planning;
(b) operational planning;
(c) control.

Indicate against each item of information which operational task of the business generates it, or whether it comes from the business's environment (e.g. customers or suppliers).

2 List the main records that need to be kept by Sales, Purchasing, and Wages, and briefly state the purpose of each. Indicate the data recorded on each record and the source of that data.

3 Draw a diagram to show the data movements that take place when a supplier supplies goods to a customer. Include stock record adjustments and the payment procedure in the diagram.

(Fifteen minutes.)

HINT

The answers to all of these questions can be found in the text. The first part of a possible answer to question 3 is given in figure 7.

Supplier		*Customer*
	inquiry	
	quotation	
production/dispatch	order	entry on purchase
schedule drawn up	goods delivered	records
	receipt note	
	invoice	entry in purchases
entry in sales ledger	etc.	ledger

Figure 7. Data movements between supplier and customer

The flow of data

Systems

Figure 2 represents Mike's business as something which operates on certain inputs received from its environment to convert them into outputs. We can describe many things in this way. A cabbage in your garden, for example, converts inputs of water, nutrients, carbon dioxide, and sunlight into outputs of vegetable for your dinner and oxygen. Anything which converts inputs to outputs is called a *system*.

A system can be broken down into a collection of subsystems. The subsystems of your cabbage, for example, include the root system and the leaf system. These subsystems can be further broken down into the individual cell systems, and these in turn can be broken down into protein systems, chromosome systems, and so on, and ultimately into the atomic systems that make up all matter. By the same token your cabbage is part of the larger ecological system of the earth, which in turn is part of the planetary system of the sun, and so on.

The systems approach to business Mike's business is very like your cabbage. It can be broken down into a number of subsystems – purchasing, wages, sales, and so on – and it is itself a part of a wider economic system consisting of other businesses, consumers, and the government. Just as Mike's business converts inputs received from its economic environment to outputs transmitted to that environment, so each of the subsystems of his business converts inputs received from its environment (which includes other subsystems of his business) to outputs transmitted to its environment.

So it is possible to break down Mike's business into a number of subsystems, each of which is bounded by a set of inputs and a set of outputs. Figure 8 shows the wages system represented in this way.

Input	*Operation*	*Output*
Hours worked Wage rates PAYE and NI rates	Calculating and paying wages	Paycheques Payslips PAYE and NI payments Information on wage costs

Figure 8. The wages system

Now turn to figure 32 on page 206. You will see there a number of subsystems of a manufacturing business linked by various inputs and outputs. You can see that what is an output of one subsystem is the input of another. 'Stock levels', for example, is an output of Stores and an input of Production Planning. So far as Stores is concerned it is information that it has produced, so far as Production Planning is concerned it is data that it will use.

Each of these systems can be subdivided into further subsystems, of course. The sales system, for example, includes the sales order processing subsystem (which involves receiving customer orders and producing the sales documentation), and the collection of payments subsystem (described on page 29, and also in the subsection below).

This technique of analysing a business into its constituent subsystems, each bounded by inputs and outputs, is an extremely useful tool. It is something that must be done before computerisation can be carried out. The reason for its value is that any business – even a small business like Mike's – is very complex, and it is difficult to handle it in one chunk. Splitting it down into subsystems makes it more manageable. As we shall discover later in the course, each subsystem will be computerised in turn, often over a number of months or years, and when this process is complete the individual computerised procedures will be amalgamated into an integrated whole.

Self-check

Draw diagrams like figure 8 for the sales and the purchasing systems of a business.

HINT

Use the information in figures 4 and 5 and in your answers to the related self-check questions. For example, the input box for sales will include inquiries, orders, and payments.

Flowcharts

This is a terminator. It shows the starting point and finishing point of the procedure.

This represents an input to or an output from the procedure.

This shows an operation in the procedure.

This is a decision box. It indicates an either/or situation, and it always has two exits. A question will always be asked, a 'yes' answer indicating one exit, a 'no' answer the other.

This is a connector. It shows where one flowchart connects to another.

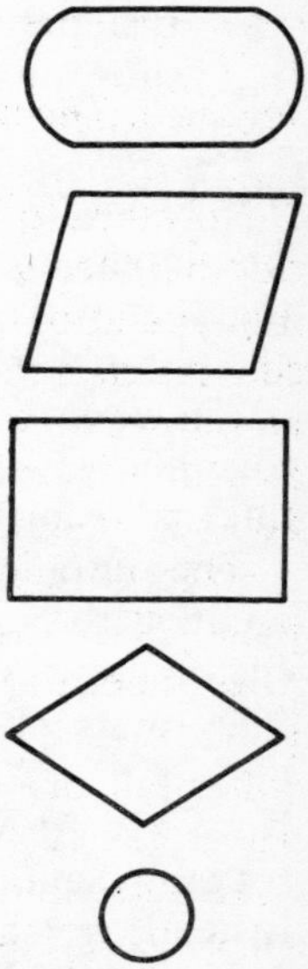

Figure 9. Flowchart symbols

The systems diagrams you have just drawn do not provide sufficient detail to be of much practical use. They tell us what the inputs and the outputs of each subsystem are, but they tell us nothing about the operations, i.e. what has to be done to the inputs to convert them to outputs. We need some way of showing the steps in the flow of data through the system – in other words a *flowchart*.

There are a number of flowchart symbols, but for our present purposes we need the five main ones only, shown in figure 9. Study these now. They are widely used in data processing work.

Flowchart of the collection of payments procedure On page 29 we described the steps in the collection of payments from customers. Read through this list of steps again – we are going to use it now to illustrate flowcharting.

Self-check

List the inputs, the operations, and the outputs of this subsystem.

ANSWER

The inputs are: lists of goods or services supplied to customers together with prices, names and addresses of customers, and cheques plus remittance advice notes from customers.

The operations are: calculations and checks of various kinds, together with entering data into and reading data from the internal records such as the sales ledger.

The outputs are: invoices and statements to customers, payments with paying-in slips to the bank, reminder letters to any customers who are slow payers, entries to the cash book, and sales totals for management and tax purposes.

If we wished, we could represent these inputs and outputs on a systems diagram like figure 8, but there is no need to do this. Instead, we shall go straight to the more detailed (and useful) flowchart. This is shown in figures 10 and 11, and you should study this in conjunction with the explanation that follows.

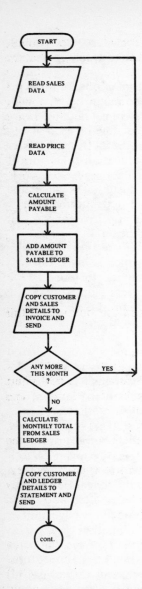

```
START
  │
  ▼
READ SALES DATA
  │
  ▼
READ PRICE DATA
  │
  ▼
CALCULATE AMOUNT PAYABLE
  │
  ▼
ADD AMOUNT PAYABLE TO SALES LEDGER
  │
  ▼
COPY CUSTOMER AND SALES DETAILS TO INVOICE AND SEND
  │
  ▼
ANY MORE THIS MONTH ? ──YES──▶ (back to READ SALES DATA)
  │ NO
  ▼
CALCULATE MONTHLY TOTAL FROM SALES LEDGER
  │
  ▼
COPY CUSTOMER AND LEDGER DETAILS TO STATEMENT AND SEND
  │
  ▼
cont.
```

```
cont.
  │
  ▼
ANY OVERDUE AMOUNTS ? ──NO──▶
  │ YES
  ▼
CHASE
  │
  ▼
READ REMITTANCE ADVICE NOTE
  │
  ▼
CHECK WITH AMOUNT PAID
  │
  ▼
ENTER AMOUNT IN SALES LEDGER AND CHECK WITH STATEMENT AMOUNT
  │
  ▼
ENTER AMOUNT IN CASH BOOK
  │
  ▼
ANY MORE TODAY ? ──YES──▶
  │ NO
  ▼
CALCULATE TOTAL RECEIPTS TODAY
  │
  ▼
ENTER AMOUNTS IN BANK PAYING-IN BOOK AND DEPOSIT IN BANK
  │
  ▼
STOP
```

Figure 10   *Figure 11*

Flowcharts always begin and end with the 'start/stop' symbol, as shown in these figures. This identifies the beginning and the end of the procedure.

Our procedure begins with reading lists of goods (or services) supplied by the firm to a customer (these might be on a sales order), and prices (perhaps from a price list or catalogue). These are the first inputs. In Mike's case the documents used at this point in the procedure would be the time sheets (for the labour costs of the job) and suppliers' invoices or price lists (for prices of materials used).

From this the amount payable by the customer is calculated (by adding up the amounts for each item listed, subtracting any discount that might be offered, and adding on 15% for VAT, if applicable). This is the first operation on the data.

This sum is then entered in that customer's section of the sales ledger (a further operation), and the invoice is made out and sent to the customer (this is the first output). Included in the invoice are the customer's name and address (copied from the sales ledger), the quantities and description of each item purchased, the unit price of each, the VAT, and the total amount payable.

This procedure is repeated for all customers who purchased goods or services until the end of the month is reached. The decision box in the flowchart shows what happens. Up to the end of the month the 'yes' exit takes us back to the start of the procedure and the next batch of sales data, at the end of the month the 'no' exit takes us on to the next step in the procedure, which is to produce and send off the second output, the statement. This is compiled from the sales ledger by copying on to it customer details and all unpaid invoiced amounts. The total amount due is calculated and entered in the ledger and on the statement.

Our flowchart has now reached the bottom of the page, and so a connector is shown linking it to the continuation on the next page. Here we find another decision box. If, from the sales ledger, a customer is seen to owe any outstanding amounts from the previous month, then these must be chased. Otherwise, no further action is taken until the next input is received, namely the cheque settling the amount owing, together with a remittance advice note. (Of course, we are now in the next month, and the invoicing procedure described in the first section of the flowchart is taking place for that month at the same time that payments are being received for the previous month's invoices.)

The amount entered on the remittance advice note by the customer is checked with his cheque, and the details on this note identify the corresponding sales ledger entry. The fact that this sum has now been paid is noted in the ledger. The remainder of the flowchart is constructed in a similar way from the information on the collection procedure given on page 29.

Activity

Construct a flowchart for the task of boiling an egg. (Five minutes.)

HINT

Your flowchart might begin as follows. First, there are two input boxes, 'Get eggpan', and 'Put water in pan'. Next, there are two operation boxes, 'Put pan on cooker', and 'Switch on cooker'. Now try drawing the chart, then check your answer with figure 12.

Review

1 State in a few lines what is meant by 'system', and write down in your own words the value of splitting up a business into subsystems.
2 List as many of the main subsystems of a manufacturing business as you can, and draw a systems diagram (like figure 8) of the production subsystem. (For help with the first part of this question, see figure 32.)
3 Explain what a flowchart is. Try drawing a flowchart for the paying procedure described on page 32. To help you on your way, figure 12 shows how the flowchart should start.

(Twenty minutes.)

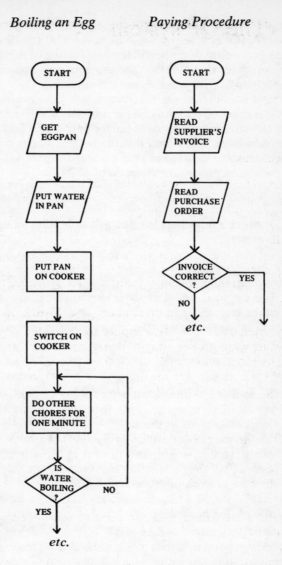

Figure 12

2 | The DP system

Introduction

You have listed the main subsystems of a business (see review **2** on page 43), and in the last chapter we looked at some of these (production, sales, purchasing, and wages). You learned that a system (or subsystem) is something that converts inputs received from its environment to outputs transmitted to its environment. Every subsystem that you listed has some data inputs, and it produces some information outputs. The task of converting these data inputs to information outputs is called data processing, or DP for short.

In many businesses nowadays much of this DP work is carried out by computer. The data inputs to the sales department, purchasing department, wages department, etc. are all processed by the one machine, which produces the required information outputs. So DP is thought of as a further business (sub)system, processing data inputs on behalf of the other business subsystems.

We must now home in on Mike's DP system. In this chapter we are going to look at the inputs, the processing, and the outputs of that system, and in Chapter 3 we are going to look at the way in which Mike exercises control over the system. The questions we shall be answering under each of these headings are:

- *Inputs*: what data does Mike need to run his business, and what are the sources of that data?
- *Processing*: what methods might he use for recording, storing, communicating, and otherwise operating on this data?
- *Outputs*: what information does Mike want to produce by this processing?

- *Control*: how can Mike ensure that the outputs are correct?

Remember that at the moment Mike does not have a computer, and all of his processing is done manually.

The story so far

Data processing is carried out in the 'office', and so associated with every business subsystem there is some office work. That is why we speak of the sales office, the buyer's office, the wages office, the production control office, and so on. Let's begin by recalling what you learned in Chapter 1 to be the main features of the office work that Mike has to do. You saw there that it can be divided into clerical work and managerial work.

Self-check

Jot down two or three sentences explaining these two types of office work.

Clerical work is to do with the actual data processing – producing, from customer orders, the sales documentation, filling in purchase orders for stock items that are running low, calculating wages from clock cards or time sheets, and so on. As a result of this work, information is produced and is communicated to other parts of the business and to the business's environment:

- Documents are sent actioning the various business operations (invoices are sent to customers to generate payments, orders are sent to suppliers to generate purchases, and so on).
- Reports are produced which give Mike information on the state of his business and its subsystems (its profitability, sales trends, etc.).

Managerial work is to do with making decisions on the basis of these reports. Strategic plans are drawn up using, for example, information from market research surveys carried out in the street or from government statistical data held in libraries; operational plans are drawn up on the basis of orders received and on the basis of sales forecasts; control is exercised using feedback information on the performance of the business.

Decision-making is central to all of Mike's activities, and we begin our survey of his DP system by analysing this task.

> ## *Self-check*
>
> To refresh your memory, explain in a sentence or two the difference between a document and a report. Turn back to page 26 and revise what is written there.

OUTLINE ANSWER

A document, or 'action document' as it is sometimes called, contains information on an individual transaction. A report, or 'management report', contains information in a summarised form on many transactions. You will be learning more about action documents and management reports and their uses in this chapter.

Decision-making

Information and decision-making

You are now well aware that Mike's managerial work centres on decision-making. However, even when Mike is wearing his clerk's hat he is making decisions about individual transactions, like:

How much should I buy of item A to replenish my stock?

How much should I pay supplier B this month?

To make a clerical decision about a transaction Mike must refer to the document(s) relating to that transaction.

> ## *Self-check*
>
> Note down the documents that Mike must refer to for the two decisions listed above.

ANSWER

They are (1) the stock record, and (2) the purchase ledger and the supplier's statement.

So all Mike's office activities, whether managerial or clerical, involve decision-making, and to make decisions Mike needs information: information contained in reports for his managerial decisions, information contained in documents for his clerical decisions.

> ### Self-check
>
> Write down three managerial decisions that Mike has to make and three clerical decisions. (Think of decisions other than those given above – if necessary refer to the sections in Chapter 1 on managerial and clerical work.)

ANSWER

You will find a number of decisions listed in figure 16 (pages 60–61). One managerial decision is: *What wage rates should I pay my workers?* (This requires information on wage rates paid by other employers in the industry.) A clerical decision is: *What should I pay them this week?* (This requires information from clock cards or time sheets on the hours worked this week.) These decisions are both part of decision 7 in figure 16.

Programmable and non-programmable decisions

The sort of decisions that Mike makes when he is wearing his clerk's hat are called *programmable decisions*. This does not mean that the decisions are made by means of computer programs (although they may be). It means that they can be made in a mechanical way by following a set of rules. *What debts should I chase?* is a decision that can be made simply by comparing entries on the credit side of the sales ledger with entries on the debit side. A clerk with no knowledge of the business could make this comparison and produce an aged debtors list, as could a computer. (An aged debtors list is a list of customers with overdue accounts, analysed by age of account, e.g. one month overdue, two months overdue, three months overdue.)

Self-check

Look at the three clerical decisions you wrote down in the last self-check. They should be programmable. Try writing down the rules (just a sentence or two) by which each of these decisions is made. For example, the *What should I pay my employees this week?* decision is made by multiplying the hours worked (as shown on the clock cards or time sheets) by the wage rates.

Decisions that cannot be made by following set rules but instead require the exercise of human judgement are called *non-programmable decisions*. These are the sort of decisions that Mike makes when he is wearing his manager's hat, and you will find three examples in your answer to the last-but-one self-check. The question *What wage rates should I pay?* cannot be answered by a machine; it requires a manager's judgement.

We can contrast programmable and non-programmable decisions in other ways also:

- Programmable decisions normally relate to individual transactions (such as a sale or a purchase), and they are therefore made frequently, as each transaction arises. A programmable decision is made on the basis of information contained in a document or record relating to that transaction. An example is the *How much should I pay employee A this week?* decision, which is made each week on the basis of the hours worked recorded on the clock card and the wage rate recorded on the employee's record.
- A non-programmable decision normally relates to a large number of transactions, and is therefore made infrequently. It is often based on information contained in a report. An example is the *What wage rates should I pay?* decision, which is made maybe once a year on the basis of wage rate information obtained from other employers in the industry, perhaps contained in a report in a trade magazine or government publication.

Self-check

Both the wages decision and the wage rates decision given above result in an information output on a document or record. Write down for both cases what the information is and the document/record.

Procedures

The programmable decision *What should I pay employee A this week?* results in an amount entered on a payslip and a paycheque and recorded on the payroll. The non-programmable decision *What wage rates should I pay?* results in an amount entered on all the employee records.

So in the end all Mike's office work, whether managerial or clerical, results in outputs contained in documents and records. You can see some of these outputs written alongside the list of decisions in figure 16.

Now look at figure 13. It shows as a flowchart the steps leading up to a decision, and the output that follows that decision. We call this sequence of steps a *procedure*.

Let's apply this flowchart to both the programmable and the non-programmable decisions discussed above. You will note that the programmable case bypasses the 'information output' box in the figure.

Procedure for the programmable decision *What wages should I pay this week?*

- Input: data on hours worked recorded on a clock card.
- Store: the clock card data is temporarily stored, and then retrieved together with data held on the employee's record (wage rate, tax code, other deductions).
- Decision: the *What wage?* decision is made by multiplying the hours worked by the wage rate and subtracting the deductions.
- Output: the results of this decision, together with data from the employee's record, is printed on the payroll, the wage slip, and the paycheque.

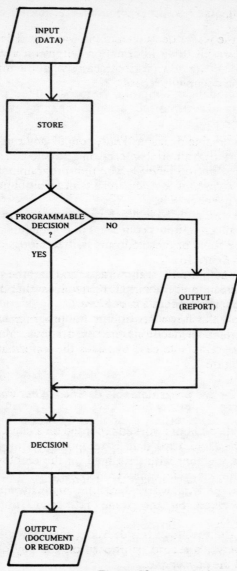

Figure 13

Procedure for the non-programmable decision *What wage rates should I pay?*

- Input: data on wage rates paid by other employers in the industry is collected (either by Mike, or by an outside agency, such as the government).
- Store: this data is temporarily stored, added to, and then retrieved and summarised (again, this might be done by Mike or by the outside agency).
- Report: the summarised data (i.e. information) may be printed out in a report.
- Decision: Mike calculates, on the basis of this information, what wage rates to pay (he must bear in mind how much he can afford to pay, and also how the wages he will pay this year compare with those paid last year, taking into account inflation).
- Output: the wage rates are entered on the employee records.

Notice that in both the programmable and the non-programmable procedures the decision-making involves computations (i.e. calculations). A computation is a processing operation, and so decision-making is shown as an operation box in the flowchart. We shall be speaking about processing operations in detail later on.

Activity

1 When a purchase is made, the buyer in a company compares alternative suppliers by asking for a quotation or, in the case of repeat orders, by looking at the purchase record for the item in question. Find out more about the procedure used in your company, or alternatively read again page 31. Then list the steps linking the input (the purchase requisition) to the output (the purchase order) in the way that is done for the programmable decision above.

2 Carry out a similar exercise for the non-programmable decision *What should I make/supply?* (Assume that the decision is based on market research data.) The output

is a product specification (in the case of goods) or a
planned level of service (in the case of a service).

ANSWER

1 Input: data on purchase requirements. Store: data temporarily
stored, and then retrieved together with data on alternative
suppliers. Decision: the buyer decides from this data which
supplier is most suitable for this purchase. Output: details of
the required purchase and the chosen supplier are printed on
the purchase order.

2 Input: market research data collected. Processing: the data is
stored, added to, then retrieved and summarised. Report: the
summarised data is printed out in a report. Decision: the *What
product/service?* decision is made on the basis of this information. Output: the final output is a product specification.

Self-check

A procedure is a subsystem of the DP system. Can you
explain in a sentence why this is? (Look at page 37 if you
are not sure.)

The chain of procedures

A procedure converts inputs to outputs, and so by definition it is
a system. The sort of procedures we are talking about in this
book convert data inputs to information outputs, and so they are
subsystems of the overall DP system of a company.

As you learned on page 38, the output of one subsystem is the
input of another. So the information that is output by one
procedure is the data that is input to another procedure. If you
are involved with the first procedure you will call the piece of
paper containing the information you have produced an *action
document* – it is generating action elsewhere in the system. If you
are involved in the second procedure you will call this same piece
of paper a *source document* – it is the source of the data that you
are going to use.

Figure 14 shows part of the chain of procedures that takes
place when customer *B* makes a purchase from supplier *A*. The

procedures shown are the supplier's invoicing procedure and the customer's paying procedure. The invoice is the output of the first procedure and the input of the second.

Study this figure now. Both procedures follow the pattern given in figure 13. There are, of course, other procedures in the chain. There is a procedure that precedes the invoicing procedure (which results in the input of the sales order to supplier *A*), and a procedure following the paying procedure (which inputs the remittance and produces a deposit paid in the bank).

Self-check

State two other procedures in the chain of transactions between a supplier and a customer, and give the inputs and outputs of each. (Turn to your answer to review question **3** on page 36 for help.)

ANSWER

1 Making an inquiry – the inputs are the purchase requisition and the supplier's address, the output is the inquiry document.
2 Producing a quotation – inputs are the enquiry document and price data, the output is the quotation.

Review

1 Explain why clerical decisions are made frequently and managerial decisions are made infrequently. Distinguish between the information needed for these two types of decision. Give examples of three clerical and three managerial decisions.
2 List the inputs (documents and reports) needed for the decisions you have listed in question **1**, and state the source of each.
3 Review the procedures described in this section and make out a list of operations that must be carried out on data when it is processed. Your list should begin 'Input (i.e. record) data', and it should end 'Output (i.e. print) information'. Check your answer with page 81.

(Ten minutes.)

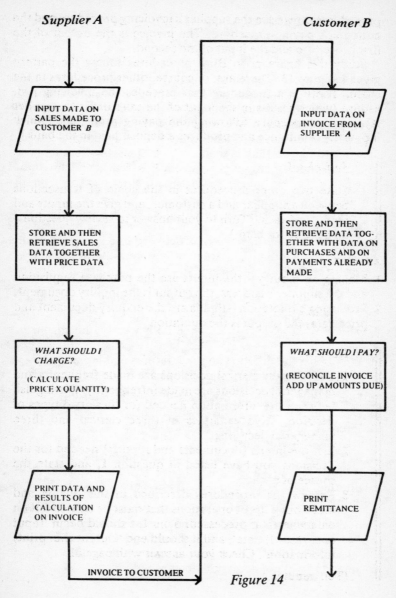

Figure 14

Inputs and outputs

Types of input and output

In the last subsection you learned that the output of one procedure is the input of another. Depending upon where you are in the chain of procedures, you might regard a certain document or report as an output, or you might regard it as an input. As far as Mike is concerned, his final outputs are the documents plus the one or two reports that he sends to his business environment (i.e. to people and organisations outside his firm), and his initial inputs are the documents and reports that he receives from his business environment.

However, within his business there are a large number of outputs and inputs which do not pass between the business and its environment but instead pass between one subsystem of his business and another. The wage rates entered on the employee records (page 50) is one example – these rates are output from the *What wage rate?* procedure and then input to the *What wages?* procedure. There are also the reports that are some of the outputs he produces when he is wearing his clerk's hat – these are some of his inputs when he is wearing his manager's hat.

We can list the different sorts of outputs and inputs of Mike's business as follows:

1 Documents sent to environment: *output* from business.
2 Documents received from environment: *input* to business.
3 Internal documents and records: *output* and *input* between subsystems of business.
4 Reports sent to environment: *output* from business.
5 Reports received from environment: *input* to business.
6 Internal reports: *output* and *input* between subsystems of business.

Note: remember that Mike does not yet have a computer. When he has one, many of his internal documents and records will be in electronic form, i.e. they will exist within the computer system, and will not necessarily be printed out.

Self-check

Go through the lists of outputs and the lists of input documents and reports given in figure 16 and indicate which of the above categories each one belongs to, by writing against it the appropriate number (**1** for documents sent to the environment, etc.). For example, against the first output (purchase requisition) you should write **3**, since it is an internal document; against the second output (purchase order) you should write **1**, as it is sent to the environment; against 'accounts' (in the input column) you should write **4** and **6**, as these are required by the external tax authorities and they are used internally.

Your biggest single group of inputs/outputs in this self-check is category **3**, internal documents and records. For example, purchase records, sales records, stock records, and clock cards are all in this group. The information contained in these consists mainly of names and numbers – suppliers' names, part code numbers, quantities, prices, and so on. Information appearing in this form is referred to as *data*, the term being used here in a restricted technical sense to distinguish this type of input/output (numbers and names) from the other types (see next paragraph).

Smallest in size is category **4**, reports sent to the environment. The borrowing proposal (made to the bank manager or other potential sources of funds) belongs to this group. This will certainly contain data (for instance numbers in the cash flow forecast), but it will also contain *text* (written verbal matter), possibly *image* (i.e. diagrams and graphs), and certainly *voice* (i.e. spoken information when the proposal is presented to the bank manager). All inputs and outputs will be in one or more of these four forms.

Notice the 'source' column in figure 16. Information that Mike receives from within his business is called *internal*, that which he receives from his environment is called *external*.

Self-check

Look up the items of information you have listed in your

answer to review question **1** on page 36, and enter each item in the appropriate box(es) in figure 15. To start you off, some items have already been entered. (The explanations in brackets after these entries indicate why they have been put in the boxes shown. For example, job times have been measured and appear as numbers (data) on a job card.)

	Internal	*External*
Data	Quality achieved (measurement). Job times (measurement).	Government statistics (tables). Market research (questionnaire entries).
Text		
Voice		Market research (interview).
Image		Government statistics (charts).

Figure 15

Figure 16 You have already looked at figure 16. It shows a range of decisions that have to be made in a business, together with the outputs of those decisions and the inputs. The inputs are analysed under three headings: input information required (column 3), input document or report containing the information (column 4), and the source of the information (column 5). Study the figure again now.

Note that most of the decisions listed in the figure can be broken down into two or more subsidiary decisions. For example, decision 7 involves both the non-programmable *What wage rate?* decision and the programmable *What wages this week?* decision (see page 49). Similarly decision 5 contains both the non-programmable *What should I charge for this product?* decision (i.e. price-fixing) and the programmable *What should I charge this customer for his purchases?* decision (i.e. invoicing).

Activity

1 Write down what proportion of the documents and reports used by the business (as shown in the input column of figure 16) comes from internal sources, and what proportion comes from external sources. Then look at the documents and reports you obtained in the activity on page 28 and note which are internal and which external.

2 Note that the documents all contain data rather than information in the form of text and image. Can you find any exceptions to this rule, either in the documents you have collected or in figure 16?

3 Reports contain data, text, and image. The data often takes the form of numbers entered in tables, and the image is in the form of charts and graphs. Try to find and read one or two reports containing information in these forms. Good examples of reports produced externally can be found in the government statistical publications *Economic Trends* and *Social Trends*, obtainable in a college or public library.

Decision	Output	Input
1 *What should I buy?*	Purchase requisitions	Materials required Plant required
2 *Whom should I buy from?*	Purchase orders	Prices, credit terms, quality, delivery, reliability of alternative suppliers
3 *How much should I pay?*	Remittance advice, notes, cheques	Amount of cash available Amount owed to each supplier
4 *What should I make/ supply?*	Product specifications Works orders	Consumer preferences Customer requirements
5 *What should I charge?*	Price list, catalogue Sales invoices	Demand for product or service Competitors' prices Labour, materials, and overhead costs Profit required Customer orders
6 *Whom should I hire?*	Job offers	Attributes needed for job (knowledge, skills, etc.) Attributes of applicants
7 *What wages should I pay?*	Wage rates Wage slips, paycheques	Wage rates in industry Hours worked, wage rates Deductions
8 *How much money should I borrow?*	Borrowing proposal	Future cash needs

Figure 16. Business decisions, together with the outputs produced and the inputs required

Input document or report	Source
Stock records	Internal
Reports	Internal (production engineer)
	External (trade journals)
Purchase records	Internal
Catalogues	External (suppliers)
Quotations	External (suppliers)
Accounts, budgets	Internal
Purchase invoices, suppliers' statements	External (suppliers)
Trade statistics, reports, questionnaire forms	External (libraries, consumers, journals)
Sales reports	Internal
Sales orders, telephone calls, visits	External (customers)
Sales reports	Internal
Trade statistics, reports, questionnaire forms	External (libraries, salesmen, consumers)
Catalogues, salesmen's reports	External (exhibitions, traders, salesmen)
Time sheets, job cards, costings, estimates, accounts records	Internal
Budgets	Internal
Sales orders	External (customers)
Personnel specification, based on job description	Internal
Application forms, references, interviews	External (applicants, referees)
Trade statistics	External (libraries, journals)
Clock cards, employee records	Internal
Tax codes, NI rates	External (tax office)
Cash flow forecasts	Internal

Reports

The only document in figure 16 containing anything other than data is the product specification (decision 4), which may contain diagrams of the product. Reports, in contrast, often contain a great deal of text and image, and any data that they do contain will usually be in the form of tables of figures.

The reason for this difference is that whereas documents contain data relating to individual transactions, reports may relate to many hundreds or thousands of transactions, and their purpose is to present in the clearest possible way an overall picture of the situation. To appreciate a picture you do not study each individual brushstroke; you stand back to gain an overall impression of the totality of brushstrokes.

Take the *What should I make/supply?* decision as an example. To determine what his product mix should be, one piece of information the businessman needs is the trends in sales of his various products. You might think that he should therefore look at all the sales orders received over the past several years, but this is not so. Not only would it take him weeks to read through all this data, but he would be no wiser when he finished than when he started.

What he wants is information in the form of a few meaningful summaries of this data. These could take the following forms:

- *Data* (i.e. *numbers*): a table showing the total sales in each year of each of his products.
- *Image*: a diagram presenting the same information on a graph or in chart form so that the trends can be more easily seen (see figure 19 for an example).
- *Text*: a written report stating how the sales of each product have altered.
- *Voice*: a verbal report giving the same information.

All of the reports given in figure 16 present information in one or more of these forms.

Self-check

You have to explain to a friend how to reach a certain destination by car. Using the above categories as a guide, write down the various ways by which you might convey this information, and give the advantages and disadvantages of each. Which method is the most suitable in this case?

PART-ANSWER

The methods are: **1** data (i.e. numbers) – an ordnance survey reference; **2** image – a sketch map; **3** text – a written description of the route; **4** voice – a verbal explanation.

Data processing

In the next section we are going to look at the ways in which the inputs to a procedure might be processed and the decisions made to produce the outputs. For most of his programmable decisions Mike can use a computer. The inputs to programmable decisions are always documents, the information in these documents being in the form of data (i.e. numbers and names). This is the reason why this type of processing is called 'data processing', and the reason why the inputs are always referred to as 'data' (see page 57). ('Names' here include names of items, parts, streets, etc.)

Many of Mike's decisions are non-programmable, however. These cannot be made by a computer, and the inputs are normally in the form of reports, not documents. The information in these reports will take the form of data and text and image. Our interest in this type of decision-making lies in the fact that any internally produced reports will be outputs of data processing procedures.

Note that any processing that is carried out by human labour instead of by computer is called *manual data processing*.

Review

1 List five programmable decisions made by a business, and write down the source documents used in each case. Use figure 16 as a guide, remembering that many of the decisions listed there can be broken down into two or more subsidiary decisions, some of which will be programmable.

> Write down the outputs of these decisions, separating them into action documents and reports.
>
> 2 Explain why the inputs to a DP system are referred to as data, whereas the outputs are referred to as information.
>
> 3 80% of information reaching management in the typical business comes from internal sources, the reason being that this type of information can be produced automatically by the computer from the data within the system, whereas external information has to be collected manually by e.g. visiting libraries or carrying out market research. Study figure 16 and state whether you think that this proportion is appropriate. If not, what proportion do you think should come from external sources?

(Seven minutes.)

ANSWERS

2 Inputs to a DP system always take the form of numbers and names, whereas outputs can be numbers, text, or image, which are collectively referred to as information.

3 About half.

The processing

What about a computer?

We are now in a position to start thinking about computers. In deciding whether he should have one, Mike must determine exactly what he is going to use it for, and whether computer processing is preferable to his present manual processing for those uses, bearing in mind the cost of acquiring a computer and the problems of changing from manual to computer processing. So he, or an adviser, must:

1 decide for each of his procedures whether it should be done manually or whether it could be done by computer;

2 add up the benefits that will be obtained from computerising the latter sort of procedure and compare these with the costs of computerisation.

We shall be looking in detail at change-over problems, costs, and benefits of computerisation later in the book.

Fortunately for Mike, computers have been applied to so many businesses that it is now possible to apply standard solutions to most of his data processing problems. As you will learn in Chapter 5, he can buy a small business computer system, together with off-the-shelf 'packages' of programs to carry out his invoicing, stock control, general accounting, and other DP tasks, and in a fairly short space of time he can convert many of his procedures from manual processing to computer processing.

However, it has not always been like this, and for many business applications of computers it still isn't this easy. Mike's needs will not be quite the same as other business's needs, and some modifications may have to be made to the packages to meet these needs. And then he has to think about getting his business data into a form which is suitable for computerisation (see Chapter 3). Also, Mike may have applications for which standard packages are not available, such as producing estimates for jobs, and if he wants to computerise these he will have to pay an expert to produce some tailor-made programs.

So you can see that Mike cannot simply walk into a shop, buy a computer system, and immediately start using it. Quite a lot of preliminary work needs to be done.

Activity

At this point in the course you should obtain three or four leaflets on a selection of the microcomputers that are available for home and business use. Apple, Commodore, Tandy, Acorn, Sinclair, and Dragon are some well-known names. If you can, visit a microcomputer exhibition and get the leaflets there; failing that, visit one or two microcomputer shops, or look through some of the many microcomputer magazines that are sold at newsagents.

You will need these leaflets for several of the activities in this book. For this activity you should find out prices for the three or four systems that you have leaflets for, including the prices of disc drives and printers (more about these later in this section). Try to find out why a cheap home

|| system is not suitable for business use. (There are several reasons, as we shall see later.)

What Mike needs to do

Mike's immediate task is to decide whether a computer is feasible for his business (points **1** and **2** at the start of the previous subsection). The procedure that he (or his adviser) must go through to make this decision properly is as follows:

1 List all the business decisions that he has to make, and the outputs that should result from those decisions (columns 1 and 2 of figure 16 show some of these).

2 Divide the decisions into programmable (i.e. capable of being made by a computer) and non-programmable (i.e. must be made by the exercise of human judgement).

3 Decide what data inputs are required for the programmable decisions, and whether these inputs should be processed by computer or manually.

4 Decide what management information (reports) he needs for the non-programmable decisions.

5 Decide which of this management information is to be obtained from internal sources, and which from external sources.

6 List the data that is to be input to produce the internal information, and decide whether it should be processed by computer or manually.

7 And for completeness, although this has little to do with his decision to acquire a computer, he should at the same time decide the best way to obtain the external information (libraries, market research, etc.).

We have already looked at a number of business decisions that Mike has to make and the outputs that result from those decisions, and we have looked at the inputs required to make those decisions. What we haven't done is look at the way in which the processing is carried out (points **3** and **6** above), in other words how the steps shown in the flowchart in figure 13 are carried out. We must now look at these steps, seeing how they are done by Mike's present manual DP system, how they might be done if he acquires a computer, and what are the advantages and disadvantages of these two processing methods.

> *Self-check* ،
>
> To refresh your memory, jot down the term by which these steps are known, and explain what each of the steps involve.

The DP operations

The steps in a procedure are called operations. From figure 13 you can see that we can list them as input, store, decision, and output. We could construct a more helpful list from this figure. Think about the *What wage?* decision. The list is:

1 *Record* the hours worked by each employee (this is the 'input' step).
2 *Store* this data temporarily, then *retrieve* it together with the wage rate data (this is the 'store' step).
3 *Calculate* (i.e. *compute*) the wages from this data (this is the 'decision' step).
4 *Print* (i.e. write, type, or print out) the wages documentation (this is the 'output' step).

We should also add a fifth essential operation which links one procedure in a chain with another (see page 53):

5 *Communicate* (i.e. send) the wages documentation to the users (employees and also other procedures such as a bank's direct debit procedure if wages are paid this way).

> *Self-check*
>
> Write down the DP operations that make up the procedure used by a selling business for invoicing a customer, using the above headings.

ANSWER

1 *Record* the details of the customer's order (items ordered and quantities).

2 *Store* this data until invoicing, then *retrieve* it together with price data.
3 *Calculate* the amount to be charged.
4 *Print* the invoice.
5 *Communicate* the invoice to the customer and to the sales ledger procedure.

Self-check

You should now be able to write down a precise definition of 'data processing'. Try writing down also the reason why the various data processing procedures in a business together form a DP system.

The DP system

Data processing is the task of recording, storing, and retrieving data inputs, and calculating, printing, and communicating information outputs. As we have seen, all DP procedures in a business follow this same pattern of operations. It follows that the same equipment and the same human skills can be used for every DP procedure, whether it is sales order processing, payroll, or stock control. So the data processing in a business can be regarded as a system of common equipment and skills that operate on every data input to produce the information outputs.

Figure 17 represents this by means of a systems diagram.

Inputs	*Processing*	*Outputs*
Sales orders Hours worked Goods received, etc.	DP operations converting inputs to outputs	Amounts payable Wages slips Sales analyses, etc.

Figure 17. Mike's data processing system

Activity

Write down how each of the DP operations are carried out in a manual data processing system, listing against each operation three items of equipment that are used for that operation. If necessary, use one or two offices in your workplace as a guide, or get help from an office equipment catalogue or from an office/secretarial textbook in your library.

Manual data processing

Manual DP methods

In the past, businesses used manual methods of data processing. This meant that clerks carried out the work using pen and paper and limited mechanical assistance. Let's see how the DP operations are carried out in the traditional manual office, and the sort of equipment that is used.

1 *Record*: recording (or *posting* as it is sometimes called) is normally done by pen or typewriter on paper.
2 *Store and retrieve*: the paper record is stored temporarily in in- or out-trays, or more permanently in a filing system, in a way which assists later retrieval.
3 *Calculate* (or *compute*): calculations are carried out by hand or by calculator.
4 *Print*: the results are handwritten or typed on paper.
5 *Communicate*: this paper output is sent by messenger or post to the user.

You will find other items of equipment described in Chapter 4.

Activity

Describe the way in which a manual procedure is carried out in your workplace using the above list of headings as a guide. Find out whether there are any advantages in doing this procedure by manual rather than computer methods, and whether there are any disadvantages.

It might seem surprising that these rather old-fashioned methods are still widely used in business. However, manual data processing has some advantages over modern computer processing, and in certain situations it is superior to computer processing. Mike would be very foolish to install a microcomputer in his business just because it is technically so advanced. He must weigh up the advantages and disadvantages of each method of data processing and then decide which is the best for him.

Let's look first at the advantages of his present manual methods.

Advantages of manual methods

- The equipment is cheap – just a pocket calculator, a small typewriter, some lever-arch files, and accounts books. To justify the relatively high cost of purchasing a microcomputer system, Mike must have a reasonable volume of data processing work. A tiny business issuing a handful of invoices a week and making few purchases could not justify such a purchase.
- The equipment is unlikely to break down, and even if it does Mike can still carry out his data processing. For example, if his calculator fails he can do the sums in his head. If a computer fails, on the other hand, all of the data processing that it handles will stop, and it may be several hours or even days before the system will be up and running again.
- The methods are flexible – Mike can easily change any of his data processing procedures, and the procedures do not have to follow a set of rigidly defined and invariable rules. This is not so with computer processing, where a change in procedures may involve expensive reprogramming of the machine, and the procedures must be capable of being precisely defined in a computer program (i.e. made to follow an exact sequence of rules – see Chapter 6).
- Manual methods are well tried and tested – which isn't always the case with computer methods!

Self-check

In spite of the advantages of manual methods the use of computers in business is becoming widespread. From the

|| above list of points, can you see two reasons why this is?

The reasons are that many business procedures involve the processing of large volumes of data, and the procedures themselves can be precisely defined. Where this is the case the computer offers a number of advantages, and to appreciate what these are let's now turn to the disadvantages of manual methods.

Disadvantages of manual methods

- Manual methods are labour-intensive. Because of this they are (a) costly to run, (b) prone to human error, (c) slow. A computer does not suffer these disadvantages. It does for the office what automation does for the factory: it reduces the need for human labour in procedures by carrying out the operations automatically, thereby reducing costs, eliminating mistakes, and speeding up the process.
- Data has to be re-entered many times. For example, in the invoicing procedure described on page 67, data already recorded (on price lists etc.) has to be copied (i.e. re-entered) on to the invoice form, then re-entered into a calculator, and the result of the calculation has to be copied on to the invoice. Some details are also copied into the sales ledger and on to the monthly statement. This repeated entry of the same data is not only inefficient, it also introduces the possibility of error. With a computer system, on the other hand, data is normally entered once only, stored, and then retrieved from the store whenever it is needed.
- Manual storage of documents is expensive in terms of space. Roomfuls of shelves may be needed to hold an organisation's records. Computers, in contrast, can store vast quantities of data in a compact way on magnetic discs or tapes (see Chapter 4). The entire text of this book, for example, could be stored on a single tape or hard disc; everything that you have read up to this point could be stored on one of the small floppy discs used in microcomputer systems.

|| *Self-check*

|| Should Mike buy a computer? Write down what he would

gain, what the disadvantages of a computer are, and what your advice to him is. (Three minutes.)

ANSWER

If he buys a computer, Mike will avoid the above disadvantages of manual processing. He will save on labour, reduce his space requirements, and process data faster and more accurately. The question is, will these savings offset the cost of buying and installing a computer, and the problems that arise if the computer breaks down?

If he is processing a reasonably large amount of data, then the savings probably will offset the costs. In a business such as his, employing several people, DP probably takes a number of hours a week by manual methods, and a computer is almost certainly a worthwhile acquisition.

For detail on how Mike should compare the costs of computerisation with the benefits, see Chapter 6.

Review

A number of activities, review questions, and assignments in this text are based upon the Pinecrafts case study in the Appendix, which you should now read. These are the first. Like all the exercises, they are based on the situation that will face the firm after it has expanded.

1 Consider the following decisions, as they apply to Pinecrafts:
   (a) *What should I buy?*
   (b) *Whom should I buy from?*
   (c) *What should I make/supply?*
   (d) *What should I charge?*

For each decision write down, under the headings 'internal' and 'external', the source documents or reports required, and state for each whether the subsequent processing and decision-making should be done manually or by computer. In each case note down the reasons for your choice of method.

2 For decision (a), outline the procedure for determining

what materials should be ordered (from the stock records). Use the headings 'record', 'store and retrieve', 'calculate', etc. as a guide.

(Ten to fifteen minutes.)

HINT FOR Q 1

Figure 16 will be of some help here. Your answer for decision (a) might be:

Internal	*External*
Material requirements on stock records – by computer (rigidly defined sequence of operations, programmable decision).	Recommendations for plant in journals – manual methods (operations not precisely defined, non-programmable decision).
Recommendations for plant in O&M report – manual methods (not rigidly defined, non-programmable decision).	

ANSWER TO Q 2

- Record: receipts and issues of stock.
- Store and retrieve: store on stock record and retrieve together with item details.
- Calculate: test whether balance in stock is less than reorder level.
- Print: if so, print reorder quantity and item details on reorder suggestions list.
- Communicate: pass to production manager.

Electronic data processing

'Electronic data processing' (EDP) is the term by which processing involving computers is generally known. The reason why it is called this rather than 'computer data processing' is that a number of pieces of electronic equipment besides computers may be involved in the processing. We begin our survey by examining the essential difference between the equipment used in an electronic system and that used in a manual system.

Electronic equipment

What is the difference between the electric typewriter and the electronic typewriter? The electric typewriter is, in essence, a mechanical typewriter powered by an electric motor. Pressure on one of the keys of the keyboard is transmitted via a system of levers to the typeface hammers, which strike the ribbon and paper to create the character impression. Such a machine has a large number of moving parts, it is relatively expensive to manufacture, and it is subject to mechanical wear.

An electronic typewriter is quite different. There are no moving parts linking the keys to the typing (printing) mechanism. Instead there are electric wires linking the keys to a tiny *microprocessor* (i.e. silicon chip), which is in turn linked by wire to the printing mechanism. The printing mechanism itself is an electro-mechanical device, but the rest is electronic.

It is this electronic part that is revolutionary:

- There are no moving parts, i.e. it is *solid-state*. It is therefore relatively inexpensive to manufacture, it is extremely reliable, and it will not wear out.
- It is *intelligent*, meaning that it incorporates a *processing unit* (i.e. the microprocessor) able to carry out some of the routine mental tasks previously done by the secretary or clerk. For example, it can automatically centre headings. Note that the word 'intelligent' as applied to computers does not suggest the ability to think creatively or originally.
- It can *communicate* electronically with other electronic equipment by sending the electrical impulses generated by the microprocessor down a connecting cable. This means that an electronic typewriter can send messages electronically instead of printing them out on paper, and it can act as a computer terminal (see later in this section). (However, many electronic typewriters lack the necessary output sockets to make these connections.)

Many pieces of office equipment are now electronic, which means they are solid-state and possess the sort of intelligence and communications capabilities described above. This equipment is making a revolutionary impact on the work of the office.

Self-check

From what has been said above, give three reasons why electronic equipment is revolutionising office work.

My answer would be:

1 It is relatively inexpensive, compact, and very reliable. Even a small businessman like Mike must consider using it.
2 Its intelligence enables it to do some of the jobs that were previously carried out by clerks, secretaries, and managers.
3 The fact that one piece of equipment can communicate electronically with another means that data need only be entered into the system once. It is then stored in electronic form and communicated to any part of the system whenever it is needed.

Electronic data processing methods

Here's how the DP operations involved in the *What wages this week?* procedure could be carried out if Mike used electronic data processing.

- *Record* The hours worked by each man will be recorded on clock cards or time sheets as at present, but this data will subsequently be entered into the electronic system.
- *Store and retrieve* The data will be stored within the system, and it will be retrieved and communicated to the processing unit in the system at the time when the payroll calculations are carried out. Data on wage rates and on deductions will be retrieved from the employees' records (also stored in the system) at the same time.
- *Calculate* The processing unit will calculate the gross pay, the tax, and the net pay, and it will communicate the results of these calculations, together with the relevant employee details, to the printing part of the system.
- *Print* The printer will print these details on the payroll, the payslips, and the paycheques, in accordance with instructions received from the processing unit.
- *Communicate* The payslips and the paycheques will be handed to the employees.

Only the initial recording of the data and the final handling of the paycheque are carried out by traditional manual methods.

> *Self-check*
>
> Using the above headings, outline the sequence of operations for producing invoices by electronic means. Use the answer to the self-check on page 67 as a guide.

The computer

If Mike decides to process his data electronically he will buy a *microcomputer*. This is the commonest sort of computer, and you should have acquired leaflets describing some microcomputers in a previous activity. As its name implies, a microcomputer is very small, and it can in fact be housed on an ordinary desk-top.

We often think of a microcomputer as a single piece of equipment. In fact it is a complete system for processing data consisting of:

- *keyboard*, to enter, or 'key in', the data;
- *disc-drives*, to store the data on magnetic discs (the cheaper home systems use tape cassettes for storage);
- *processing unit*, to control the system and carry out the calculations;
- *screen*, to display what is keyed in as well as the output of the system;
- *printer*, if the computer is to print the output on paper (as 'hard copy').

In many microcomputer systems each of these items of equipment, apart from the printer, is housed in a single cabinet, and you will probably find this to be the case in the leaflets you have of small business systems. This results in a compact system which can be operated by a single individual seated at a desk.

A large business needs a much bigger computer to handle its data processing. In this case the various parts of the system will be housed in separate cabinets. The biggest computers are called *mainframes*, which was the name originally given to the large cabinets in which the processing units were housed. A vital difference between a large computer system and a microcomputer is the fact that in the former many people can use the system simultaneously, keying in data and receiving output via *terminals* (i.e. keyboard and screen units) linked by wire to the mainframe. We shall be explaining this in more detail later in the book. The cost of a mainframe computer is about £100,000.

Other types of computer

There are several other varieties of computer. One is the *minicomputer*, which is really a small version of the mainframe computer, with processing unit, disc and tape drives, and printers housed in separate cabinets, and a number of keyboard and screen terminals. It is less powerful than a mainframe, which means that it cannot work at such high speeds and it cannot support so many terminals, but it is very much more powerful than a microcomputer. It is suitable for use in medium-sized firms. Minicomputers can cost anything between £10,000 and £70,000 or so.

Another version of the computer is the *word processor*. You can think of this as an electronic typewriter with the addition of a large internal memory for storing text currently being worked on, disc drives for longer term storage of large quantities of text, and a screen displaying up to a full page of text. It is used by secretaries for the production of letters, reports, and other textual material, and like other computers it comes into its own in situations where there is a reasonable volume of routine, well-defined work.

Besides carrying out the functions of an electronic typewriter, the word processor can store large amounts of text for later editing (on the screen) and then printing; it can insert standard paragraphs in an otherwise variable document; it will 'personalise' standard letters (by automatically inserting the name and address and other personal details); and much more.

A word processor is very similar to a microcomputer, although it will use a high-quality printer so that the letters and reports it produces look good. It costs in the region of £4,000.

Like electronic typewriters, microcomputers and word processors can communicate electronically. This means that an organisation using them can send messages by wire instead of on paper, so that the messages are displayed on the recipients' screens instead of arriving in in-trays. It also means that these devices can be used as terminals to large computers. Where microcomputers are used in this way they are able to access all the information held in the large computer's store while at the same time being able to carry out any data processing themselves. In effect they are adding to the data processing capabilities of the system. You will learn more about this in Chapter 8.

Information processing

You can see that nowadays computers are used not just for processing data, but for processing text also. Additionally, many computers have powerful graphics facilities, which means that they are able to present information in the form of charts and graphs. As a result they can present business trends and make comparisons in a vivid and meaningful way, and managers find this very useful.

Because computers are now used to handle not just data but information in a variety of forms, we use the term *information processing* to describe their work.

Review

1 List the main items that make up a computer system, and explain their purpose.
2 List four types of computer and note against each its area of application.
3 What advantages has the computer over manual data processing methods? (See the section on the disadvantages of manual methods.) Explain why manual methods will continue to be used for some office work for a long time to come. (Look at your answer to Review 1 on page 72, and read again the section on the advantages of manual methods.)

(Ten minutes.)

Pinecrafts assignment 1

(This assignment and those located at the ends of Chapters 4, 6 and 8 are based on the Pinecrafts case study in the Appendix. You have already read this case study in a previous activity. You should spend between one and two hours on this assignment – you will find most of the answers in this chapter. If you experience difficulties with this or later assignments see *Model Answers to Business Administration Assignments* by R. Carter, published by Heinemann.)

Six important decisions that have to be made in a business like Pinecrafts are:

a For *sales*: pricing; advertising policy (i.e. level and type of advertising).
b For *production*: work schedules; equipment replacement policy (i.e. when to replace).
c For *purchasing*: reorder quantities; sources of supply.

Sales, *production* and *purchasing* were described in Chapter 1. For each of these three operations carry out the following exercises:

i Write down another decision that has to be made.
ii List the information needed to make each of the three decisions.
iii Indicate against each item of information whether it can be obtained from the firm's internal records, or whether it must be obtained from external sources.

In each case state briefly the procedure to be used in obtaining the information (assuming for the purpose of this exercise that the firm will not be using a computer system).

3 | Controlling data

Introduction

The story so far

In Chapter 1 you learned that a system consists of the following parts:

- *inputs* received by the system from its environment;
- *processing* of the inputs;
- *outputs* produced by the processing.

Also in Chapter 1 you learned the distinction between the prime inputs and outputs of a system and the non-prime inputs and outputs.

Self-check

List two prime inputs and two prime outputs of Pinecrafts (see the Appendix), and two non-prime inputs and two non-prime outputs. Revise pages 21–2 if you can't remember the distinction between prime and non-prime.

ANSWER

Pinecrafts is in the business of making fitted pinewood kitchens, and to carry out the operations required for this it needs prime inputs of wood and labour. Two prime outputs will be the fitted kitchens it makes and the wages it pays it workers. Non-prime inputs and outputs are data relating to the business operations, such as data on customers' requirements (on sales orders), data on materials received (on stock records), data on the amounts to be paid by customers (on invoices), and data on the earnings of the company (in the accounts).

In Chapter 2 you learned that the procedures for converting data inputs to outputs were themselves a part of a system, namely the data processing system of the business. Like any system, this consists of inputs, processing, and outputs, but we found it helpful to use headings which more aptly describe what's going on in the system, namely:

- *record* the input data;
- process the data, i.e.
  (a) *store* and *retrieve* the data,
  (b) *calculate* the output;
- *print* and *communicate* the output.

The next step

In this chapter you are going to learn how systems, in particular DP systems, are controlled. You already know something about this, for in Chapter 1 we saw that control is exercised over a system by adjusting its inputs. In the case of Mike's data processing system, he controls it by ensuring that the data inputs are suitably presented and accurate.

So in the pages that follow you will be finding out:

- how to present data, which includes how to code data and how to design and control the forms (i.e. documents) on which it is recorded; and
- how to ensure the accuracy of the data.

We begin by looking at what's involved in controlling a system.

Activity

Think about a central heating system in a home. What are the prime inputs and the prime output? What device controls the system so that the prime output is maintained within the planned limits? What does this device do? (Two minutes.)

Controlling a system

System control

Up to this point we have drawn systems diagrams with three boxes only, showing input, operations (or processing), and output. Figure 17 is one example of such a diagram. However, this is not the whole story, for a control element should be included. In fact a system has four boxes, as shown in figure 18.

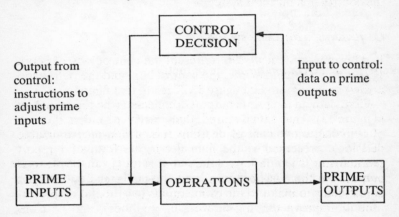

Figure 18. A system showing the control box

Let's apply this figure to your answer to the above activity. The prime inputs are the fuel to heat the water and the electricity to operate the pump. The prime output is the hot air from the radiators. The control device is the thermostat. To analyse what this device does, recall what you learned about control in Chapter 1 (go back to page 19). Control involves:

● comparing the actual output of the system with the planned output; and
● adjusting the inputs if the planned output is not being achieved.

Now think about what your thermostat does. First, it measures the prime output of the central heating system, i.e. the temperature of the air in the room. This temperature data is represented by the upward arrow on the right-hand side of figure 18. Second, it switches on the pump (i.e. adjusts the prime input 'electricity') if the temperature falls below the planned temperature range, or switches off the pump if the temperature rises above that range. This switching command is represented by the downward arrow on the left-hand side of figure 18.

This process of output measurement and input adjustment applies to the control of any system. In particular it applies to the control of a business system.

Controlling a business system

In a business system we can represent the control loop of figure 18 (i.e. the left-hand arrow, the control box, and the right-hand arrow) by a diagram like figure 13. Turn to that figure now.

First, data on the prime outputs is collected (the top input box in figure 13). That data is stored, then retrieved, and, in the case of a management control decision (i.e. a non-programmable decision), presented to the manager in the form of a report summarising the variations of the actual output from the planned output. On the basis of this report the manager decides what adjustments to make to the prime inputs (e.g. to increase over-time or improve training or working methods), and he communicates those adjustments either verbally or by instructions on output documents (the final output box in figure 13).

So you can see that the procedure for control decisions involves the same DP operations as the procedures for any other sort of business decision.

Example of business control

Two important types of control that are carried out in business are *quality control* and *quantity control*. The purpose of the former is to ensure that the quality of work in the factory or office conforms to the accepted standards; the purpose of the latter is to ensure that the planned output volumes are achieved.

Let's think about quality control in the factory, taking the simple example of a machine set up to produce metal bolts of a certain length. This length is called the 'process mean length'.

Every so often a sample of the bolts produced by the machine will be selected, the length of each bolt measured, and the sample mean (i.e. the average length) calculated and plotted on a quality control chart. An example of such a chart is shown in figure 19. Over a period of time a series of plotted points builds up across the chart, and if a fault develops in the machine these points will start to diverge from the process mean. If they reach the 'action limits' on the chart (i.e. the limits beyond which action should be taken) the machine is stopped and adjusted.

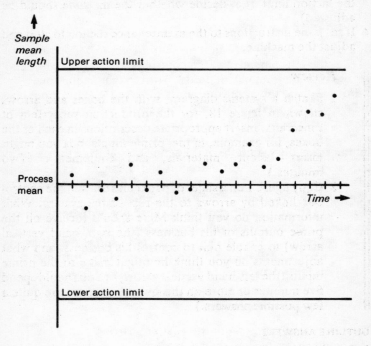

Figure 19

Self-check

Using figure 13 as a guide, sketch a flowchart showing the

steps involved in the above quality control example. The input will be the sample mean lengths (the calculation of these mean lengths will be a previous procedure), and the decision will be programmable.

ANSWER

1 Record the sample mean lengths.
2 Store the data on the chart.
3 Test whether the trend of the plotted points is passing outside the 'action limit' (i.e. decide whether the machine should be adjusted).
4 If so, issue instructions to the maintenance section to stop and adjust the machine.

Review

1 Sketch a systems diagram, with the boxes and arrows shown in figure 18, for the production subsystem of Pinecrafts. Insert appropriate descriptions in each of the boxes; for example, in the 'prime inputs' box you might insert 'labour, materials, and equipment'. (Two minutes.)
2 Copy figure 1 on a sheet of paper and draw in the control box linked by arrows to the rest of the system. What information do you think Mike should receive on the prime outputs of his business (the right-hand vertical arrow) to enable him to control his business, and what adjustments do you think he might make to the prime inputs (the left-hand vertical arrow)? (You should spend five minutes or more on this question – there are quite a few possible answers.)

OUTLINE ANSWERS

1 Possible inserts in the various boxes are: 'processing' box: production operations; 'prime outputs' box: assembled and finished fitted kitchen units; 'control' box: production manager; 'input to control': data on finished kitchens (quality and whether completed on time); 'output from control': instruc-

tions to foremen if quality standards are not being achieved or work is falling behind schedule.

2 Mike is the overall controller (i.e. general manager) of his business. To exercise this control he needs firstly to check the quantity and quality of his men's output. Are they achieving their work schedules, and is their quality of workmanship satisfactory? If standards are not being maintained he will investigate causes and perhaps adjust inputs by exercising tighter supervision, introducing improved methods and equipment, or giving additional training. He also needs to check financial aspects (such as his overall profitability) and marketing matters (such as his sales trends). If these are below expectation he may try to make adjustments such as cutting costs and increasing efficiency, seeking additional or different work, or altering his pricing policy.

Controlling a DP system

We must now turn to our main topic in this chapter, namely the control of the data processing system itself. As with any other system, control involves adjusting the inputs to obtain the required outputs.

Self-check

Think about the work of a clerk. How is 'control' applied in this case?

As you have already learned, two major aspects of control are quantity control and quality control. So my answer to this self-check is:

1 Quantity control – a given volume of work must be completed within a given time.
2 Quality control – the work must be carried out accurately, and the presentation should be satisfactory.

Both of these aspects of his work must be monitored, and suitable input adjustments made (e.g. overtime working, more training, improved methods) if the required outputs are not being achieved.

Controlling DP

These two types of control must be applied to any DP work. Quantity control means organising and adjusting the labour inputs (i.e. the staff) so that the required volume of work is got through in the required time. We shall be looking at the organisation of labour inputs in Chapter 8. Quality control means organising the data inputs so that the information outputs are accurate. It is this type of control that you will be learning about in this chapter.

> *Activity*
>
> Jot down in a sentence or two the process by which you control your bank account.

ANSWER

You record all receipts and payments on the cheque book stubs, and you subsequently check these entries with your bank statement to ensure that the bank has made no mistakes.

Control in a manual DP system For his present manual system Mike (or an office employee) will operate the following quality controls:

- He will scrutinise all documents (cheques, invoices, etc.) produced by the system to ensure that they are presentable (neat, legible, etc.) and that there are no obvious errors.
- He will check the accuracy of all calculations. He will possibly use a calculator which produces a hard-copy print-out on a paper roll so that all data keyed in can be checked.
- He will check the accuracy of any copying of data from one document or book to another.
- He will check that the record of receipts and withdrawals on his bank statement matches the record in his cash book. He will also check that invoices received from suppliers match his records of goods purchased and received, and that the invoice calculations are correct.

Control in an electronic system In an electronic system the whole emphasis of quality control is on the presentation and accuracy of the input data. The reasons for this emphasis are:

- The subsequent processing is automatic and error-free, and no human controls are therefore necessary.
- Because there is no human involvement in the subsequent processing, any errors that are introduced when the input data is keyed in will remain unnoticed in the system and will ultimately affect the output – the only point at which it is possible to pick them up is at the input stage.

In the remainder of this chapter, therefore, you will be learning about, first, the *presentation of data*, which includes coding data as well as the design of the forms on which the data is recorded and, second, *accuracy*.

Review

1 State in a few words what you understand by 'system control', and then give three examples of the use of data processing to assist the control of business operations. (One example is stock control – ensuring that stock item quantities are maintained within predetermined limits, using a system of stock records.)
2 Give two reasons why control of accuracy of input is important in a computer-based system.

(Three minutes.)

Presentation of data: coding

Coding is most important in data processing, and if a business intends to install a computer one of the first things it must do is devise suitable coding systems for its stock records, employee records, and all the other records that it wants to computerise. Let's start off by finding out what we mean by 'coding' and why it is so important.

The purpose of codes

Men set up primitive manufacturing and trading enterprises before writing and paper were invented, and we might wonder how data was processed in those days. In fact people used their inbuilt biological data processing abilities, namely:

- eyes and ears to record data;
- the brain to store data and to calculate;
- voice to output and communicate data.

However, this is not a very efficient way of processing business data – the brain is notoriously forgetful, and voice is often not a convenient means of communication – and so writing on paper or other media was developed specifically to assist business and trade. Its impact on data processing in those days was at least as great as the impact of the computer in our own day.

Writing is a way of describing data by means of 'codes' consisting of alphabetic and numeric characters. There is nothing secret or mysterious about such codes; we all use them unthinkingly every day of our lives. Let's list the codes used by Mike for his customer records, writing against each the purpose that it serves:

- the customer's name (alphabetic characters) – to identify him;
- his address (alphabetic and numeric characters) – to pinpoint where he lives;
- his telephone number (numeric characters) – to enable Mike to contact him by phone.

These codes are doing two jobs;

- identifying the customer;
- giving information about him.

This is true of most codes used in business: they identify and they inform.

The 'international standard book' (ISB) number on the back cover of this book is another example of a code. It identifies this book uniquely – no other book has this particular ISBN – and it also provides useful information. For example, the digits 330 at the beginning of the number identify the publisher as Pan Books Ltd.

Activity

Write down three codes that you are familiar with, giving the purpose of each and any information that they contain.

My answer would include my own Department of Education and Science reference number (74/96570), which identifies me in the department's files. The first two digits give the year in which I took my teacher's training course.

Coding systems

A person's name and address are a very useful code for everyday purposes. However, the large number of characters in a name and address can be a drawback in business data processing. The Post Office, for instance, finds postcodes consisting of six or seven letters and numbers much more convenient.

Although Mike finds it easy at the moment to identify his customers, suppliers, stock items, etc. by their names, as his business grows and the volume of data processing grows the inherent disadvantages in this everyday sort of code will become more and more obvious to him.

Self-check

Can you think of two disadvantages?

1 A name and address takes much longer to type than a code number, and they occupy much more space in the record.
2 The larger number of keystrokes needed to type a name or address means that a typing error is more likely to be made. This may not matter too much in a manual system, but in an electronic system it will result in the computer failing to recognise the name that has been keyed in.
3 There are a number of ways of writing a name, but a computer will recognise only one of them. For instance, if my records

are stored under the name 'Roger Carter', the computer will not recognise 'Carter, Roger', 'R. Carter', 'Mr Roger Carter', or any other variant. A code number, on the other hand, can be keyed in in one way only, and this problem does not arise.

There are three sorts of coding system used in business. They are:

Numeric codes These are codes consisting of numbers only. One-digit numeric codes offer ten different combinations (0 to 9), two-digit codes offer 100 (00 to 99), three-digit codes offer 1,000, and so on. This compares unfavourably with the number of possibilities offered by the other two sorts of code described below, but numeric codes have one advantage not possessed by the others. It is possible to add a 'check digit' to the end of such a code whose value can be calculated mathematically from the other digits. When the code number is keyed into the system the computer can check whether the other digits do in fact yield this value, and if they do not it means that a keying error has been made. (See page 105 for a fuller explanation.) Thus the code number itself contains a built-in error check.

Alphabetic codes These codes consist of alphabetical characters. One-digit alphabetic codes offer twenty-six different possibilities (A to Z), two-digit alphabetic codes offer 676 (AA to ZZ), and so on. This is more than the possibilities offered by numeric codes.

Alphanumeric codes These are codes consisting of both alphabetic and numeric characters. One-digit alphanumeric codes offer thirty-six combinations (A to Z, 0 to 9), two-digit codes offer 1,296, and so on. Such codes offer the most possibilities, and their use of both alphabetic and numeric characters means that they can be highly informative. (See the example of a coding system given at the end of the next subsection.)

Self-check

Examples of each of these three types of coding system are given on pages 89–90. Write down another example of each type.

POSSIBLE ANSWER

Numeric: your bank account number; alphabetic: examination grades (A, B, C, etc.); alphanumeric: car registration numbers.

Devising a coding system

You have learned that codes have several advantages in data processing, especially in electronic data processing. Businesses need to code their suppliers, their customers, their employees, their stock items, and much more. If Mike decides to have a computer, he will have to introduce coding systems into his business.

In devising a coding system he should ask the following questions:

- Should the code be descriptive, i.e. informative to humans? One example of descriptive codes is air-flight codes, where the alphabetic characters indicate the destination (LN = London, NY = New York, etc.). This is obviously helpful to passengers and airline staff. Mike must consider the use that his employees or customers will be making of his codes, and devise them accordingly.
- How short should the code be? A short code will result in fewer keystrokes when entering the data via a keyboard, and it occupies less space in the record. However, it provides fewer possible combinations of characters than a longer code (and it therefore limits the number of records). For example, a two-digit numeric code for coding employees is short, but what will happen if the number of employees rises above 99? Also, short codes cannot be as descriptive as long codes.

Example of a coding system

A light engineering company (described in the case study on page 259) had to devise a coding system for its stock records in preparation for computerisation. It decided that the system should have the following characteristics:

- The code should indicate the supplier and the product-group (i.e. type of product), as well as identifying the particular stock item.
- It should contain some descriptive alphabetical characters to help staff identify the item.
- It should contain less than ten characters.

The system the company came up with was a nine-character code embodying the following features:

Characters 1–3 were alphabetic, indicating the product-group.
Characters 4–6 were numeric, indicating the supplier.
Characters 7–9 were numeric, uniquely identifying the stock item.

The system proved so logical and effective in practice that staff were often able to work out the part code of an item without needing to look it up in the parts catalogue.

To illustrate the system, the code number of one stock item was ARC123001. Characters 1–3 showed that the type of product was *Anti-Rust* for *Cars*, characters 4–6 indicated the supplier (F. Stevenson & Co. had been given the code number 123), and characters 7–9 indicated the capacity in litres. So ARC123001 is the code for a one-litre can of Stevenson's Anti-Rust Treatment for Cars.

Other examples of coding systems can be found on pages 115–17.

Self-check

Imagine Pinecrafts want to put their employee records on to a computer. Decide two items of data (besides the name) that they will want to store for each employee, and suggest coding systems that they might use in each case. Also write down the coding system they might use to identify each employee uniquely (i.e. the works number assigned to each person).

ANSWER

A two-digit numeric code will be suitable for the works numbers – there are less than forty employees at the moment, and such a code will allow up to ninety-nine employees. One item of data that should be stored is the sex – a one-digit alphabetic code (M or F) is suitable – and another item is the date of birth – a six-digit numeric code (two for the day, two for the month, and two for the year) is suitable. So part of the employee record might look like this:

01	SMITH	JOHN	HENRY	M	09/08/65
02	JONES	DAVID		M	11/01/53

etc.

Activity

In this and in one or two subsequent activities in this chapter you are asked to imagine that you are setting up a computer dating bureau for arranging introductions between single people of the opposite sex. In this activity I want you to list the items of data about each person registered with you that you will want to store in your computer records, and the codes that you might use for this data.

PART-ANSWER

You may decide to use a numeric code to identify each individual. Data will be required on relevant characteristics such as their sex, age, height, and occupation. An alphabetic code might be used for occupation: MN for manual worker, CL for clerk, SC for secretary, MG for manager, and so on.

Review

1 If Pinecrafts install a computer, they will have to apply coding systems to many of their records. Explain why.
2 Pinecrafts make a number of standard kitchen units in a variety of finishes. Outline a suitable coding system for these units. State why you think your code is suitable.

(Five minutes.)

PART-ANSWER TO Q 2

A descriptive code might be useful, especially as the units will be described in a catalogue (see case study in the Appendix). Two digits will be sufficient to identify the units (e.g. SU for sink unit, WC for wall cupboard), and perhaps two for the type of finish. This code requires only four keystrokes.

Presentation of data: forms

You learned in the last section that Mike has to devise suitable coding systems before he can put his data processing on to computer. In this section you will learn that he also has to revise the system of forms on which he records and presents his data. Many of his manual records will be replaced by electronic records, and so some forms will be eliminated, and other forms may be filled in by a computer printer instead of by hand. You will also be learning how he should tackle the task of revising the forms.

What is a form?

We have talked about source documents (meaning documents containing input data), action documents (meaning documents containing output data), and reports (meaning documents containing management information). All these documents consist of data and information recorded on paper. The paper can be blank sheets, or it may contain pre-printed headings and instructions. If the latter, it is called a form.

Activity

You have already collected some forms in the activity on page 28. The data that would be entered on those forms could also be recorded on blank sheets of paper, thereby saving on printing costs and on the need to store many different sorts of forms. So why are forms normally preferred to blank sheets of paper in data processing? Try to write down three reasons. (Hint: imagine you are Mike, and you are writing out an invoice for a customer. What would be the disadvantages of using a blank sheet of paper?)

The purpose of forms

Forms are the almost universal way of recording, storing, and presenting data and information in manual systems, and they are also widely used in electronic systems. The advantages that forms have over blank sheets of paper for Mike are:

- Fixed data, such as his name and address, is pre-printed, so that he has to enter only the variable data.
- They ask a sequence of pre-defined questions, which helps him to complete the forms, ensuring that he won't forget anything and that the data will appear in a logical sequence.
- A completed form presents data in a standardised format, which makes it easier to read and process (since it is logically laid out, and an item of data – such as the date, or the code number – always appears on the same spot on the paper).

Of course, not every form is well designed, in which case some of these advantages are lost. Also, there may be unnecessary duplication of some data on the forms used in a company (i.e. the same item of data may appear on several forms). It is important to a business that its forms are properly designed and that they do not lead to unnecessary duplication of data.

Forms control

Many larger companies operate a system of forms control. The purpose of forms control is to monitor all the forms used in the company, checking whether any data is being collected unnecessarily or duplicated unnecessarily. When forms control is first set up in an organisation, it often results in a reduction of 25% in the amount of paperwork. This is achieved by cutting out unnecessary data collection, by redesigning forms so that one form satisfies two or more purposes, and by producing copies of forms for different users instead of re-entering data on different forms.

Forms control is normally carried out by one individual in the organisation (e.g. the office manager), or by a small team of people (e.g. the O&M section). Even in a tiny business, such as Mike's business or Pinecrafts, forms control can contribute to efficiency.

X-charts The starting-off point in forms control is the *X-chart*. This is drawn up to show which items of data appear on which forms, and from it can be seen which items are duplicated. Figure 20 shows an X-chart with some of the forms used by Pinecrafts. The forms are listed across the top of the chart, the data down the side. The *x*'s indicate which data appears on which forms, and as you can see there is a lot of duplication. One way of avoiding this would be for Pinecrafts to produce several of the forms as a single 'set' (i.e. an original plus copies).

Form / Data	Quotation	Sales order	Installers diary	Works order	Receipt note	Invoice	Sales ledger
Date	X	X		X	X	X	X
Reference/ Delivery date	X	X	X	X	X	X	X
Customer details	X	X	X		X	X	X
Product details	X	X		X	X	X	
Price	X	X				X	X

Figure 20

Activity

Devise a system of forms that would enable Pinecrafts to do just that (i.e. produce the various copies in one operation). State in your answer the purpose of each form and how it would be used. You will find it helpful to read through the 'administrative procedures' section of the case study in the Appendix, particularly paragraphs 2, 3, 9, and 10. You will also find it helpful to examine similar systems of forms that may be used in your own firm. (Ten to fifteen minutes.)

ANSWER

As described below, a single set of forms could be produced for the procedures described in the case study, copies being obtained either by using carbon paper or by printing the forms on 'no-carbon-required' paper (in which case copies are produced by a chemical-impregnated in the paper).

The original (i.e. the top copy) of the set could form a combined sales order and invoice and could be held in the sales department in code number order and handed to the customer at the time of delivery and installation of the kitchen. (Since it is planned to produce and deliver kitchens at the rate of one per day, the code number could be the planned delivery date. This would be useful in subsequent stages of the procedure.)

The customer could retain the second copy for his own records, and the general office would need the third copy to maintain the customer accounts. The fourth copy could be on card, and this might form the works order for the production department. (Coding by delivery date will ensure that the order of the cards corresponds to the order in which jobs should be scheduled through the workshops.)

This fourth copy could ultimately form the receipt note – it will be signed by the customer at the time of installation and returned to the general office. If held there in code number (i.e. delivery date) order it could form the basis of a credit control system – cards could be removed from the file as customers settle their accounts, those remaining at the back of the file representing customers with overdue accounts.

Forms design

The task of designing the individual forms can now be carried out. To do this properly you should ask the following sequence of questions:

- *Who* is going to fill in the form? The wording used on the form and the instructions printed on it must be appropriate to the level of staff dealing with it.
- *How* is the data going to be entered on the form and how will the form be processed? If the form is to be filled in at a factory bench then it should be printed on stiff paper or card; if it is to be filled in by typewriter or printer then the line and character spacing must match the characteristics of the machine. You should decide at this stage how any copies are to be produced, and what size the form should be (bearing in mind the width of the machine roller, file jacket sizes, and sizes of other forms).
- *What* data is to go on the form? To decide this you must find out what the user of the form needs to know. The list of data should meet these requirements, omitting no essential data and including nothing superfluous.
- *Where* on the form is each item of data to go? You must put the data in your list in the most logical order, bearing in mind the order used on other forms in the firm (standardisation is desirable, so that date, code number, and other common data appear on the same spots in each form).

Now you can draw up the form. If the data is to be entered on the form by a typewriter or printer, then the form should be drawn up on a *spacing chart*. This can be obtained from suppliers of office stationery, and resembles graph paper. Make sure that the grid size of the chart you use matches the line and character spacing of the typewriter or printer that is to enter the data. You should calculate and allow for the number of spaces required for each item of data, as well as any margins needed at the edge of the form. Note that any instructions should appear at the top rather than the bottom of the form, so that they are read before the form is filled in.

Activity

Design the invoice copy of the set of sales documents described in the last activity. In arriving at your design you should answer each of the four questions listed above. (Ten minutes.)

Designing forms for computers

All the above principles apply if you are designing forms for computer-based systems, though you must observe the following special points.

Source documents The order in which data is presented on a source document must correspond with the order in which the data is to be keyed into the computer. Also, the number of character spaces allowed for each item of data must correspond to the number allowed in the computer's store, and must be clearly marked on the source document. You will be learning more about designing these documents in Chapter 7, and you can see part of the design of a source document in figure 36 in that chapter.

Action documents and reports The design of these forms must match up with the computer's instructions about where to print each item of data on the paper. Sometimes a computer is programmed to print out the form (i.e. the headings, etc.) at the same time as it prints out the data, in which case the form design is held in the machine's electronic memory and blank sheets of paper are used.

Action documents and reports will usually be printed out on *continuous stationery*, which means that the forms or blank sheets come in very long lengths, each one separated from its neighbour by a row of perforations (rather like giant-size toilet paper). This avoids the need to feed each sheet individually into the printer. The forms are separated at the perforations after they have been filled in.

Review

1 Briefly explain why every business uses forms in its data processing.
2 Outline the steps that Mike (or an adviser) must follow in designing forms for the procedures in his business that are to be computerised.

(Ten minutes.)

Accuracy

Remember that we said at the start of this chapter that controlling data processing means controlling the presentation and the accuracy of the data that is input to the system. We have completed our survey of data presentation, and so we are now going to look at the procedures that Mike must adopt to ensure that his data is accurately entered into his DP system.

The control of accuracy

You have learned that once Mike has a computer DP errors can creep in only when the data is input, not in the subsequent (computer) processing. It is at the input stage, therefore, that he has to make his accuracy checks. These checks are of two kinds:

- Checking whether the input data is invalid (i.e. 'impossible'). This kind of check is called *data validation*. An example of invalid data in Mike's case is if he keys in an employee code number of 81, when the actual code numbers lie in the range 01 to 15. Any number lying outside this range is invalid, and if he attempts to key in 81 the computer will reject it.
- Checking whether valid data has been correctly keyed in (data may be valid yet incorrect). This second kind of check is called *data verification*. In some situations a 100% check will be carried out, which means that a second operator keys in data previously entered by the first operator. The computer checks each of the second entries as it is keyed in with the corresponding data previously keyed in and stored in its memory. If there is a discrepancy it will signal this, and the second operator must check the entries and indicate which is correct before he or she can key in further data.

In this section you will be learning about the various validation and verification checks that may be carried out on input data.

Self-check

Write down possible validation checks that Mike might use for the following items of employee data: name, age, hours worked in a week.

ANSWER

Name – possible checks are: must be less than thirty characters, these being letters, spaces, and hyphens only; age – must be two numeric digits only, within the range 16 to 70; hours worked – must be two-numeric digits only, less than sixty.

Batching

In a DP procedure the source documents may be allowed to accumulate over a period of hours or even days and then processed altogether, i.e. in a single 'run'. This is called *batching*.

Batching has a number of advantages:

- A single 'batch' of documents is easier to handle and control than many individual documents handled separately.
- The work to be done on the documents can be carried out more efficiently.
- Useful accuracy checks can be carried out on data which is input in batches.

The important advantage for us here is the last one, and we shall be looking at these checks shortly.

| *Self-check*
|
| Write down two or three everyday jobs around the house
| that involve batching.

You batch your washing up – you don't wash up the odd teacup or teaspoon, instead you let the articles accumulate and then wash them up in one go. In a similar way you 'batch' your shopping, your gardening, and many other activities.

Mike will likewise batch much of his paperwork in his present manual system. He may, for instance, let his suppliers' invoices accumulate for a couple of weeks and then deal with them in one go. The chief advantage in this is the second point above: he gets his chequebook, envelopes, stamps, remittance advice notes, cash book, invoice file, and pen together just the once, and puts them all away just the once, instead of repeatedly setting up for the job as would be the case if he processed the invoices as soon as they arrived through the post.

There is no hard-and-fast rule about batch sizes, though twenty to fifty forms in a batch would be fairly typical. It depends on the situation. Mike finds it convenient to deal with suppliers' invoices in fortnightly batches; the wholesaling business described in Chapter 5 finds it convenient to deal with sales documents in batches of eighteen.

> ## Activity
>
> Look at your answer to the activity on pages 97–8 and decide at what points in the procedure, and with what frequency, work should be batched. You may find it helpful here to look at one or two examples of batching in your workplace.

ANSWER

Works orders could be passed to production once a week (the production work could be planned on a weekly basis). Copies of the documentation could also be passed to the general office in batches, where it could be dealt with on a batch basis. Also, checking of overdue customer accounts could be carried out once a month.

Accuracy checks

Some of the main data validation and verification checks are:

Informal checks The starting-off point for many DP procedures is the completion of a source document. For example, hours worked might be recorded on clock cards, customer orders might be recorded on order forms, and consumer responses to a market survey might be recorded on questionnaire forms. If the data is being entered manually on these forms, then errors can occur, and it is the responsibility of the person filling in the form to make informal checks on his work to try to avoid errors. There are usually no formal checks at this stage, though formal validation checks on the recorded data (such as the range checks described below) may be applied later on.

Batch totals Next, the documents are normally batched for further processing. For example, clock cards might be collected at the end of the week and put into batches of fifty. It is obviously important to check that (1) cards do not go missing from the batch, and (2) the data recorded on the cards is keyed into the computer system accurately.

So verification procedures begin at the point where the documents are initially batched, by calculating one or more *batch totals*. In the case of the clock cards, for example, the employees' code numbers (which appear on the cards) might be added up, and the result written on the *batch control slip* that is attached by a rubber band to the batch. The hours worked by the employees might also be added up and the result written on the batch control slip, and this would be a second batch total.

Later, when the clock card data (i.e. the code number and hours worked of each employee) is keyed into the computer system, the computer will calculate these batch totals again. If the results agree with the figures on the batch control slip, then the computer operator knows that (1) the batch is complete, and (2) the code numbers and hours worked have been keyed in correctly.

If the figures do not agree, then an error has been made which must be rectified, either by keying in the batch again, or by comparing the data on the source documents that make up the batch (i.e. the clock cards in this case) with the keyed-in data and so locating the incorrect entry.

The first batch total in this example – the sum of the code numbers – has no use or meaning other than an error check. We call a non-informative total such as this a *hash total*. Some batch totals are not hash but are useful in themselves. The second batch total – the sum of the hours worked – is a useful figure to have, for it can be used for purposes such as calculating the total hours worked in a department.

Self-check

You are given the task of adding up 1,000 numbers correctly. How would you make use of batching to check correctness and locate errors?

My answer would be to split the numbers into batches of e.g. thirty numbers, and run a 100% check on each batch total (i.e. calculate each batch total twice). Any errors that arise are thereby restricted to certain batches and they can be quickly tracked down and corrected.

This self-check illustrates the importance of choosing an appropriate batch size. If you chose large batches, say of 500, then you would have to re-key or check through 500 numbers to find the mistake, which would be very time-consuming. If, on the other hand, you chose small batches of three or four numbers, then the batching process itself would be rather time-consuming (you would have several hundred batch totals to write down), and you would end up with a large 'batch' of batch totals to add up to get the final result, which again would lead to very lengthy checks to isolate an error that might arise in the final adding process.

Check digits This is a validation check commonly applied to numeric code numbers. The method is to build into each item's code number a digit known as a check digit, which has a certain mathematical relationship with the other digits in the number. When the number is keyed in the computer will check that this relationship holds. If it does not, a keying error has been made, and the computer will warn the operator.

One check digit method is to locate the check digit at the end (i.e. the right) of the number and to fix its value so that the following relationship holds:

$1 \times$ (right-most digit, i.e. the check digit) plus
$2 \times$ (next digit) plus
$3 \times$ (next digit) plus
$4 \times$ (next digit) plus . . .
equals a number which is divisible by 11.

Self-check

Suppose the part code of a particular stock item has six digits, and the first five digits are 32305. Using the above method try to work out what the sixth (check) digit is.

If you find this self-check difficult, here's how it is done, step-by-step. Begin by calling the check digit x, and then carry out the calculation:

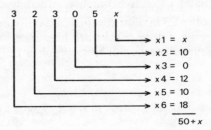

$$3 \quad 2 \quad 3 \quad 0 \quad 5 \quad x$$

$$x\,1 = x$$
$$x\,2 = 10$$
$$x\,3 = 0$$
$$x\,4 = 12$$
$$x\,5 = 10$$
$$x\,6 = 18$$
$$\overline{50 + x}$$

Now $50 + x$ must be divisible by 11, and so x, the check digit, must be 5. Hence the code number is 323055. If you operate on this number in the way described above, you will find that the result (55) is exactly divisible by 11.

The last digit of the ISBN on the back cover of this book is a check digit. You may like to check that the above calculation works on this number. You will be doing exactly what a computer does when it validates input data containing check digits.

Range checks This is another type of validation check. The computer checks that the data keyed in does not lie outside certain limits. In the clock card example the computer might compare the hours worked for each employee with the figure of 60. If the operator keys in a number larger than this, indicating that an employee has worked for more than sixty hours in the week, then the computer will request confirmation that this is in fact correct. In a similar way the computer will check that any code numbers keyed in are feasible, i.e. that they lie within the range of possible code numbers.

Other checks A common type of verification check is the *100% check*, already referred to at the start of this section. This is obviously a very time-consuming check (involving keying in each item of data twice), but it is often worth doing since in a computerised system errors can only arise at the keying-in stage, but any that do creep in at that stage will remain undetected in the system (since humans are not involved in the subsequent processing).

Another type of check is *parity checks*, carried out by the computer itself each time it moves data around from one part of its store to another. This ensures that data is not degraded during these movements. Parity checks are discussed in the section of the text dealing with computer storage (page 139).

Error action

Errors that might arise when data is keyed in can be divided into two types:

1 Errors that will affect the action documents that are produced as well as any reports.
2 Errors that will not affect the action documents but will affect the reports.

In some retail establishments both the price of a purchase and the product code is entered at the check-out till. If the price is entered wrongly the customer will be charged incorrectly and any subsequent sales analyses will also be wrong (type (1) error). If the product code is entered wrongly the customer will be charged the correct amount but the sales analyses will be wrong (type (2) error). Obviously any errors in the price should be corrected immediately, if they are spotted, but errors in the product code can be adjusted later.

If type (1) errors are detected at the data entry stage in a computer system the processing will stop and the computer will request new data. If type (2) errors are detected at the entry stage during a batch processing run (see page 121) the computer may be programmed to accept the data but it will later print out an 'error report' containing this and any other type (2) errors for subsequent correction. This avoids holding up the run and the production of action documents.

Activity

Assume that a computer is to be installed in Pinecrafts (see the Appendix) and that the employees are to be given numerical code numbers consisting of three digits. The payroll system is to be computerised, which means that instead of a clerk working out the wages manually they will be worked out by computer, on the basis of clock card data keyed in each week. (Employee details such as name, department, and tax code will be stored on the employee records in the computer store.) State what data will be keyed in from the clock cards, what accuracy checks might be carried out, and what action might be taken by the computer if it detects an error. (Three minutes.)

ANSWER

For each clock card the employee code number and the total hours worked in the week must be keyed in. (The name will not be keyed in – one of the purposes of coding is to remove the need to key in lengthy names or descriptions.)

The employee code might incorporate a check digit, a range check might be applied to the hours worked (e.g. check that the number of hours entered is less than sixty), and a batch total (the sum of the hours worked by all the employees) might also be entered and checked.

If there is any error in any of these the computer will stop processing and request new data. This is because each of these items of data is entered on the wages documents, and an error in either the code number or the hours worked will result in the worker receiving incorrect wages.

Review

1 Explain in a sentence what 'data validation' means, and give two reasons why it is widely used in electronic data processing.

2 Give three reasons why source documents are often batched in data processing.

3 Jot down two-line explanations of each of the following: *hash total*; *check digit*; *range check*.

4 | Processing data

Introduction

So far you have learned that Mike's data processing system consists of data inputs, processing, and information outputs. We have looked in some detail at the outputs he needs in order to run his business, and at the data that he must input to produce these outputs. We have also looked at the coding of input data, at the design of the forms on which it is presented, and at the checks that might be applied to make sure that it is entered correctly into a computer. Now we are going to look at the way in which it is processed.

Self-check

Can you remember what the data processing operations are? Write them down. (Look at figure 14 if you are not sure.)

Mike's data processing system records, stores, and retrieves the input data, and calculates, prints, and communicates the output information. We shall be examining the equipment used for these operations later in the chapter. To begin with, let's find out how the computer organises the data within its store and how it accesses (i.e. finds) items of stored data.

Organising data

Self-check

Think about how Mike organises his data in his present manual storage system. Jot down some of the documents on which the data is held, and how those documents are

‖ organised so that he can retrieve them easily.

Records

Mike stores his data at present on invoices, stock record cards, and on other documents. Each of these documents is a *record*.

Of course, a record does not necessarily have to be held on a sheet of paper or a card. It can be held electronically in a computer system. A definition of a 'record' which applies equally to a manual or electronic system is:

the set of data relating to an individual customer, supplier, employee, stock item, or piece of plant or equipment, or to an individual transaction such as a sale or a purchase.

A record is subdivided into what are known as *fields*. These are the spaces within the record occupied by the various items of data. Look back at the self-check on page 93. The fields shown in the answer are the employee code, the name, the sex, and the date of birth.

Keys Some records contain a special field known as the *key*. The data in this field uniquely identifies the record and distinguishes it from other records, enabling the computer to retrieve the record from amongst the mass of records in its store. In most instances a specially devised code number will be used as the key – in the example given in the last paragraph the employee code will be the key. However, an existing data field may sometimes be used as the key – Pinecrafts could use the employee name as the key in the example referred to above, filing and retrieving the records by name instead of by number.

‖ *Self-check*

‖ Study the stock record shown in figure 21. Which field is
‖ the key?

Field lengths

The first field (the stock item code number) is the key. You will notice in figure 21 that the field lengths (i.e. the number of characters in each field) are stated. In a computer system these lengths must be carefully worked out when the records are designed. Fields which are too long use up storage space unnecessarily; fields which are too short can't hold the required data. We have all filled in forms where there is more than enough space for our name, but not nearly enough for our address. On a form you can use very small handwriting to squeeze in the data, but a computer system does not allow that sort of flexibility.

Activity

Refer to your answer to the computer dating bureau activity on page 94. Some of the fields for a record held on the bureau's files might be as follows:

NAME	ADDRESS	PHONE	SEX	DATE OF BIRTH	HEIGHT	WEIGHT

Complete the list of fields and write down the length of each.
    Write down the data that would have to be keyed in if you were registered at the bureau.

HINT

You will find the examples of records and fields given in figures 21 and 22 helpful in answering this activity. For any codes that you might use, refer to your answer to the activity on page 94.
    To allow enough room for people with long names, you will probably need a name field thirty characters in length. The sex field, on the other hand, need be only one character long (for M or F), and the height field only two characters long (if height is recorded in inches).

Files

My answer to the second part of the self-check at the start of this section (on how Mike organises his documents) includes the following:

- He holds his invoices from suppliers in a lever-arch file or a ring binder marked 'Purchase invoices'.
- He holds copies of his invoices to customers in a lever-arch file marked 'Sales invoices'.
- He holds his stock record cards in a small card index system.

If Mike installs a microcomputer, then these physical boxes or folders of documents will be replaced by computer files, which are areas within the computer's storage system in which the records are held in electronic form (more about this later in the chapter). Some of the files which he will have on his computer might be:

- A sales file (containing records of customers' orders).
- A purchases file (containing records of his orders to suppliers).
- A stock file (containing his stock records).
- A customer file (containing his sales ledger records).
- A supplier file (containing his purchase ledger records).
- An employee file (containing his employee records).

Self-check

Mike has several hundred customers, each of whom use his services from time to time.

1 Write down what items of data Mike will enter on an invoice for one of these customers.
2 Distinguish between items which: **a** have no long-term use and which instead relate only to this particular transaction (one such item is the date of the job for which the customer is being invoiced); and **b** are used over a long period of time in the processing of a number of transactions (one such item is the customer's name, which will appear on all documents relating to transactions between Mike and the customer).

ANSWER

Items of data on this invoice which relate solely to this transaction are the date of the job, the description of the job, the price, and the invoice number and date.

Items of data which have a long-term use and which relate to a number of transactions are the customer's name and address (and also of course Mike's name and address and VAT number).

Transaction files and master files

The first sort of data in the above self-check, which relates to that transaction only, is called *transaction data*. The second sort of data, which is used over and over again in the processing of a number of transactions, is called *standing data*. Corresponding to these two sorts of data there are two sorts of files:

- *transaction files*, which hold the transaction data;
- *master files*, which hold the standing data.

Let's look at these in turn.

Transaction files For each type of transaction that is processed by the computer, there will be a transaction file. So there will be, for example, a transaction file for the sales, and another transaction file for the purchases.

Transaction data is added to a transaction file at the time when (or shortly after) the transaction takes place, and it is deleted from the file after the transaction has been processed. The data on transaction files is therefore impermanent, and it changes daily.

Self-check

Jot down how you think the transaction data will be organised on a transaction file.

As with all files, transaction files organise the data into fields in records. There will be a record for each transaction of the day, containing the data for that transaction. The computer always processes these records in the order in which they have been keyed on to the file – it never searches through the file for a particular record – and so transaction records do not need keys.

The first two files in the list given in the previous subsection are transaction files. Other transaction files are stock receipts and issues, and cash receipts.

Master files These hold the standing data on the business's customers, suppliers, employees, and stock. The last four files in the list in the previous subsection are master files.

Unlike transaction files, the computer often needs to pick out an individual record from a master file. For example, the computer will need to look up particular items on a product file when an invoice is being produced, in order to enter the product details and the price. So the records on these files must contain keys, and they will be held on these files in key order. (If you are not sure why, revise the subsection on keys on page 110.)

Two kinds of standing data

The standing data held on master files is of two kinds:

- reference data;
- master data.

Reference data is fixed data, i.e. it does not change from week to week. Customers' names and addresses, and stock descriptions and prices, are examples of reference data. This data is used in the processing of transaction data but it is not altered by that processing. Customer names and addresses, for example, are printed on sales documents when customer orders are processed, but are otherwise unaffected by the processing.

Master data, on the other hand, is data on the master files which is updated during processing. Stock levels are an example of stock file master data – they must be adjusted as a result of filling customers' orders.

Self-check

What transaction files and master files will a firm like Pinecrafts use in preparing the payroll and employees' payslips, and what transaction data, reference data, and master data will these files contain?

ANSWER

Transaction file: a file containing the week's clock card data; transaction data: works number and hours worked of each employee; master file: the employee records; reference data: includes works number, name, wage rate, tax code, and fixed deductions for each employee; master data: cumulative gross pay, cumulative taxable pay, cumulative tax paid for each employee.

Example of a master file

Figure 21 (overleaf) shows the data that might be held on a stock file. The figure lists the fields contained in each stock record, together with a description of the data held in each field and the field sizes. An example is given in the first column of the data for one particular stock record.

The complete record for the particular stock item is:

WID234-010SILVER WIDGETS – BOX OF 10
COMM12300000050000001250000100000020000005.

(NB The description field is thirty characters long, hence the gap of four spaces after 'BOX OF 10'.)

The complete file will consist of many hundreds or thousands of such stock records.

Self-check

Which of the data in figure 21 is reference data, and which is master data?

ANSWER

The first six fields in the figure contain reference data, the last three contain master data.

Example of a transaction file

Figure 22 shows the data held on records in a stock transaction file. An example transaction for the stock record given above is included (column 1).

Field	Description	Field type	Field length
Stock number (e.g. WID234-010)	A code uniquely identifying this part	Alphanumeric	10
Stock description (e.g. SILVER WIDGETS – BOX OF 10)	The description of this stock item	Alphanumeric	30
Product group (e.g. COMM, this stands for COMponents Misc.)	The code of the broad product category into which this stock item falls	Alphanumeric	4
Last supplier (e.g. 123)	The code of the supplier from whom this item was last purchased	Numeric	3
Cost price (e.g. 50p. This will be written 00000050)	The cost value of this item	Numeric	8 (££££££pp)
Selling price (e.g. £1.25)	The price at which this item is sold	Numeric	8 (££££££pp)
Quantity in stock (e.g. 10)	The quantity currently in the warehouse	Numeric	6
Quantity ordered (e.g. 20)	The number of units required to fill existing sales orders	Numeric	6
Quantity allocated (e.g. 5)	The number of units earmarked against specific orders	Numeric	6

Figure 21. Design of a master file

Field	Description	Field type	Field length
Transaction date (e.g. 840623, this is 23 June 84)	Date of keying	Numeric	6 (YYMMDD)
Transaction type (e.g. R)	Type of transaction: R – stock receipt A – stock adjustment S – stock-take amendment I – stock issue	Alphanumeric	1
Transaction ref. number (e.g. 00027)	Unique number assigned serially by the computer to this transaction	Numeric	5
Batch number (e.g. 020)	The number of the batch of which this transaction is part	Numeric	3
Stock number to be changed (e.g. WID234-010)	The key of the stock item to be adjusted on the master file	Alphanumeric	10
Change quantity (e.g. 000035)	Quantity by which 'Quantity in stock' field on master file changed	Numeric	6 (can be positive – for receipts – or negative – for issues)
Unit cost price (e.g. 50p)	Cost of each unit purchased	Numeric	8 (££££££pp)
Comment field (e.g. 5 DAMAGED, RETURNED TO SUPPLIER)	Operator's comment (optional)	Alphanumeric	30

Figure 22. Design of a transaction file

Self-check

Write down the transaction record for the example shown in figure 22.

PART-ANSWER

The record begins: '840623R00027 . . .'

Review

1 Write two-line notes explaining each of the following terms: record, field, key, file.
2 Explain in two or three sentences the distinction between transaction files and master files.
3 Design the employee master file for Pinecrafts. Your design should follow the format given in figure 21. (The records will include the reference data and master data given in the answer to the self-check on pages 114–15; look at a payslip to get an idea of what each item of data will look like and the field lengths.)

Accessing data

So far in this chapter you have learned how the computer organises the data in its store. In this section you will learn how the computer *accesses* (i.e. finds) stored data so that it can retrieve and process it. (Note that, in contrast to a manual system, retrieval does not mean that the records are removed from the files. It means that they are copied into the working area of the computer system. You will be learning more about this later in the chapter.)

In a computer system there are two access methods:

● sequential access;
● random access.

Let's look at these in turn.

Sequential access

In this access method the computer accesses every record in the file, starting at the first record and reading the rest in the sequence in which they are stored until it reaches the last record. In the case of a master file this means accessing the records in key sequence (since that is the sequence in which they are stored), while in the case of a transaction file it means accessing them in chronological sequence (since in these files each new record is simply added on to the end of the rest).

Sequential access is used in applications where all the records in a file have to be accessed and processed. An example in the case of master files is the production of monthly statements. Every customer's account details held on the customer file must be accessed in order to produce the statements. Another example is stock reporting – every record on the stock file must be accessed to produce a full stock report. Records on transaction files are usually read in the order in which they are stored, and so transaction files lend themselves to sequential access.

Self-check

Write down another computer application requiring sequential access from a master file.

ANSWER

There are several. One is producing the payroll (every employee must be included), another is printing an aged debtors' list (every customer's account must be checked).

Random access

Random access allows the computer to pick out individual records from a file. The access device in this case is able to go straight to the spot in the store where the record is held (see page 141). Transaction files are not usually accessed randomly, but master files generally need to be accessed both randomly (in some applications) and sequentially (in others). An example of a random access application is stock adjustment, where the computer has to pick out particular stock records for updating with the latest receipts and issues.

Self-check

What is the sequence in which non-fiction books are stored in a library? Jot down how you would go about finding a particular book – for example this book – on the library shelves.

The non-fiction books in a library are held in key sequence (i.e. code number order). To locate a particular book you don't have to search through every shelf, you can look up the code number of the book you want in a card index and go straight to the spot on the shelves where the book is held.

A common computer random access method works in a similar way. It is called *indexed sequential access*. The records are stored in key sequence in the file, but an index is provided which allows the computer to pinpoint the location of a specific record without needing to read through all the preceding records in the file. If necessary, of course, the records can be read off the file sequentially.

Self-check

Which of the following applications require random access, and which require sequential access: printing paycheques, checking the credit status of a customer, checking the quantity in stock of a stock item?

ANSWER

Sequential access should be used for paycheques – the employee details are read off the file in key (i.e. employee number) sequence. The other two applications are random access – they require the computer to pinpoint a specific record on the file.

Review

Briefly explain what you understand by sequential access and random access. In what sequence are records stored on transaction files, and in what sequence are they commonly stored on master files? Why are transaction files normally accessed sequentially, and master files both sequentially and randomly? (Half a page.)

Processing data

Having looked at the ways in which the computer organises and accesses the data in its store we must now turn to the way in which it processes that data. To begin with, you need to understand the two ways in which computer processing can be organised:

- batch processing;
- real-time processing.

Batch processing

This is the type of processing that the computer carries out when it handles data in batches. One batch processing application is the production of management reports, which involves retrieving and analysing large quantities of data. Another is the production of monthly statements, where the computer prints out all the firm's statements in a single 'run'.

It is important that you understand how the computer handles the input and storage of transaction data in batch processing applications. The input data is keyed in and temporarily stored as transaction records on transaction files. Over a period of time large 'batches' of transaction records accumulate on these files, and periodically (perhaps once or twice a day) the computer processes these batches in a single 'run'.

This way of organising the handling of transaction data has the advantage that the batch 'runs' can be scheduled for times in the day when the computer is not heavily used, leaving peak periods clear for work that cannot be handled in this way, but it has the disadvantage that the master data on the master files is normally slightly out of date.

Self-check

Explain in a sentence or two why the master data on the stock file will be slightly out of date if goods inwards data is processed in a batch way. (Read the explanation of master data on page 114 if you are not sure.)

The master data on the stock file is the stock balances. In batch processing the transaction data on stock receipts (in the goods inwards department) will be held initially on a transaction file, and it is only later in the day that that data will be processed and the master file updated. So in the period between the receipt of particular items of stock and the updating of the master file during the batch processing run, the stock balances will be out of date.

During or after the batch run the data on the transaction file is used to print out an *audit trail*, i.e. a record of transactions. This helps the auditors later on when they want to trace transactions through the system (see page 229). It is at this time also that error reports are printed listing any invalid data (page 104). After these tasks have been carried out the transaction data is deleted from the file.

Real-time processing

This is the type of processing that the computer carries out when it inputs and handles items of data individually rather than in batches. In this case the items of transaction data are not first accumulated on transaction files; they are immediately processed and used to update the master data on the master files. After this, however, they are copied to transaction files, the purpose of these files being solely to produce the audit trails.

This processing method has the advantage that the master files are always up to date. The disadvantage is that it makes heavy use of the computer during busy periods. However, the steadily increasing power of computers is lessening the importance of this disadvantage, with the result that there has been a shift in recent years away from batch processing towards real-time processing for many applications.

Self-check

Think about and jot down how sales order processing (i.e. input of sales orders, production of sales documents, and update of master files) might be carried out using each of these processing methods.

Example: sales order processing

Sales order processing can be carried out either in a batch manner, or in a combination of batch and real-time, or in a real-time manner;

1 *Batch* In this the orders are keyed on to the transaction file, with a batch run of this file later to update the master files and print out the sales documentation and the picking list (i.e. the list of stock items to be picked off the warehouse shelves to fill orders).
2 *Batch/real-time* In this case the orders are keyed in in a real-time manner, so that the master file is updated immediately. There will be a batch run later to print the sales documentation and the picking list.
3 *Real-time* In this case the orders are keyed in in a real-time manner, updating the master files and printing the sales documentation and a picking list for each order immediately it is keyed.

Data processing activities

From what I have said so far you can see that files are central to data processing. Every DP procedure involves storing data on files and retrieving it. Not only must the sort of activities mentioned in the above example be carried out, but periodic management reports must be produced from the data on master files, reference data must be kept up to date, and inquiries have to be dealt with. The complete list of DP activities is as follows:

1 Transaction processing This includes the activities in the above example – recording transaction details on transaction files, updating master files, and printing audit trails. It also includes looking up (i.e. 'referencing') data on master files in order to process the transaction data, and printing out action documents. For example, to process a customer's order the product details (such as price) must be looked up and these will be used in the invoice calculations and will ultimately be printed on the invoice and on other sales documents.

2 Reporting That is, referencing data on the master files to produce reports.

3 Inquiries Looking up data on master files when queries arise. For example, when a sales order is received it may be necessary to look up the credit status of the customer on the customer file or check the stock balance of an item on the stock file.

4 File maintenance Keeping the reference data on the master files up to date. Customers' addresses may change, new parts may be added to stock and other parts deleted, new employees may join the firm and old employees leave. All these changes must be noted on the files. This is not part of transaction processing (for the changes are not transaction data), but it will be done as a special file maintenance job.

Self-check

Read the description of the procedure for paying a supplier on page 32. The master file used in this procedure is the supplier (i.e. purchase ledger) file. Write down the activities that will be carried out on this file. (Refer to the above list of activities to answer this.)

ANSWER

The amounts invoiced and the amounts paid must be entered on this file, and these amounts must be looked up when checking suppliers' statements and making payments (transaction processing). Supplier information such as names and addresses must be kept up to date (file maintenance), and queries will sometimes arise on the amounts owed to certain suppliers (inquiries). Monthly supplier activity reports analysing purchases will also be produced (reporting).

Self-check

To carry out these activities the computer must perform the basic DP operations of recording, storing, retrieving, calculating, printing, and communicating data. For each of the above four activities list the operations that the computer must perform.

You will be learning how the computer carries out these operations in the rest of this chapter. My answer to this self-check is:

1 Transaction processing – all of the operations.
2 Reporting – retrieving, calculating, and printing.
3 Inquiries – retrieving and printing.
4 Maintenance – recording and storing.

The operation of communicating data is involved in each one, for each part of the computer system must communicate with the other parts in order to carry out the activities. Thus data that is input to the recording device must be communicated to the storage device, which in turn will communicate it to the calculating part of the system and to the printing device.

Review

1 Explain in two or three sentences the difference between batch processing and real-time processing.
2 Outline the activities that will be carried out on the customer file in a computer system. (Write your answer in the way that I have written my answer to the last-but-one self-check.) You will find the description on what's involved in collecting payments from customers on page 29 helpful here.

How computers work

What is a computer?

To understand how a computer carries out the DP operations (record, store, retrieve, calculate, print, communicate) you must first appreciate what computers are and how they work.

Computers and other electronic gadgetry sometimes seem mysterious and incomprehensible. At their heart, however, is something very simple: lots of tiny switches. The microprocessor (or silicon chip) is, in fact, thousands of minute switches embedded in a sliver of silicon.

A switch is either 'on' or 'off'. Thus it allows an electrical current either to flow or not flow. An item of data is stored inside a computer as a sequence of switches in various 'on'/'off' positions, and it is communicated by a sequence of electrical pulses down a wire, an 'on' switch allowing a pulse to flow, an 'off' switch resulting in the absence of a pulse. Thus the switch sequence 'on/off/on/on' results in a pulse/no-pulse/pulse/pulse sequence flowing down a wire.

This can be converted to a sequence of magnetised/demagnetised spots on the surface of a magnetic disc or tape, or into a sequence of holes/no-holes on paper tape or cards. (You will be learning about magnetic discs, etc. later in this chapter.) So the above sequence would appear as a hole/no-hole/hole/hole sequence on paper tape.

Binary code

To store data as a switch, hole, or magnetised spot sequence the computer must first convert it to a code consisting of two digits only, one digit representing an 'on' switch (or magnetised spot, or hole), the other representing an 'off' switch (or demagnetised spot, or no-hole). This two-digit code is called *binary code* ('binary' comes from the Latin for 'two'), and each digit is called a *binary digit*, or 'bit' for short. The two digits that are always used in this code are the numbers 0 and 1. 0 represents an 'off' switch, 1 represents an 'on' switch.

Self-check

Write down the switch sequence given above in binary code.

The 'on/off/on/on' sequence is 1011 in binary code. This code number does not mean 'one thousand and eleven'. Let's see what it does mean.

Numbers in binary

Binary code can be used to represent either numbers or letters. If it is used to represent numbers, then the coding system is:

```
   0 represents zero
   1 represents one
  10 represents two
  11 represents three
 100 represents four
 101 represents five
 110 represents six
 111 represents seven
1000 represents eight
1001 represents nine
1010 represents ten
and so on
```

Any number can be represented in this way by a sequence of 0s and 1s. You can add, subtract, multiply, and divide numbers in binary, just as you can in our everyday number system, and computers do in fact do this when they carry out calculations. However, you do not need to be able to do this yourself to understand computers.

Self-check

Study the above list of binary numbers, and try to spot the pattern. Then write down what the binary number 1011 represents. Write down the number twelve in binary digits.

ANSWER

1011 is eleven, twelve is 1100. The pattern in binary numbers is the same as the pattern in our everyday numbers, except that all numbers which include any of the digits 2 to 9 are omitted.

Text in binary

Alphabetical characters, and therefore text, can be similarly represented in binary code. A simple way of doing this would be to represent A by 0, B by 1, C by 10, and so on. Various systems have been adopted, the one used on microcomputers being the ASCII system:

A = 1000001
B = 1000010
C = 1000011
and so on.

Other symbols such as brackets, £, etc. can be similarly represented in binary code.

Self-check

When you strike a key on a computer keyboard a sequence of pulse/no-pulses is sent down the wire to the computer. Representing a pulse by 1 and a no-pulse by 0, write down what sequence of bits (binary digits) will be sent when you key the word MIKE.

ANSWER

1001101
1001001
1001011
1000101

Image and voice in binary

If you look at a photograph in the *Radio Times* or in one of the national dailies you'll see that it is made up of lots of tiny dots. It is, in fact, a very long sequence of dots which, if suitably coded, could be converted to a sequence of electrical pulses sent down a wire. The surface of a videodisc, under a microscope, can be seen to consist of an enormously long sequence of holes/no-holes. Both of these are examples of image converted to binary digital form.

Moving on to hi-fi, you have probably heard of digital recordings. (The word 'digital' normally means 'binary digital'.) To produce these, speech and music are converted to (binary) digital form, and recorded as a sequence of holes/no-holes on the surface of a disc.

So you can see that all forms of information – numbers, text, image, and voice – can be handled in the same way using the same equipment. They can be sent down a wire, and they can be stored inside a computer.

Analogue systems

In the everyday world information doesn't normally come to us in digital form. Visual information reaches us by light waves, spoken information reaches us by sound waves. A conventional disc recording is produced simply by duplicating the sound waves in the air by minute waves along the groove of disc. As the disc rotates these waves move relative to the stylus and so can be converted back into sound waves. (The old-fashioned '78' records could be played simply by moving a pin attached to a paper cone along the groove.) The word 'analogue' is used to describe information and devices of this sort.

Self-check

Write down three commonly used analogue devices.

ANSWER

Traditional watches (i.e. those with hands, not the digital variety); rulers; ordinary kitchen scales; the telephone; tape recorders; cameras.

Digital and analogue systems compared

In essence, analogue devices measure things, whereas digital devices count things. For example, a sundial measures the movement of a shadow, and a traditional watch measures the movement of tiny cogwheels, but a digital watch counts the oscillations of a quartz crystal. All of the devices in the answer to the above self-check measure things: time, length, weight, sound, and light.

For every analogue device there is often a digital device that will do the same thing and will do it better. For example, the traditional slide-rule has been replaced by the electronic calculator, traditional scales by electronic scales, traditional watches by digital watches, and so on. The advantages of digital devices over analogue devices are:

- Counting is absolutely accurate, but measuring is not. You can count the number of people in the room in which you are now sitting and be completely certain that you have the right answer, but if I asked you to measure the height of the person sitting next to you you could not do it accurately. In the same way digital recordings give faultless reproduction because the equipment is counting holes, whereas analogue recordings involve measuring waves and give imperfect results. Using digital equipment you could copy a recording over and over again and you would still get a faultless result, even on the hundredth copy. This is because a hole is always copied to a hole is always copied to a hole. With a conventional recording there is a drop in quality when a copy is made.
- Analogue equipment usually has moving parts in it, it is expensive to manufacture, and it wears out. Digital equipment is based on solid-state electronic devices which are usually cheap to manufacture and which don't wear out. The computers used in business are digital devices, and so they are cheap, reliable, and completely accurate.

Review

Explain in a couple of sentences why word processing equipment (for handling text) is virtually identical to small business computer equipment (for handling data). Give two reasons why this equipment is replacing traditional office equipment.

OUTLINE ANSWER

Text and data can both be converted to digital form, and so can be handled by the same digital equipment. Digital equipment is accurate and reliable, and is relatively cheap.

Recording data

In the rest of this chapter we're going to look at how the DP operations are carried out, both in Mike's present manual system and in the computerised system that he hopes to install. Manual processing is important, even today, and some office tasks are best done manually.

Self-check

Before we start, jot down what the DP operations are, and what 'manual data processing' means.

The first DP operation is recording the input data. This is always done by either

1 writing it by hand, or
2 entering it via a keyboard, or
3 dictating it.

Manual data processing includes the use of mechanical equipment such as typewriters and dictating machines, but it excludes computers and associated electronic equipment.

Later in this chapter you will be learning about storing, calculating, printing, and communicating data.

Manual methods for recording data

In manual data processing, options (1) and (2) above always involve filling in a form which is then used for further processing. Even in electronic data processing systems the first step often involves completing a source document by hand. Handwriting is often an appropriate method if forms are filled in on the factory bench or in the cab of a lorry or elsewhere outside the office. However, if neatness is important, then the form should be filled in by typewriter.

The electronic typewriter is starting to replace the traditional 'office electric' for reasons that I have already outlined (see page 74). We can class this as a piece of 'manual' equipment since it is normally used as part of a manual DP system. (We can class the electronic calculator similarly.)

If text rather than numerical data is to be recorded then dictation systems may be used. The recording medium is normally tape cassettes, and these allow up to an hour's recording on each side and they can be used in recorders as small as 6 cm by 11 cm. The recorded text will normally, of course, be transcribed on to paper by an audio-typist.

One DP option which should be investigated by Mike is the *posting board*. This is a large board (about 70 cm by 50 cm) with a row of metal pegs down one side. The forms that are used with posting boards have a row of matching holes at the side, and this allows them to be accurately aligned on top of each other on the board. The forms may be carbon backed, or they may be the 'no-carbon-required' variety (see page 98), and entries made on the top form will be reproduced automatically on the forms below. If Mike uses this system for his payroll, for example, he will be able to record entries simultaneously on the paycheques, the wage slips, and the payroll sheet. This system obviously saves a lot of time, and it eliminates the possibility of introducing errors through copying. Of course, the various forms must be designed so that common data appears in the same location on each.

Self-check

Write down what other applications a posting board might have in Mike's business.

PART-ANSWER

The sales ledger might be kept in this way. The customer's

statement and the entries to the ledger can be completed at the same time.

Electronic methods for recording data

Handwriting Data can be handwritten into an electronic system by means of an *electronic writing pad*. In some versions of this device the characters (capital letters and numbers) have to be written in defined squares on a pressure-sensitive surface. The electronic gadgetry connected to the sensors beneath the surface recognises the characters and converts them to binary digital form for entry to the computer. The latest version of the pad detects not pressure but low frequency signals emitted by the point of a special pen, and it can recognise ordinary handwriting written (neatly) on any area of the surface.

It is also possible to convert a sheet of handwritten data (capital letters and numbers) to digital form for computer entry by feeding it into an *optical character reader*. This device works by scanning each line of text and recognising the characters written there. However, it is mainly used for reading typed rather than handwritten text, which it feeds into a word processor for editing.

Keyboards Handwritten data entry devices are expensive and not widely used. Most entry to an electronic system is by means of a *keyboard*, which converts keystrokes to electrical impulses in digital form. The traditional typewriter keyboard layout is almost always used. This is called a QWERTY keyboard, because the first six characters on it, reading from the top left, are Q, W, E, R, T, and Y. These devices are becoming so common that keyboard training for all types of office staff is now almost mandatory.

Dictation Speech recognition devices are now available which can recognise a few hundred spoken words in English and convert them to digital form for computer entry. In Japan, where the spoken language is phonetically much simpler than English, word processors are now available which can recognise any

spoken word and which therefore accept dictated text as input
and produce automatically a typed copy. Some experts claim
that similar systems for English will be available by the turn of
the century, and that keyboards will then be obsolete.

Punched cards and paper tape To complete this survey of recording methods we should also mention punched cards and paper
tape. In this case data is keyed into a special sort of keyboard
known as a *keypunch*, which translates each letter or number
into a pattern of holes across the width of the card or the tape.

Paper tape is normally eight hole positions wide, seven of
which are used to represent the letter or number, the eighth
representing a parity check digit to ensure that the character is
read off the tape correctly. The way in which this check works is
explained on page 139.

Each hole that is punched represents the binary digit 1, a no-
hole (i.e. an unpunched hole position) represents the digit 0. For
example, if I key in the number 6, this is converted to 0000110 in
binary code, i.e. no-hole/no-hole/no-hole/no-hole/hole/hole/no-
hole across the width of the tape. (Check back to page 127,
where you will see that six in binary is 110; zeros are written in
front of this number to fill up the seven positions.)

Self-check

Write down the hole/no-hole sequence for the number 8
and the letter B. (Write down first the binary codes – see
pages 127 and 128 for help – then write zeros in front as
necessary to fill up the seven hole positions. Then convert
to a hole/no-hole sequence.)

ANSWER

No-hole/no-hole/no-hole/hole/no-hole/no-hole/no-hole.
Hole/hole/no-hole/no-hole/no-hole/hole/no-hole.

Paper tape is usually an inch wide, a typical reel being about
1,000 ft long and able to hold 120,000 characters. A reel of tape
can therefore hold a large number of records. Punched cards, on
the other hand, are about 7½ by 3¼ inches, and contain eighty

columns of holes. A punched card can therefore hold eighty characters, which is sufficient for only a single record. So a reel of tape can hold the data on many invoices (for example), whereas a punched card can hold only one invoice.

A stack of punched cards, however, can be rearranged in a different order, and out-of-date cards can be removed and new cards inserted. A reel of paper tape cannot be altered.

Punched cards and paper tape were formerly widely used as a way of entering data into a computer, and they are still used in some installations. The operator keys the data on to the cards or paper tape, and later runs the cards or tape through a reader connected to the computer. This seems a roundabout way of doing things, but the point is that card or paper tape readers operate at very high speeds, and a large amount of data can be read by this means into a computer in a short time. Computer time used to be very expensive, and so considerable savings could be made.

Over the years computers have become more and more powerful, and costs have steadily fallen. Since the 1970s it has been economical to enter data directly via a keyboard without the intermediate stage of cards or paper tape. This is known as *direct entry*. The data in this case is usually stored on a magnetic disc (see next section), and so the data entry method is also called 'key-to-disc'.

Finally, you should note that a machine which does a computer-related task (such as punching cards) while not connected to the computer is known as an *off-line* device. A machine which does its job while connected to the computer is known as an *on-line* device. A card reader is an example of an on-line device.

Self-check

Which of the following are on-line devices? A microcomputer keyboard, a keyboard for typing source documents, a disc drive.

ANSWER

The first and last.

Review

What are the three main ways of recording data? Write a couple of sentences on each briefly explaining how it is applied in electronic data processing.

Storing data

Earlier in this chapter you learned that data is stored in records on files. In this section you will learn about the methods and equipment used for this. We are now, of course, into the second DP operation (storing and retrieving). We shall follow the pattern adopted in the previous section, and look at manual methods first, then electronic methods.

Activity

Obtain an office equipment supplier's catalogue, and look through the pages dealing with filing systems.

Manual storage methods

The records that make up a manual file may be stored in folders, lever-arch files, card indexes, or record books. In a small business like Mike's, lever-arch files will be used to hold invoices and other documents, and books will be used for records of sales and purchases and of cash received and paid. A larger business, however, has many more records to look after, and requires a more complex storage system. The manual records in this case will normally be held in folders, usually called *file jackets*. For example, there will be a file jacket for each employee, with his name and code number on the spine, holding all records and correspondence relating to him.

During its lifetime this file jacket (plus contents) will be housed in three kinds of storage system:

Temporary storage during processing When the records in this jacket are being referenced (e.g. an employee is being considered for transfer or promotion), it will be held temporarily in an immediately accessible place, such as an in-tray on a desk.

Current mass storage This term is used to describe systems for holding the mass of files which are 'current' (i.e. likely to be called up at any time) but which are not presently in use. Although the files in this system are not immediately to hand as are those in temporary storage, they are being constantly withdrawn and the system must provide for their rapid retrieval. To assist this the files will be held in an orderly way, for example alphabetically (by name) or numerically (by code number), and the physical storage method will allow for easy access to the files.

There are several possible current mass storage methods:

- *Lateral storage*, in which the file jackets are stacked like books on shelves and withdrawn laterally. Lateral storage equipment ranges from simple open shelves to lockable cabinets in which the files are held in pockets suspended from rails. In the latter system each jacket is assigned a specific pocket, so minimising the possibility of replacing the jacket in the wrong location.
- *Vertical storage*, in which the files are stacked in cabinet drawers and withdrawn vertically. Again, the files will normally be held in suspended pickets.
- *Rotary storage*, in which the containers that house the files rotate horizontally or vertically, thus allowing the office worker to insert or extract files while sitting down.

> *Optional activity*
>
> Lateral storage is reckoned to be the best option for most offices. Next time you visit your library try to find out why. Look in the secretarial studies section of the library, or if possible read the article on filing in the February 1983 edition of *Mind Your Own Business*.

Archival mass storage Files which are no longer current and therefore likely to be referred to only infrequently in the future will normally be held in a low-cost storage system. Mike, for example, may keep lever-arch files containing previous years' invoices in his roof. These records have such little usage that the long retrieval time is of small consequence. Records on computer files which are more than a few months old and unlikely to be referred to in the future may be printed out on paper and stored in this sort of system. They are then deleted from the computer files, so keeping the files down to a manageable size.

Of course, records which are known to have no further future use should not be stored but destroyed. (Note, however, that there is a legal requirement to keep invoices and books of account for at least six years.) Many organisations review records in rotation – perhaps a shelf each week – and weed out those whose usefulness has lapsed.

Activity

Think about the ways in which you store your household and other bills. Can you classify the storage stages in the three ways given above?

Going through your old records and weeding out those that are no longer needed is obviously a time-consuming process. What problems would arise if it were not done?

Microfilm

Some large organisations store their records on *microfilm*. This involves taking tiny photographs of the records, each one being a 16 mm black-and-white transparency, called a 'frame'. The original documents are then destroyed, and the microfilm can be stored in a very small amount of space. You can view the frames on a microfilm viewer, or print out a hard copy (an enlargement on paper).

There are several microfilm formats. Like ordinary photographic transparencies, they can be held sequentially in long rolls (in cassettes or cartridges) or they can be held individually in cardboard mounts (called 'aperture cards'). The most popular format, however, is *microfiche*, a sheet of film of A6 size (105 mm by 148 mm) holding some 200 frames. This book could be produced on a single microfiche, for a fraction of conventional printing costs.

Microfilm systems are sometimes used for archival storage only, but with the right equipment they can be very efficient and suitable for current mass storage. Photography of the original documents and indexing of the frames is fast and automatic, and with computerised retrieval systems any frame can be located in under thirty seconds. It might be thought that microfilm frames suffer from the disadvantage that they cannot be updated (because photographs can't be altered), but in fact it is possible, with one type of microfilm, to erase out-of-date data and over-write new data.

However, the disadvantage of microfilm for current mass storage is the high cost of the sophisticated retrieval equipment, and in practice only large organisations use it for this purpose.

Electronic storage methods

As with manual storage, I shall discuss these under the headings temporary storage, current mass storage, and archival mass storage.

Temporary storage This refers to the internal working area of the computer, or 'memory', which holds data during processing. In modern computers this is in the form of silicon chips. As I mentioned earlier, a silicon chip is made up of what are in effect many thousands of tiny switches, each of which can store one binary digit (bit).

These switches are organised in groups of eight, each such group being known as a *byte*. So one byte contain eight bits. The largest binary number that can be stored in a byte is 11111111, which is 255 in our everyday number system. To store larger values than this it is necessary to group two or more bytes together. A commonly used group consists of four bytes, and this is called a *word*. A word contains $4 \times 8 = 32$ bits, and this will store values up to almost 43 million.

A byte always contains one bit which is used as a parity check. The purpose of this is to ensure that no errors occur in copying data from one part of the computer system to another, and it works like this: if the number of 1s in the binary number is odd, then the parity bit will be set at 1, but if the number of 1s is even, the parity bit will be set at 0. So there will always be an even number of 1s in a byte, and the computer will check that this is the case each time it copies data from one part of its store to another. If this condition is not fulfilled, the computer will copy the data again. The parity check digit on paper tape, mentioned in the last section works in the same way.

In some parity check systems the number of 1s in a byte is required to be odd, in which case the parity bit setting will be the opposite of that described above.

Chips and other electronic storage devices are rated according the number of thousands of bits they can hold. A thousand bits is a Kbit, normally shortened to K. A popular chip size is 64K, meaning that it can store around 64,000 bits. Chips are available that can store up to 256K.

Chips are normally installed in microcomputers in groups of eight. Since 8 bits = 1 byte, this means that a microcomputer with eight 64K chips (for example) has a total memory capacity of 64,000 bytes, i.e. 64 Kbytes. As a guide to what this means in concrete terms, a byte will hold one alphabetical character, the average word of text is four or five characters long, and a chapter of this book averages around 10,000 words, i.e. 40,000 to 50,000 bytes.

Self-check

How much of this book will a group of eight 256K chips hold? How many bytes of storage would be needed to hold this page of text?

ANSWER

About five chapters. About 1,500.

Current mass storage Memory chips are not used for the long-term mass storage of data. One reason is the limited storage capacity of chips compared to other devices; another is the fact that everything stored on a chip is lost when the electricity is turned off. Solid-state memory devices are being developed which can hold very large amounts of data and which don't lose their contents when the electricity is off – these will therefore be suitable for long-term mass storage. One example is the bubble memory, which uses minute magnetic 'bubbles' to store the data.

At the moment, however, magnetic disc and magnetic tape

are the only feasible mass storage media, although disc and tape drives are not solid-state and so are relatively expensive and subject to wear. With these you can store an indefinitely large amount of data, simply by adding discs or tapes.

Magnetic tape is the most inexpensive way of storing data. This is why the typical home computer stores data on ordinary cassettes using ordinary cassette recorders. The disadvantage of tape as a storage medium is that the data has to be accessed sequentially, in other words in the order in which it was recorded. As you have learned earlier in this chapter, it is often necessary to access data randomly, i.e. in any order.

Magnetic discs, and in fact the memory chips I spoke of above, allow you to access data randomly. With disc the tracking arm skims across the rotating surface to locate the required data. The rotation and the tracking arm speeds are very high, giving an access time measured in thousandths of a second. Alternatively the tracking arm can start at the beginning of the disc and read through to the end, giving sequential access.

However, disc drives are more expensive than tape drives (a single microcomputer disc drive costs ten or twenty times the price of a cassette recorder), and the discs are more expensive than tape. A single 'floppy disc' (the small discs used on microcomputer systems) costs about £2 and will hold about two chapters of this book, whereas a tape cassette costs about £1 and will store rather more than this. In spite of this relatively high cost, small business computer systems invariably employ disc rather than tape storage, and tape is beginning to disappear as a storage option on large computer systems. The reason is that the versatility of disc (random access as well as sequential access) is most important in business applications.

Archival mass storage Records which are no longer current should be deleted from a computer system. Once a customer's order is filled, for instance, the details of it should be erased from the order file. However, a query may arise later on that order, and so some sort of record does need to be kept. One solution is to store the original source documents (in this case the customer order forms) in a manual system.

Another option is 'computer output on microfilm', or COM for short. As its name implies, this involves copying data held in computer storage on to microfilm. The equipment available for doing this is fast and automatic, and, as mentioned previously, it is possible to update microfilm records.

Although the copying and the computerised retrieval equipment is expensive and therefore limited to large organisations (see the previous subsection), and the retrieval time can't match the extremely short times that are possible in electronic systems, COM has one important advantage over the latter. The microfilm readers (which work by projecting a microfilm frame on to a screen) are inexpensive, and it is therefore feasible to provide every potential user with one. Computer terminals, in contrast, are expensive and cannot normally be provided on this basis.

Activity

Microfilm is widely used in banks and in libraries. If you have not met this way of storing data you might go along to your local library to see one in use.

Review

Mike intends to buy a small business computer system and wonders what data storage systems he will need. Briefly explain, with reasons, why tape cassette storage and COM are unsuitable for him, and outline the equipment that he will need. (Ten minutes.)

OUTLINE ANSWER

Tape cassette does not allow random access, which is essential for most applications. COM equipment is prohibitively expensive for him, and is in any case designed for large organisations. He will need some manual files for archival storage of e.g. source documents, though the manual files he uses at present for current mass storage will be replaced by floppy discs.

Calculating data

Calculating, or 'computing', means adding, subtracting, multiplying, and dividing numbers, and also comparing one number with another. Whether Mike is sizing up a customer's room, preparing a quotation, calculating wages, invoicing customers, or controlling his financial affairs, he is computing.

'Computing' is the point in a DP procedure at which decisions are taken. Refer back to pages 50 and 52 for detail on this. For example, a clerk or a computer might compare the total amounts received from a customer with the total amount owed, and print a reminder letter if the former is less than the latter. The 'print if receipts less than amounts owing' step in the procedure is a programmable decision (see Chapter 2).

Computations are carried out in part of the internal working memory of the computer. In the case of a large computer this part is called the arithmetic logic unit, or ALU. You do not need to know how the calculations are done, but basically the switch technology allows the computer to add up and subtract binary numbers, and by carrying out these processes repetitively the computer can also multiply and divide.

However, you should have an understanding of how computers can be programmed to carry out the required calculations on data. This is a large topic, and so I am going to deal with it in a separate chapter (Chapter 6). Manual calculating methods, which form a useful introduction to computerised methods, are also discussed in that chapter.

> *Optional activity*
>
> The mathematics which describes the way in which computers carry out calculations by the use of switches is called Boolean algebra. It is not difficult to understand, and if you want to know more about the subject try your public library's computer science section.

Printing data

In data processing the term 'print' may be used to describe any method of outputting information, including writing or typing on a form and displaying on a screen. In manual DP systems the devices used for printing information are the same as those used for recording data (pen, typewriter, etc.), and there is no need to speak of these further here. In electronic systems, however, different equipment is used, and I'm going to deal with this now.

Electronic methods

In electronic systems *printers* are used if hard copy is required; a *screen* (like a TV screen) is used otherwise. Many computer terminals are visual display units, or VDUs for short, meaning that they incorporate both a keyboard and a screen, allowing the operator to input data and to receive the computer output at the same time. Some terminals are teletypewriters; these operate in a similar way to VDUs, but they incorporate a printer instead of a screen. Usually, however, printers are quite separate units, not attached to keyboards.

Let's look at printers and screens in turn.

Printers Like computers, printers vary enormously in price, from £200 up to £200,000. You pay more for higher print quality and faster print speed. For most of Mike's data processing requirements, such as printing invoices and other business documents, a low-priced printer is adequate. If he wants a higher print quality, for example for letters, then he will have to think in terms of £1,000 or so. For his volume of data processing work he will certainly want to buy a type of printer known as a *character printer*, so called because it prints one character at a time (like a typewriter).

The printing mechanism on many character printers is a small circular device called a daisy wheel. This has characters embossed on the circumference, and as it rotates, the required characters strike against a ribbon to create the printed impression on the paper. Different type-founts are obtained by changing the daisy wheel.

These printers print at around fifty characters per second. This is some ten times faster than manual typing, but very much slower than computer processing speeds. So that the computer is not tied up with the printing operation for excessive periods of time some character printers incorporate memory chips. By dumping the data for printing into these chips the computer is released for other processing work. Some microcomputers incorporate similar chips, enabling them to process one job while printing another.

Another type of character printer is the *dot matrix printer*. The printing mechanism in this case is a small cluster of tiny pins, the characters being created on the page by tiny hammers punching out a pattern of pins. This type of printer is some three times faster than daisy wheel printers, but the print quality is low.

Character printers are too slow to handle the high volumes of output produced by larger computers, and for these *line printers* are normally used. These print a line at a time, but the speed advantage that this gives them over character printers has to be set against their higher purchase price.

For very high volumes of output a *page printer* might be used. These machines cost in excess of £100,000, and print a page at a time. A page printer would print this book in thirty seconds, and the print quality is good. One type of page printer works by forming an electrical impression on special paper of the characters to be printed. The surface of the paper is then sprayed with ink, which adheres to the electrically charged areas but is washed off the rest.

Continuous stationery for printers has already been mentioned (see page 100). Its use allows printers to run for long periods unattended.

Screens Screens usually display up to twenty-four lines of computer output, with up to eighty characters on a line. They are almost always cathode ray tubes (CRTs), and therefore similar to the screen on your television set, though liquid crystal display (LCD) screens are sometimes used. (Displays on digital watches and on most calculators are of this latter type.) LCDs consume very little power and they do not wear out, but they do not emit light and so must be illuminated by the background light of the room.

To avoid eye-strain and fatigue screens must be flicker-free, and they must be able to be placed in the position and at the angle that best suits the operator. Most microcomputer screens are housed in the same unit as the keyboard, and this can result in a position relative to the operator's eyes which may be quite tiring. Screen units that are separately housed and adjustable are reckoned to be best.

Review

Outline the various types of printer that are available, and state which is best for Mike. Why should he take account of the characteristics of the screen when selecting a micro-computer? (Five minutes.)

OUTLINE ANSWER

A character printer is most suitable. If some of his output is to be high quality (e.g. letters to clients), then he should use a daisy wheel printer.

A badly positioned screen is very tiring, which is unpleasant for the operator and costly for Mike (since it reduces the operator's output).

Communicating data

Data recorded on a document must be communicated by some type of manual delivery system. Data which is held in electronic form within a computer system is communicated by sending an electrical signal down a wire, a radio signal through the air, or a laser light signal down an optical fibre. If these electronic forms of communication are carried out over a distance rather than within an installation they are known as *telecommunications*.

As in previous sections, let's look first at the manual methods, then at the electronic methods.

Manual methods

Methods for delivering documents between rooms on a single site are

- *internal post*, with collections and deliveries at fixed times; and
- *document conveyor systems*, which link the floors or rooms in

a building by continuously moving belts or wires. Documents fed into the system at one point are automatically ejected upon reaching their destinations.

The Post Office's *postal service* will normally be used for delivering documents to external addresses. Large organisations will normally have a mail room to which all outgoing mail is sent prior to posting. A mail room can reduce overall costs by providing specialised equipment (such as franking machines) and trained staff, and by collecting together a number of communications for posting to a single addressee (such as a branch office) and sending them in a single package.

Electronic methods

Electronic communication systems are of two types:

- Systems which require you to make contact with the receiving machine before sending your message. An example of this is the telephone system, where you dial the receiver's code number in order to make contact.
- Systems which don't require you to contact the receiver before sending the message. In these systems each message travels as an independent 'packet' of information. It contains the receiver's address, and the system reads this address and routes the message to its destination.

Let's look at these systems in turn.

Contact systems The telephone is the main example of equipment which requires you to establish a connection between transmitter and receiver before transmission can take place. The telephone is an analogue device (see page 129), and it works by converting voice to electrical wave form. However, data in binary digital form can also be transmitted over the telephone system by using a device, called a 'modem', which modulates the telephone carrier wave with the digital information. British Telecom offer a variety of data communications services based on this equipment.

Voice and data, then, can be transmitted over the telephone network, using telephone receivers and modems. Turning now to text and image, these can also be transmitted over this same network, using devices called *telex* (to send and receive text) and *facsimile* (to send and receive image).

A telex machine is a teletypewriter (see page 144). This consists of a keyboard for converting the typed characters to digital form, a keypunch for recording these characters in digital form on paper tape, and a printer for printing messages received from other telex machines. Also included is a paper tape reader, which transmits the messages recorded on the paper tape down the telephone line. The reason why messages are normally first recorded on paper tape rather than being typed straight down the telephone line from the keyboard is the fact that tape readers transmit the information at high speeds, and therefore low cost, down the line. Keyboarding, in contrast, is slow, and it is therefore expensive on line time.

Facsimile machines work by scanning the image on the paper (this can be a picture, or a page of text), converting it to digital form, and transmitting the digital signal down the telephone line. At the other end of the line a compatible facsimile machine converts the signal back to image. Facsimile is often used for transmitting text, the advantage being that it can be faster (and therefore cheaper) than telex. However, unlike telex, the equipment of one manufacturer may not be compatible with that of another, and there is no complete directory of facsimile users.

Packet systems These systems are still being developed. They are the electronic equivalent of the Post Office's postal service:

- Each message is sent down the wire as a self-contained unit of information called a packet, and it includes the coded address of the receiving device.
- The system 'reads' the address and routes the packet accordingly.
- The cost does not depend upon the distance travelled but upon the volume of data in the packet.

These systems are designed to transmit data in digital form at high speeds, and they have several advantages over the conventional telephone-based technology.

Self-check

Think about what these advantages might be, and list them. Refer back to what was said about contact systems for help with this.

The advantages are: lower cost of line time, modems are not needed, and contact does not have to be established with the receiving device.

Two types of packet system are being developed:

Local area networks for use on a single site, such as a building or group of buildings. An LAN (as it is normally abbreviated to) consists essentially of a loop of coaxial wire laid around the site, with sockets located at convenient points for connecting the various pieces of electronic equipment. As a message travels along the wire it passes all the machines connected to the system. Each one 'reads' the coded address, but takes no action if it does not recognise that address as its own. The machine with the right address plucks the message off the wire and deposits it in its internal memory.

Public packet switched networks (PPSNs) linking the many sites in a country. The British PPSN is being installed by British Telecom. It is known as System X, and it will shortly link up the main areas of this country as well as connecting the networks of other countries. The technology employed will convert the electrical impulses in digital form from the transmitting device to laser light pulses, which will be transmitted along optical fibres. This technology is so powerful that a single hair-like fibre will be able to carry all the telephone conversations going on at this moment in the country. The network will be computer controlled, which means that the address on each packet will be read by the system and the packet routed automatically to its destination. The network will temporarily store the packet if sections of the route, or the receiving device, are engaged.

Activity

Obtain leaflets from British Telecom describing their various data communications services and their text communications service (Telex). Find out also about the Post Office's facsimile service. Get what information you can about the proposed public packet switched network (you may need to refer to your library for information). List and compare the main applications, transmission rates, and costs of each of these.

Review

1 Explain briefly (in two or three lines) why facsimile, in spite of its advantages over telex, is not widely used as a text communication service.
2 Give three reasons why public packet switched networks are likely to be the main data and text communications service in the future.

OUTLINE ANSWERS

1 Machine incompatibility; no directory of users.
2 Increased volumes of data and text communications require a more powerful service than is presently available; PPSNs are cheap in use, do not require modems, and avoid problems caused by engaged receiving devices.

Shared facilities

Finally, you should note that the communications capabilities of electronic equipment mean that data processing and word processing systems can consist of a variety of items of equipment linked in a variety of ways. This variation is particularly marked in word processing, where systems are labelled either *stand-alone* or *shared facility*.

● A stand-alone system consists of a single keyboard, screen, processing unit, disc unit, and printer, none of these items being linked to or shared with other systems.
● A shared facility system consists of a number of keyboard and screen units sharing common equipment such as a central processing unit, disc drives, and printer.

A stand-alone system is ideal for the smaller office, but larger offices will normally install a shared facility system, with obvious savings in cost. In some arrangements the printer only is shared, whereas others may share common processing and disc storage.

The latter sort are called *shared logic* systems, and the processor may in fact be a large computer carrying out data processing jobs as well as word processing. In shared logic systems messages can be sent electronically from one operator's keyboard to another's screen, avoiding the need for traditional memos on paper (see pages 270–1).

Pinecrafts assignment 2

Refer to the 'administrative procedures' section of the Pinecrafts case study in the Appendix, and consider the following sequences of steps:

a 1, 2, 3, 9, and 10
b 4, 5, 6
c 7, 8.

In the next assignment (at the end of Chapter 6) you will be examining the implications of installing a microcomputer in Pinecrafts. In this assignment assume manual data processing, and carry out the following exercises on each of the above sequences of steps:

  i Develop the procedure in detail and document it (e.g. by a flowchart), and design the forms required.
 ii State the purpose of each item of data that is to be entered on each form.
iii State the methods by which any copies are to be produced.
 iv State the filing method to be used for each completed form, or whether it should be destroyed after use; for example, the stock record cards might be held vertically in a card index.

You will find the catalogue of office equipment obtained in a previous activity helpful in answering this question, as well as information on similar procedures carried out at your place of work.

5 | Applications, procedures, and programs

Introduction

The story so far

Mike now has a good grasp of data processing. He knows how computers record, store, calculate, print, and communicate data, and he knows in general terms how a computer would help his business.

> #### Self-check
>
> If Mike purchases a computer, list four action documents and two reports that he will expect it to produce. For help, revise pages 60–1.

ANSWER

Documents include invoices, purchase orders, paycheques, remittance advices. Reports include sales analyses and debtor reports.

The next step

In the rest of the book we are going to accompany Mike as he finds out the practical implications for his business of what he has learned so far. We shall also, of course, be looking at the implications for larger businesses. In this chapter you will be finding out the answers to two questions which are at the forefront of his mind:

- *Is a computer a good idea for my business?*
- *If it is a good idea, how would I use it?*

The second of these questions requires a lengthy answer, so I have split it into three subsidiary questions:

- *What are the applications of a computer in a business?*
- *How does a real-life business use its computer in one of these applications?*
- *How do I make a computer carry out my applications?*

Let's begin, then, by finding out whether a computer is the right solution to Mike's data processing problems. The critical factor is not the type of business he is in, but the size of his business. Very few tiny businesses use computers, whereas large businesses use them extensively. Let's see why this is.

Business growth and data processing

A tiny business produces a very small range of action documents and reports, whereas a large business produces many. In this section we are going to look first at a one-man business, then at a firm the size of Pinecrafts, and finally at a large company. You will learn how and why their needs for action documents and reports differ, and in what way this affects their data processing requirements.

Let's look first at their need for action documents. To keep the account simple I'm going to describe purchasing only, omitting sales, wages, and other activities.

Activity

Suppose you decide to start up on your own as a one-man decorating business. List the documents you think you will need to produce for the purchasing side of your business. (Include the procedure for paying for your purchases.)

Action document requirements

A one-man business A sole trader with no employees will probably not keep purchase records, he certainly won't need purchase requisitions, he probably won't order on a specially printed order form, and he will buy in such tiny quantities that it will not normally be worth his while to send out quotation requests to determine the most suitable supplier.

Depending on the type of business, his procedure might be simply as follows. As he uses stock he notes on a shopping list those items which are low, and he periodically takes this list to a local trade supplier to replenish his shelves. He pays on the spot by cash or cheque, and he subsequently enters the purchase value (as shown on the trade supplier's invoice) in his cash book.

He therefore produces only two documents, namely his shopping list and his cash book, plus possibly a cheque, and he makes out these documents perhaps once or twice a week. A computer would be an impediment to the absolutely minimal amount of data processing he has to do.

Activity

Suppose that after a number of years the business grows to the size of Pinecrafts (see Appendix). Write down the documents you think he will now need to produce for the purchasing (and paying) side of his business. For help refer to the section on purchasing in Chapter 1.

A small business (like Pinecrafts) The much greater stock usage and purchasing requirements, and the fact that the various business functions are now split amongst a number of people, result in more formal and more complex data processing procedures. The business may now need proper stock records, and it will produce a reorder list showing all items which fall to a predetermined reorder level. It will take greater care over purchasing, and it may find it worthwhile keeping purchase records (to carry out formal supplier comparisons) as well as sending out quotation requests for some orders. It will also use specially printed purchase order forms. It will adopt formal procedures to check that goods ordered have subsequently been received, and that suppliers' invoices tally with orders and receipts. The volume of output will also be much greater, requiring more clerical labour.

A microcomputer designed for small business use would be useful in this case. This would print automatically a reorder list for use by the person responsible for purchasing, and it would maintain a supplier file with details of goods ordered and received. It would also maintain the purchases ledger file and print the cheques and remittance advice notes. It would obviously give substantial savings in clerical labour.

A large business The very high rate at which stock is used up and the fact that the above procedure is now split amongst several departments demand highly formal data processing procedures leading to the production of many more documents. These documents are:

- Purchase requisitions (from stock control and other departments to the purchasing department).
- Quotation requests (from purchasing to suppliers).
- Purchase records (internal to the purchasing department).
- Purchase orders plus copies (from purchasing to supplier, to goods inwards, and to accounts).
- Notification of goods received plus copies (from goods inwards to purchasing, to accounts, and to requisitioning department).
- Cheques and remittance advice notes (from accounts to suppliers).

A large computer system, with a number of VDUs in these various departments, is appropriate in this case. In a typical manufacturing or wholesaling business such a computer system would work as follows.

The computer will copy details of items on its stock file which fall below the reorder level on to a purchase requisition file. It will also maintain a purchase record file, showing for each item the details of goods ordered and received as well as information on alternative suppliers. Each requisition will be displayed in turn, together with the appropriate purchase record, on a VDU screen in the purchasing department, and from this information the buyer is able to make and key in his purchasing decision. The computer will store these decisions on the purchase record file, and on the basis of these decisions it will periodically print a batch of purchase orders to send to the various suppliers.

Data on goods received will be keyed into a VDU in the goods inwards department, and the computer will store this on the stock file and note the receipts on the purchase record file. Details of invoices received will be keyed into a VDU in the accounts department, and these will be held on the invoice file. The computer will automatically reconcile the invoice details with both the order details and the receipt details held on the purchase record file, and it will report any discrepancies. It will then copy the details of the checked invoices to the purchase ledger file for payment.

The volume of data to be processed in a large business is high, and to do all these tasks by manual methods is very expensive in terms of clerical labour. It is therefore worthwhile buying a large computer.

Activity

In most of the rest of this chapter we shall be looking at the way in which a computer handles sales order processing and invoicing. In preparation for this, and also to ensure that you have grasped the points made above, you should now carry out a similar exercise to the above for the sales order processing and invoicing procedure. You should list briefly the steps used for order processing and invoicing in a one-man business and in a business like Pinecrafts (the account given in Chapter 1 will help here), and you should summarise the procedure used in a large business.

To do this activity you will find it helpful to discover all you can about the sales order processing procedure used in your firm (if appropriate). Get hold of the forms that are used, and find out what files are used for the procedure and the contents of those files.

ANSWER

A one-man business will probably produce only the invoice for the customer, plus a copy for its internal records, plus cash book entries. A larger business will keep stock records, and it will check these when the customer's order is received to ensure that it can fill the order, and it will buy more stock if it can't. It will also update the stock records with the order details, and it must pass details of the order to stores so that the customer's requirements are 'picked' from the shelves and dispatched.

If it has a computer system this will automatically check the stock file and update it from the keyed-in order details, and it will also automatically produce the sales documentation (i.e. the invoice plus copies) and maintain the sales ledger. For details of what happens in a large business see the case study beginning on page 161.

Reporting requirements

Just as a business's requirements for action documents grow with increasing business size, so too do its requirements for management reports. This is because a larger business is much more difficult to manage and control, and it needs, therefore, a much greater range of management information.

A tiny business, employing perhaps one or two people, is easy to manage. The owner/manager is personally involved in every business activity, and the smallness of the operations means that he has intimate knowledge of every aspect of his business. He knows immediately if demand for his products or services is declining, or it his output targets are not being achieved, or if the quality of work is not up to scratch. A formal management reporting system would tell him only what he already knows. Furthermore, the value of any improvement in the range and accuracy of information that would result from installing such a system would not cover the costs of such a system.

Let the business grow to the size of Pinecrafts and beyond, and the picture is quite different. There are now a number of managers, each controlling and having knowledge of a small section only of the total business. The sheer scale of the operation brings with it the need for formal management reports, answering such questions as:

Which items are slow or fast moving?
How is consumer demand in the various markets changing?
What are the costs and the outputs of the various sections of the business?

The large sums of money that are now at stake justify the cost of producing these reports.

As we have seen earlier in the book, much of the information contained in these reports can be obtained from the data in the business's files. To retrieve, analyse, and summarise this data by manual methods is time-consuming and expensive in terms of clerical labour, and this is a major reason why business growth is almost inevitably accompanied by the computerisation of the data processing procedures.

Review

State, with reasons, using less than ten lines, which is best for Mike: completely manual data processing procedures, a microcomputer system, a minicomputer system.

ANSWER

Mike has a number of employees, and his business is sufficiently large to justify the purchase of a microcomputer system designed for small business use. The cost would be about £4,000. This would give him worthwhile savings in labour. A minicomputer system would be much more expensive, and quite inappropriate to his needs. Besides the savings in clerical labour, a microcomputer system would produce fuller management reports more quickly than is possible with manual DP, and with greater accuracy.

Applications

In this section we are going to answer the first part of Mike's second question (page 153), *What are the applications of a computer in a business?*

Activity

Read through the leaflets on computers that you obtained in the activity on page 65, and list all the applications given in them. Then divide your list into applications that are generally relevant to all businesses, and applications that are specific to certain types of business.

General applications

Many of the applications in your list will be general applications, which means they are relevant to almost every kind of business. Purchasing, described in the previous section, is an example of a general application. For a complete list, turn again to figure 16. Each decision listed there gives rise to one or more data processing applications. They are shown in figure 23, which you should now study.

Decision (see figure 16)	*Application*
1 What should I buy?	Stock control
2 Whom should I buy from?	Purchasing
3 How much should I pay?	Purchases ledger and paying
4 What should I make/supply?	Sales order processing and sales ledger; production planning
5 What should I charge?	Costing
6 Whom should I hire?	Personnel administration
7 What wages should I pay?	Payroll
8 How much should I borrow?	Financial modelling and forecasting

Figure 23. Business applications of computers

In Chapter 1 we looked at how Mike carries out some of these applications using his present manual system. If he used a computer, it would be doing the same sort of thing, but it would be doing it largely automatically. You will be finding out about this in an example application in the next chapter.

Activity (if your firm has computers)

Find out and write down the applications that computers are used for in your organisation. Choose one of these applications, and find out how it is carried out by computer. You should write down what is involved in getting the data into the computer, what computer files are involved, what the outputs are, and how the outputs are used.

Specialised applications

Some computer applications are specific to certain types of business. In Mike's case the most useful application could be estimating. This task, which takes him many hours a week at present, will be cut down to a few minutes using a computer. Suppose he specialises in building home extensions. The computer can store all the costs that go into the final price – the cost per square foot of the various types of flooring and roofing materials, as well as the various wall materials and finishes. All Mike has to do is key in the various specifications for the job – dimensions, materials, finishes, and so on. The computer will then automatically print out an estimate showing the individual costs and the total price.

This is obviously a specialist application for his type of business, and he might decide to buy a microcomputer because of its value to him in this application. However, having bought a computer for this purpose, he has the added bonus that it can also be used for the general applications listed in figure 23.

Self-check

In the next section we are going to find out how a wholesaling business uses a computer for its sales order processing and invoicing. In preparation for this try drawing a flowchart with about a dozen steps showing in outline what this procedure is. You will find it helpful to glance through the section on sales in Chapter 1, at figure 9 to remind yourself of the flowchart symbols, at figure 10 for detail on the invoicing part of the procedure, and also at your answer to the activity on page 156. To help you on your way, your flowchart should begin with an input box 'Read customer order' and then an operation box 'Compare order with stock records to check availability of goods'. When you have finished, check your answer with figure 24. Don't worry if it differs slightly – there are many ways of charting the same procedure!

Procedures

Self-check

You learned about data processing procedures at the beginning of Chapter 2. Refresh your memory by jotting down a simple definition of a procedure.

A procedure is the sequence of DP operations that are performed on data inputs to produce information outputs. When a computer is used for any of the applications listed in figure 23, it must carry out certain procedures. You also learned in Chapter 2 that these procedures all follow a common pattern: record, store and retrieve, calculate, print, and communicate.

Because these procedures are broadly similar, you do not have to study how a computer is used in each one of the applications in figure 23 in order to understand data processing and computers in business. You have to study just one application, and the others will be rather like it. The input data will come from different sources, different files will be used, and the output documents and reports will be called by different names, but the same general sequence of DP operations will be carried out. That's why the same piece of equipment – a computer – can be used for so many different applications.

Case study: sales order processing

The application we are going to look at is sales order processing. Figure 24 (overleaf) shows an outline flowchart of what this involves, and you should study this figure now.

So that you can see clearly how this works in practice, we are going to look in detail at the use that an actual company makes of a computer in this application. The company is Mastercare Ltd (Components Division) of High Wycombe, a large wholesaler of electrical and electronic components supplying both retail shops and companies which service electrical goods. It has recently installed a minicomputer, and at the time of writing most of the sales order processing procedure has been computer-

Figure 24

ised, while other procedures will be computerised in due course.

At present the data processing section consists of a data processing manager and five data entry clerks operating five visual display units. You will be learning about the sort of work they do in Chapter 8.

The sales order processing procedure can be split into three parts:

- receipt of orders;
- invoicing;
- invoice confirmation.

Flowcharts for each of these are shown in figures 25, 27, and 28, and you should study these in conjunction with the explanations given in the next subsections. As a result of these procedures the computer prints the following action documents: the invoice, the dispatch note, and Mastercare's internal copy. These are referred to as sales documents in figure 27, and they are described in the accompanying text.

Periodically a number of reports are produced from the computer files. This is not part of the sales transaction processing. However, it is a related activity, for the computer produces these reports by analysing and summarising the sales transactions, and so I have included a section on reports towards the end of the case study. File maintenance, another associated activity, is also included. You may find it helpful to revise at this point the section on transaction processing, reporting, and file maintenance on page 124.

Self-check

Read the flowcharts in figures 25, 27, and 28, and note down two major differences between these and figure 24.

Figures 25, 27, and 28 are much more detailed. Figure 24 was an outline flowchart only. Flowcharts are practical tools, and should be drawn at whatever level of detail is best for the purpose in hand. Later in this chapter we shall be looking at program flowcharts, which are even more detailed.

The other difference is the omission of the accounting part of

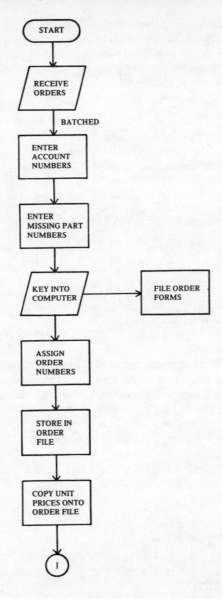

Figure 25

the procedure (adding the invoice value to the customer records and producing the statement). This is done by a separate division of the company, located on a different site.

Let's now look at the first stage of the sales order processing procedure, namely, receipt of orders.

Stage 1: Receipt of orders

Orders arrive through the post, on customers' own purchase order forms. The first step in the procedure is to put these forms into batches of about twenty. Refer back to page 100 to revise the reasons for this. This is done by the order receiving section in the company, which also looks up and enters on each form the customer's account number (i.e. their code number). These steps are shown at the start of the flowchart in figure 25.

Next, the order receiving section scrutinises the orders for missing part numbers. Customers often enter the part name only, in which case this section must look up the number in the parts catalogue and enter it on the form. The order receiving section then passes the batch to the DP section.

Here, the data entry clerk handling the batch keys in the data on each order form into her visual display unit in the following sequence:

1 The customer account number. The computer responds by displaying the customer's name and address on the VDU screen (it gets these details from the customer file). By comparing this display with the order form the clerk can check that she has keyed in the correct account number.
2 The type of order. Mastercare classifies orders under five headings ('replacement under guarantee' is one heading, 'chargeable catalogue item' is another), and each order type is coded by means of two alphabetic characters. It is these codes that the clerk keys in.
3 Whether a handling charge is to be applied. The computer displays a question to this effect on the screen, and the clerk responds by keying Y or N (for 'yes' or 'no').
4 The part number and quantity of each item ordered. The part number incorporates a check digit to ensure correct keying (see page 105).

5 Any discounts to be applied.
6 The due date (when the order is required by the customer).
7 Hash totals (see page 104). The clerk adds up the number of
   lines on the order, she also totals the quantities, and she keys
   in the two numbers obtained. The computer compares these
   with its own similar calculations and so checks whether the
   clerk has made any keying errors.

> ### Self-check
>
> List three coding systems and two verification checks that
> are used in these procedures. For help, revise pages 90 ff.
> and 101 ff.

ANSWER

Coding systems are the customer account number, type of order,
and part number. Verification checks are the comparison of
display with form in (1), and the batch total checks in (7). The
check in (4) is a validation check, not a verification check.

Before reading any further turn back to page 123 and read the
subsection headed 'Example: sales order processing'. Mastercare has adopted the second type of processing procedure listed
there, namely batch/real-time processing. If you have forgotten
what batch and real-time processing involve, revise the whole
'Processing data' section of Chapter 4 (pages 121–5).

The computer processes each order immediately it is keyed in,
in a real-time manner. The processing steps are shown in
abbreviated form in the lower part of figure 25. The computer
first codes the order by assigning it a number which it calculates
by adding 1 on to the previous order code number (in other
words, it codes the orders in straight numerical sequence). Then
it copies the order details on to its order file under this number,
and at the same time it copies the order code number on to its
customer file under the customer's name. (Both of these files are
master files.) It also displays the order code number on the VDU
screen, and the clerk copies this on to the original order form.

Next, the computer looks up in its stock file the unit price of
each item listed on the order, and it copies this price on to the
order file against the item. It also calculates the value of the

order (by multiplying the unit price for each item by the quantity and adding the results), and it enters this value against the order on the order file.

When the details of each order in the batch have been keyed into and processed by the computer, the clerk stores the original order forms in the appropriate customer sections of a manual file. This serves as the archival storage system – see the first paragraph of the subsection headed 'Archival storage' on page 141 for details.

Self-check

As a way of fixing the data processing procedures described in this case study in your mind, itemise the various steps in the above account under the headings 'Record', 'Store/retrieve', 'Compute', 'Print', 'Communicate'. Do this in the form of a table, as shown in figure 26, and indicate on it which steps are carried out manually. The next two self-checks will ask you to extend this table.

	Record	Store/retrieve	Compute	Print	Communicate
1	Key in order (manual)				
2			Assign order number		
3		Copy to order file			
4				Display order number	
5	Copy order number on to order form (manual)				
6		Retrieve item price from stock file			

Figure 26. Part-answer to self-check question

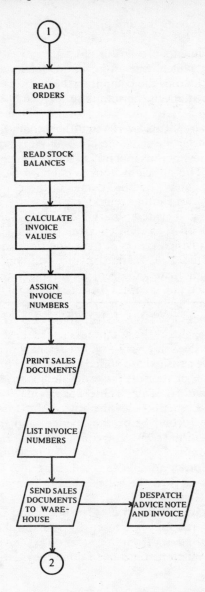

Figure 27

Stage 2: Production of sales documents

The sales documents are not produced in a real-time manner, i.e. immediately each order is keyed in. Instead, they are produced in a batch processing manner, i.e. during a sales document 'run' done twice daily by the computer. Figure 27 shows the steps in this run.

The computer begins by reading the orders that have been added to the order file since the previous run and looking up in the stock file the amount currently in stock of each item ordered.

There should be sufficient stock in hand for most orders to be satisfied immediately, and the details of these are copied from the order file on to another temporary file which is used to hold data for printing. This temporary file is known as a 'spool file', and data held on it is deleted after printing. The computer calculates the invoice values at the same time and copies these on to the spool file. It also assigns invoice numbers to the invoices (in straight numerical sequence, by adding 1 to the previous invoice number), and it copies these to the spool file.

Orders which are left over from the run because there is insufficient stock available to fill them are known as 'back orders'. Once each day the computer checks these with the stock file (in exactly the same way as it checks new orders), and any that can now be satisfied are added to the spool file.

The computer next prints the order details from the spool file on to the sales documents. These documents are in three-part sets, the top documents being the advice note that accompanies the goods, the second being the invoice, and the third being Mastercare's internal copy. The computer also prints out a list of the invoice numbers of all the documents printed, with the corresponding order numbers printed alongside. The DP section uses this list to record the subsequent movement of the sales documents (see below).

The DP section now sends the sets of documents to the warehouse. Here, they are used by the warehouse staff for 'picking' items of stock from the warehouse shelves to fill customers' orders. When this has been done they detach the advice

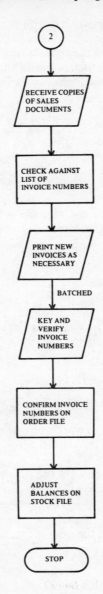

Figure 28

note from the set and dispatch it with the goods to the customer. If the customer's invoicing address is the same as his delivery address they also detach the invoice and send it with the goods; otherwise it is posted to the invoicing address.

Self-check

Add the steps described above to the table you started in the previous self-check question. (There are about twelve steps in total in this subsection.) Under the 'Communicate' heading, which you have not yet used, you should put the steps described in the final paragraph above, e.g. 'Send documents to warehouse'.

Stage 3: Invoice confirmation

The warehouse staff now return the remaining copy of the sales document set to the DP section for 'invoice confirmation', which is the final part of the procedure (see figure 28). The purpose of this is to confirm on the order file that the goods have been dispatched and the customer invoiced.

As a first step in this procedure a clerk in the DP section ticks each document returned on the list of invoice numbers (see previous subsection). This enables her to check that no sales documents have gone missing.

The warehouse staff may have been unable to completely satisfy some customers' orders (owing to unforeseen shortages caused by breakages or pilferage). In these cases they amend the documents by hand at the warehouse and return them to the DP section, where the revised details are keyed into the computer and a new set printed.

The DP section next batches the documents. Mastercare finds that a batch size of eighteen is convenient in this case, though, as explained in page 103, there is no hard-and-fast rule about batch sizes. Taking each batch in turn, the clerk keys the invoice numbers that appear on the documents into the computer twice.

Self-check

Why does she do this *twice*?

This is the 100% check described on page 106. On both occasions the computer adds up the invoice numbers to produce a hash total, and if the two hash totals agree it proceeds with the next part of the procedure. Failure to agree indicates a keying error, and the clerk has to rekey the numbers.

The computer now notes on the order file that the orders represented by these invoice numbers have been satisfied. This is called 'invoice confirmation'. At the same time it deducts the quantities of items used to fill these orders from the balances recorded on its stock file.

The final step comes at the end of the month, when the computer uses the records of satisfied orders on the order file to print the statements that are sent to customers.

Self-check

Add the ten steps described above to your table.

The reports

Besides the three computer procedures described above (receipt of orders, document production, and invoice confirmation), the computer carries out a number of associated reporting procedures. As a result of these it prints a variety of reports from the data held on its files. These are of two sorts:

1 Operational reports. These are really action documents, for they contain data on individual items and they generate action at the operational level in the business. (If necessary you should revise action documents on pages 26 and 46.)
2 Management reports, which are used by management for decision making (revise page 62).

We will now look at some of these reports, to see the sort of report produced by DP procedures, and the reasons for them. (Don't worry if you find the account a little technical.)

Operational reports

- *General stock report* The computer produces this daily. This lists all stock items for which customer orders exceed the balance held in stock, and it generates immediate action by the purchasing department, which will contact suppliers urgently for more stock.

- *Reorder level report* The computer produces this weekly. It lists all stock items that have dropped below the reorder level. Like the general stock report, this is sent to the purchasing department. It generates the routine (non-urgent) work of that department.
- *Customer order report* This is produced as and when required, and it lists all unsatisfied orders for named customers. It is used in the event of a query by the customer, or if the customer is going to visit the site (so that if stock is available he can be supplied with his requirements at the time of his visit).

Management reports

- *Daily service statistics* This report shows two things:

    (a) The number of satisfied lines (i.e. individual orders that have been filled) expressed as a percentage of the total number of lines ordered. This is called the percentage service level. Too low a service level indicates a high proportion of unsatisfied orders, which will cause customer dissatisfaction and lost trade. A general increase in stock reorder levels would then be called for. Too high a service level on high-cost items would indicate over-generous stock levels, which is expensive in terms of both cash and storage space.

    (b) The distribution of orders over the ranges £0–£5, £5–£15, £15–£25, over £25. This shows whether customers are tending to order large amounts (and therefore using Mastercare as their main supplier), or whether they are tending to order small amounts (indicating that they are using Mastercare to supply parts that their other main supplier is not holding). If there is a trend towards smaller orders then management should consider revising company policy and strategy. This information on the distribution of orders is also useful if management wishes to find out how altering the price at which handling charges are waived will affect revenue.

- *Customer activity report* This is produced weekly, and it shows for each customer the cost value of sales, the sales value, and the profit percentage. These measures are useful for the customer relations department, and for planning the structure of discounts offered.

- *Order activity report* This shows the number of sales by type of order, the average number of lines per order of each type, the average sales value per order of each type, and the handling costs per sales order and per £ of sales value. The last of these provides a guide to the handling charge structure that the company should adopt, and it also provides a measure of operating efficiency. The other statistics allow management to compare sales of each type of order as a guide to the long-term product-strategy of the company.
- *Stock gross margin report* This shows, for each line of stock, the cost price, the selling price, and the profit margin. It highlights high profit lines and low profit lines, and management uses it to adjust the range of stock held and the prices charged.
- *Stock valuation report* This shows the value of the stock held of each line, and it also shows the total value of each product-group. This information is used in profit calculations and in calculating the value of the company's assets.
- *Cost of sales report* This shows the annual cost to the company of each line stocked. It is used in calculating profits and to control costs.

File maintenance

The three files used in the sales order processing procedure are:

- the order file;
- the customer file; and
- the stock file.

These are all master files, and as you learned on page 124, any reference data held on such files must be kept up to date by keying in alterations. This is called file maintenance.

Self-check

Try listing the alterations that will have to be made from time to time to the reference data on the customer file and the stock file. (The order file has master data only, no reference data.) For help, reread the subsection a few pages back headed 'Stage 2: Production of sales documents'.

ANSWER

Alterations to reference data on customer file include: adding or deleting customers, change of customer's address, change of customer's discount status, blocking further supplies if customer is a bad debtor. Alterations to stock file include: adding or deleting lines, receipts of stock, non-sales issues of stock, changes in description or price of stock, changes in reorder levels.

Activity

The company will eventually computerise its procedure for purchasing stock items. Construct a flowchart showing the main steps in this procedure, and state one report that you think might be produced. For help, use the section that described computerised purchasing procedures in a large company on page 155, and if possible find out about the procedure in your own company.

PART-ANSWER

The first steps of your flowchart might be as shown in figure 29. One of the reports will be a supplier activity report, summarising the company's expenditure by supplier. This will indicate to the management if the company is becoming overdependent on a few main suppliers – a safer policy is to spread its purchases amongst several suppliers, so that if one has a shortage it can obtain stocks from others.

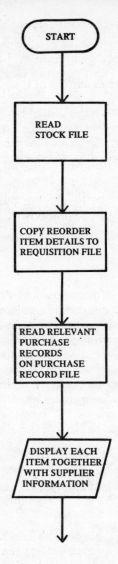

Figure 29

Review

1 State the two main reasons why a business requires more formal and more complex data processing procedures as it increases its scale of operations.
2 In many respects one DP procedure is much the same as any other. List the main activities described in the case study that apply generally to data processing procedures.

(Five minutes.)

OUTLINE ANSWERS

1 The procedures must produce a wider range of action documents and a wider range of reports.
2 *Recording*, i.e. keying in data from source documents, and applying error-checking procedures; *storing and retrieving*, i.e. looking up data in files, and storing the keyed-in data on files; *calculating*, i.e. serially numbering transactions, calculating amounts for action documents, and calculating totals for reports; *printing* action documents and reports; *communicating* action documents to staff and to people outside the company who use them, and communicating reports to management.

Software

Let's now turn to the final question that Mike asked in the introduction to this chapter, *How do I make a computer carry out the applications I have in mind – my invoicing, stock control, purchasing, general accounting, and other procedures?* The answer is to buy the appropriate software.

What is software?

In Chapter 4 we looked at the computer hardware, i.e. keyboards, chips, disc drives, screens, printers, and other tangible bits and pieces of computer systems. We shall now look at the software, that is, the sets of instructions, called *programs*, held in the computer store that tell the computer what operations to perform and how to perform them.

Self-check

In Chapter 4 you learned that a computer system holds data in two sorts of storage system. Remind yourself what these are and jot them down.

A computer holds data in its long-term storage system (on magnetic disc or tape), but when it is operating on the data it copies it into its internal memory (in a silicon chip). The same is true of software. If Mike buys some software to enable him to use his computer for his payroll (for instance), he will buy a magnetic disc with the instructions recorded on it. To make the machine perform the operations needed to produce the payroll for his firm he must insert the disc in the disc drive and copy (i.e. 'load') its contents into the computer's internal memory.

That done, he can remove the software disc and insert another disc containing his employee file, and then he enters the clock card data into the machine via the keyboard. The software tells the computer how to perform the necessary operations to print the payroll, the payslips, the paycheques, and the wage analysis.

Some software can be purchased permanently recorded on a chip. In this case the chip is plugged into a socket in the computer and if necessary it remains there permanently. This has the advantage that it is not necessary to load in the software each time it is needed, and the software does not occupy space in the internal memory. The disadvantage is that the software cannot be modified to suit the individual user; with magnetic disc, on the other hand, instructions can be deleted and new ones inserted.

Two sorts of software

The sort of software that tells the computer what operations to perform to carry out the procedures involved in an application is called *application software*. The sort of software that tells the computer system how to perform the operations is called *system software*.

Self-check

Application software is almost always held on magnetic disc, whereas system software permanently resides within the computer on a chip. Explain in a few sentences why this is.

ANSWER

Software on disc can be modified, whereas software on a chip cannot. The user may want to modify the way in which the computer handles an application, so that it produces more, or different, outputs. In this case he will want the application software on disc. It is only for applications such as word processing, that the user will not want to modify, that the software is sometimes on a chip.

The user will not want to alter the way in which the system performs its various operations, and he will want the instructions that tell it how to perform the operations permanently available. So he will want the system software on chips.

System software

This type of software is an essential part of a computer system, for without it the computer can't do a thing. It is therefore supplied by the manufacturer along with the machine, and it is included in the purchase price.

There are three types of system software needed to make the computer work:

- A group of programs, called an *operating system*, which tells the computer how to operate the various pieces of hardware, such as disc drives and printers. In essence, these programs supervise the complex switching procedures that take place within the system when application software is run.
- Another group of programs, called *utilities*, which tell the computer how to carry out the file handling required by the application software.
- A third group of programs, called *compilers* and *assemblers*, which translate the language in which the application software instructions are written into a form that the machine can

understand. As you will learn at the end of this chapter, these instructions are written using words such as 'input', 'read', and 'print', and these must be converted into a detailed code that the computer can understand and act upon.

Self-check

System software is included in and purchased with the computer system, whereas application software is purchased separately. Explain in a couple of sentences why this is so.

Application software

Although each application of a computer involves the same DP operations and therefore uses the same system software as every other application, it uses different input data and different files, and it produces different outputs. It therefore requires different application software. Furthermore, the requirements of one business may differ somewhat from those of another, and so parts of the application software may have to be individually tailored. Because of this, application software, unlike system software, is usually bought separately from the computer system.

It is possible for someone like Mike to write his own application software, and later in this chapter you will be learning how to write a simple program to produce an invoice, but the enormous number of man-hours he would have to spend on it would be prohibitive. Instead, he will buy commercially available software.

Commercially produced software for an application consists of a package of programs, and so it is called a 'software package'. So Mike can buy a wages package, an invoicing and stock control package, a general accounting package, and so on. The programs in such a package tell the computer how to carry out the various data processing activities involved in the application.

Self-check

List these data processing activities. Turn to pages 123–4 for help.

The programs in a software package tell the computer how to carry out the following activities:

- Transaction processing, which includes validating the input data, updating master files, and preparing transaction files for the production of the various output documents.
- Producing the action documents and reports from the data on these files.
- Making inquiries on the data on the master files.
- Maintaining the master files.

Self-check

Why should Mike buy packages rather than hire someone to write software specially for his business? Try to give three or four reasons.

Advantages and disadvantages of software packages

Besides saving Mike a great deal of time and money, buying off-the-shelf packages rather than trying to write (or paying someone to write) his own software has other advantages:

- A commercially produced package should be fully tested and ready to run. Writing your own takes a long time and it will involve a lot of 'debugging' – ironing out faults.
- Existing users can be consulted to check that the package will do all that it is claimed to do.
- The package may include facilities which you don't need at present, but which you may need in the future if your business grows.

However, packages have some disadvantages which Mike should take into account:

- The available packages may not fully meet his business requirements.
- He may have to change his methods of working somewhat to fit in with the requirements of the package.
- The package may contain too many facilities for his business, making it unnecessarily difficult to use.

In most instances these disadvantages are outweighed by the considerable advantages of packages – particularly cost advantages.

> *Self-check*
>
> List the packages that you think Mike will want to buy. Refer to figure 23 for help, and also look at your leaflets on microcomputer systems.

ANSWER

He will probably want packages covering all the applications in the figure, other than production planning, costing, and personnel administration. Additionally, he may want some specially written software for estimating – he probably won't find a satisfactory off-the-shelf package for his business.

> *Review*
>
> Explain what is meant by the term 'system software' and give three reasons why a computer system needs this software. Carry out a similar exercise for applications software. (Five minutes.)

Programming languages

In the last section you learned that application software consists of programs written in languages with vocabularies of English words – 'input', 'read', 'print', etc. These words are used not because computers understand ordinary English – they don't – they are used to help people who write programs.

These languages are called *high-level languages*. They are called this because each word generates a whole sequence of computer actions, so that with quite a short program you can make a computer do a lot of things. You are going to learn about these languages in this section. To understand this section, you need to know a little more about compilers and assemblers.

Self-check

Explain in a sentence or two what a compiler and an assembler are and what function they perform. Check back to the last section for help.

Compilers and assemblers

A compiler and an assembler are pieces of system software which translate a program written in a high-level language into a program written in a language that the computer understands. This second language is called 'machine code'. It is a low-level language, which means that it is very long-winded, each instruction in a machine code program causing the computer to do only one thing, not a sequence of things as is the case with a high-level language.

There are a number of high-level languages, and they each need their own compiler. There are several different computer processing chips, each with its own machine code, and each machine code needs its own assembler. This is why the system software must include both a compiler (which is peculiar to the high-level language used) and an assembler (which is peculiar to the machine).

The process of translating a program written in a high-level language into machine code takes place in two stages, the first stage involving the compiler, the second stage involving the assembler. The compiler translates the high-level language program into a low-level language called assembly language, and then the assembler translates the assembly language into machine code. This takes place each time the program is run. The entire program is translated before it is run. (One exception to this is the BASIC language, described below.)

Although compilers allow us to use high-level languages, which greatly eases the task of writing application software, they occupy a large amount of memory in the computer. When designing a high-level language, therefore, there must be a compromise between the need to make program writing easy and the need to conserve storage space within the computer. This is particularly important in the case of low-cost microcomputers, which have limited internal storage (i.e. memory).

Let's look now at the most commonly used high-level languages.

COBOL

On large computer systems the most popular business language is COBOL (short for COmmon Business Oriented Language). It was developed as long ago as 1960, and it has firmly established itself as a major language for business applications. This has come about because of its three main advantages:

- It is an efficient language for handling files.
- It closely resembles English – its vocabulary includes words such as 'negative', 'value', 'divide', and 'rounded', which have obvious meanings.
- There is now an enormous body of application programs in the language, and the cost of switching to a more modern language would be very high.

It has disadvantages, however:

- It needs an extensive compiler occupying a large amount of memory in the computer, which limits its usefulness for microcomputers.
- It is not efficient at carrying out calculations, for a large number of commands are required to take the computer through a simple computation.
- It takes three or four times longer to write a program in COBOL than in other high-level languages.

FORTRAN

FORTRAN (FORmula TRANslation) was designed at about the same time as COBOL as an alternative to that language for carrying out calculations. It is very efficient at these, and complex computations can be defined by a set of very compressed statements that closely resemble ordinary mathematical formulae. FORTRAN is generally used for engineering applications (which require a great deal of maths), but not for business. Like COBOL, it requires an extensive compiler.

APL

APL (A Programming Language) resembles the language of mathematics more than the language of English. It is a mathematical shorthand which allows the user to enter and process data on the computer in much the same way as he might use a calculator. Although developed for scientific and mathematical work, it is being used increasingly for business applications. It is extremely easy to learn, it requires little in the way of programming skills, and programs in the language can be written very rapidly.

Another difference between this language and COBOL (and also FORTRAN) is its interactive nature. You can ask questions, amend instructions, and insert data during the program run.

APL's disadvantages are that its great power demands a very large compiler occupying a considerable amount of storage space in the computer's memory, and it requires the use of a keyboard with special characters. It is therefore not at all suitable for the average microcomputer.

BASIC

BASIC (Beginners' All-Purpose Symbolic Instruction Code) is a very widely used language. It is high-level and fairly efficient at file-handling, yet it needs only a fraction of the storage space required by COBOL. It handles calculations in a FORTRAN-like way. It is closer to English than the other languages, and it is therefore particularly easy to learn. Like APL it is interactive, and easy to use. It is ideal for microcomputers, where its small demands on storage, its efficiency at file-handling and calculations, and its ease of use by non-professionals have meant that it has swept all other languages before it.

These advantages have been bought at a price. Minimal storage requirements have been achieved by replacing the compiler by some system software called an interpreter. This compiles each program instruction as it is executed (during the program run) instead of compiling the entire program in advance. This means that it takes much longer to run a BASIC program than it takes to run a compiled program – about five times as long, in fact.

Another disadvantage is the large number of variations of BASIC. Each manufacturer has his own variation, so that a program written for one make of machine has to be modified for use on another.

However, for the ordinary non-professional microcomputer user BASIC wins hands-down over other languages. It is easy to learn, it is interactive, and it takes only an evening to learn how to write simple programs in the language, as you will discover in the next section.

Other languages

Other languages are available, such as PASCAL, FORTH, and AIDA. Although these are much newer and in some respects more efficient than COBOL or BASIC, the two older languages are now so entrenched that the sheer cost and scale of change-over means that they will be dominant on the business front for a long time to come.

Review

In designing a programming language the following considerations must be taken into account:

amount of memory required;
speed of execution;
file-handling efficiency;
calculating efficiency;
ease of learning the language;
speed of program-writing;
ease of debugging.

Draw up a table with COBOL, APL, and BASIC listed across the top and the above considerations listed down the side. Imagine you are buying a computer system for your own small business. Grade each language against each consideration as follows: *** = good, ** = fair, * = poor.

PART-ANSWER

Your table might begin like this:

	COBOL	APL	BASIC
Amount of memory required	**	*	***
Speed of execution	***	***	*

Programming

In this final section of the chapter you are going to learn how to write simple programs in BASIC. This language is easy to learn and it is used on almost all microcomputers. Let's begin by seeing how an electronic calculator, which in many ways is like a computer, is made to carry out a series of computations.

Computing by electronic calculator

Suppose you have to work out an invoice for 4 items costing £3.20 each, 7 items at £2.95 each, and 3 items at £5.19 each. VAT at 15% is to be added to the total. The calculator steps are these (the boxes represent calculator function keys):

$\boxed{AC}4\boxed{\times}3.20\boxed{M+}7\boxed{\times}2.95\boxed{M+}3\boxed{\times}5.19\boxed{M+}\boxed{MR}\boxed{\times}15\boxed{\div}100\boxed{+}\boxed{MR}\boxed{=}$

Try these steps out for yourself on your calculator. Then read the explanation that follows.

The AC key clears the contents of the calculator's memory, i.e. it sets the memory to zero. Switching the calculator off and then on will do the same thing. Key in 4 × 3.20, and press the M+ key. This instructs the calculator to carry out the calculation and add the result to its memory. (On some calculators it is necessary to press the = key before the M+ key.)

You now have the first result (£12.80), which you write in the 'amount' column of the invoice. Now key in 7 × 2.95, again pressing the M+ key. The calculator works out the amount (20.65), which you can write in the 'amount' column of the invoice, and it adds the amount to its memory, so that the total sum stored there is now 33.45.

Next key in 3 × 5.19 M+, and again the calculator adds the result (15.57) to its memory, and you write this amount on the invoice. Now press the MR key, which instructs the calculator to display the total sum in its memory. This is 49.02, which you can enter as the invoice total at the foot of the 'amount' column.

To add on 15% VAT, key in × 15 ÷ 100 +. This instructs the calculator to work out 15/100 of the displayed amount (= 7.353). (The + key instructs the calculator to carry out the sum and to await a further entry which is to be added.) You can write this amount (£7.35) in the space for VAT at the foot of the 'amount' column. Now press the MR key to add on the 49.02 in the memory, and the = key to tell the calculator to display the result (56.373). You can now write £56.37 on the invoice as the total amount (including VAT) to be paid.

Self-check

Write down the calculator keys that must be pressed to work out the total amount to be paid for the following items, using boxes and symbols as in the example above. Apply a 5% discount to the total (i.e. work out 95% of the total):

12 @ £4.75 each, 9 @ £7.82 each, 15 @ £6.30 each.

Carry out the exercise on your calculator. The final result should be £210.79.

Program flowcharts

The sequence of steps I have listed in the previous subsection applies only to the particular numbers given there (4 @ 3.20, 7 @ 2.95, 3 @ 5.19). It is much more useful to write the steps in a way that tells us how to calculate any invoice, whatever the quantities of items and whatever the prices. We can do this by replacing the numbers 4, 3.20, 7, 2.95, 3, 5.19 by the words QUANTITY, PRICE, or more conveniently by the letters Q, P.

The invoice in this example had three products in it, whereas we want to write the steps in a way that permits us to cope with invoices with any number of lines. We must therefore write in an instruction to repeat the QUANTITY × PRICE calculation till

the end of the data. The sequence of instructions we end up with
might look like this:

| SET MEMORY TO ZERO | Q | X | P | ADD AMOUNT TO MEMORY | REPEAT Q X P ADD TO MEMORY TO END OF DATA | SUM IN MEMORY | X | 15 | ÷ | 100 | + | SUM IN MEMORY | = INVOICE TOTAL |

(As before, the boxes represent calculator function keys.)

A much better way of showing this sequence of steps is by a
type of flowchart known as a *program flowchart*. It is convenient
to label data such as the amount, the sum in memory, and the
invoice total by letters such as A, S, and T. The flowchart is
shown in figure 30. Note that in order to avoid confusion with
the letter x the symbol used for multiplication is *. Also, the
division symbol is /, not ÷.

When you are doing the invoice computation on the calculator
you must begin by setting the value of the memory to zero. This
is called *initialisation*, and it is represented on the flowchart by
the symbol ⬡ .

Self-check

Try your hand at drawing the program flowchart for the
calculator steps you wrote down in the last self-check.
Don't look at figure 30 while you are doing this exercise –
your answer should be very like it.

ANSWER

The same as figure 30, except for the operation three boxes from
the end, which should read: T = S * 95/100.

Activity

Now try a slightly different exercise. Draw a program
flowchart to work out the average of a set of values.
(Remember: you work this out by adding the values and
dividing by the number of them.)

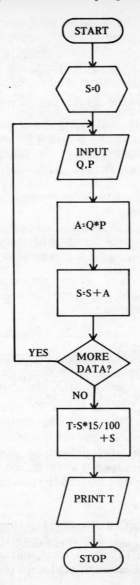

Figure 30

HINT

Don't turn to the answer – which is on page 197 – until you have completed this activity. You will find it helpful to imagine that you are doing the sum on a calculator. You might begin by clearing the working memory, then adding to it each value, then dividing by the number of values. Then press the = key to display the result. For your flowchart, call the sum in the working memory S, call each value that is to be input X, call the number of values N, and call the final answer M. (You could, of course, use other letters if you wished.) For this exercise imagine that you count N by keeping a tally as you enter each value.

Programming

A computer carries out calculations in the same way that your calculator does, by means of switches on a silicon chip. A computer differs from your calculator in that:

1 it can be programmed, so that the manual work of pressing function keys (+, −, M+, etc.) is eliminated; and
2 it can store vast amounts of data.

You have already learned quite a lot about (2); you are now going to learn about (1).

In this subsection we are going to write a computer program in BASIC to carry out the invoice calculation task. Since a computer behaves like your calculator, we can base our program on the program flowchart in figure 30. We shall use the same symbols (Q, P, A, S, and T) to represent quantity, price, amount, sum in memory, and invoice total.

The first step is to label, or 'address', the part of the memory in which the invoice amounts are to be accumulated by the letter S, and to set S equal to zero (see the first flowchart step):

10   LET S = 0

To tell the computer that this is the first step I could have labelled it with the number 1. However, it is usual to count program steps in jumps of 10 (i.e. 10, 20, 30, etc.), and so I am labelling it 10. This allows us to insert additional steps (e.g. step 5, or step 15) later on.

(Note that when you key the program into a computer you must press the RETURN key at the end of the line. This tells the computer to go to the next line in readiness for the next program step.)

Next, we tell the computer that it can expect the quantity and price of the first item on the invoice to be keyed in, and that it must accept this data for processing:

20   INPUT Q, P

What we are in fact doing here is telling the computer to label a part of its memory 'Q' and a part 'P' and put the first two values that it receives (via the keyboard) into those two parts of its memory. You can think of the computer's memory as consisting of lots of boxes, and that we have just told it to label two of these 'Q' and 'P' and to store the first quantity and the first price in them.

Next, the computer has to calculate the amount A. This will be instruction number 30:

30   LET A = Q * P

This tells the computer to multiply the value held in the 'box' labelled Q (i.e. at address Q) by the amount held in the 'box' labelled P (i.e. at address P) and to store the result in another 'box' (or address) in its memory that it is to label 'A'.

Next, we tell the computer to add the value stored in the box labelled A to the amount in the box labelled S, and then to put the answer it gets into box S. This new amount in S replaces the previous amount stored there, the previous amount being deleted. This is line 40:

40   LET S = S + A

We must now tell the computer to repeat this process for successive values of Q and P. We do this by telling it to go back to instruction 20:

50   GOTO 20

The computer will now redo instruction 20 (using the next pair of values for Q and P input at the keyboard) and all successive instructions to instruction 50.

We also need to tell the computer when it has run out of items on the invoice, i.e. when there are no more values of Q and P. If we don't it will stick at instruction 20 looking for another pair of values when there are in fact no more, and it will never get beyond instruction 50. One way of telling it that the data has come to an end is to provide it with impossible values of Q and P, such as negative values, or zero values, and to tell it to bypass line 50 when it receives these values.

Let's use zero values to tell it there are no more items on the invoice. This means that when we run the program we must key in 0, 0 as a final pair of values for Q, P. When the computer receives this it must jump instruction 50 and go to instruction 60. So we must insert after instruction 20 the following:

25   IF Q = 0 GOTO 60.

Note that it does not matter that we are writing this instruction out of sequence, i.e. after instruction 50. The computer reads and executes each program instruction or line in its numerical sequence, not in the sequence in which it is keyed into the computer.

At line 60 we tell the computer to work out the invoice total T:

60   LET T = S * 15/100 + S

Then we want it to tell us what the answer is:

70   PRINT T

If the computer's output device is a screen, this instruction tells the computer to display the answer.

And the final instruction to the computer is to tell it that it has finished what we want it to do:

80   END

Activity

If you have access to a computer you should now key in this program. (If you don't have access, study this activity anyway – it tells you how a program is run.) It doesn't matter in what order you key in the instructions, so long as they are correctly numbered. The computer will store this program in the same way as it stores data that you key in, in its internal memory.

Now tell the computer to run the program. You do this by keying in the command RUN followed by the RETURN key. First, it will carry out instruction 10, and then it will ask you to key in a value for Q and a value for P by displaying a ? on the screen. You must respond by keying in the first two values (quantity and price) shown on the invoice.

You could use the example given in the previous subsection, and key in 4, 3.20 (indicating 4 items at £3.20 each). The computer now carries out line 25 by comparing 4 with 0. Since these numbers are not identical it moves on to lines 30, 40, 50, and 20, and again it prints ? on the screen. Key in the next quantity and price (7, 2.95), and again it repeats the cycle, ending with ? on the screen. Key in the final quantity and price (3, 5.19), and the cycle is repeated once more, ending with a ? on the screen.

You have now come to the end of the data, so key in 0, 0. Line 25 now directs the computer to instructions 60 and 70, and it displays on the screen the value it has calculated for T (56.373).

Finally, line 80 tells the computer that it has completed the program run.

You have now met five BASIC programming words: INPUT, PRINT, LET, IF, and GOTO. These, together with the usual arithmetic commands $(+, -, *, /)$, will enable you to write a wide range of simple programs.

Self-check

Try writing the program to carry out the calculation represented on the program flowchart you drew for the self-check on page 189. Don't look at the program given in the previous subsection until you have finished.

ANSWER

Your program should be the same as the program in the last subsection, apart from line 60, which should read:

60   LET T = S * 95/100

> *Activity*
>
> Now have a go at enlarging the program given in the last
> subsection. Get the program to calculate and print the sum
> that you need to enter at the foot of the 'amount' column
> of the invoice before VAT is added (i.e. the £49.02 on page
> 188), as well as the VAT and the invoice total. You will
> need to replace line 60 by two other lines (which you could
> label 60 and 65), and you will need to replace line 70 by an
> enlarged PRINT instruction.
>
>   If you have access to a computer, key in and run the
> enlarged program.

ANSWER

You will need to label the VAT with a symbol – let's call it V.
The altered program lines are:

60   LET V = S * 15/100
65   LET T = S + V
70   PRINT S, V, T

> *Activity*
>
> Using the program flowchart you drew for calculating the
> average of a set of values (see figure 31), write a computer
> program to find the average of a set of invoice totals. If you
> have access to a computer, test your program on it.

HINT

I have given the answer below. Don't read it until you have had
a go at this exercise.

Much of the program will resemble the above program for
working out an invoice total. You will have to enter the data
repeatedly and add it to the stored sum S. To tell the computer
when you have run out of data you will need to key in an
impossible invoice total, such as −1. The computer will also
need to count the number of values that are input in order to
work out N. You can get it to do this by setting N = 0 at the start
of the program and writing in the instruction:

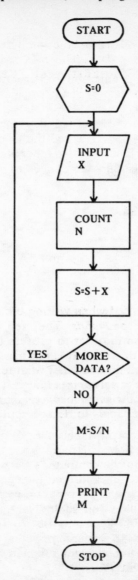

Figure 31

LET N = N + 1

immediately before you instruct the computer to GOTO the line
in the program that inputs X. This means that 1 is added to N
each time the computer goes to the INPUT X line, which has the
effect of counting the number of values.

ANSWER

10	LET S = 0
20	LET N = 0
30	INPUT X
40	IF X = −1 GO TO 80
50	LET S = S + X
60	LET N = N + 1
70	GO TO 30
80	LET M = S/N
90	PRINT M
100	END

System commands

The words that you used when writing the above program are
called *programming commands*. They tell the computer what
operations to perform in order to process the data. The command RUN is quite different. It is not used within a program,
instead it is used to tell the computer what to do with a program.
It is an example of a *system command*.

Commands vary somewhat between computers, but some
system commands that apply to ICL computers are:

- NAME – this command labels the program with whatever
  name you wish to call it. This permits you to store the program
  under that name in the computer's long-term store (i.e. on
  magnetic disc or tape), and then later to retrieve it by that
  name. If you wish to call the program you wrote in the above
  activity MEAN, then you should type in NAME MEAN
  either before or after keying in the program. On other computers (such as the BBC microcomputer) this command does
  not apply. Instead the program is named when you save it, by
  typing SAVE "MEAN".

- NEW – you can use this instead of the command NAME. Typing in NEW MEAN will cause the computer to both name the program and to delete any program lines already stored in the internal memory so that only lines keyed in after the command are included in the named program.
- SAVE – if you key in this command after you have typed in the program and named it, then the computer will store that program on disc or tape for later retrieval. On some computers you should type SAVE followed by the program name.
- LOAD (or GET) followed by the program name will retrieve the program from disc and copy it into the internal store. You can then RUN the program. Note that the program has not been removed from the disc, it has only been copied.
- KILL or WIPE followed by the program name will delete the program from the disc.
- SCRATCH will delete the program from the internal memory (but not from the disc). (Not the BBC or other microcomputers.)
- LIST will display all the lines of the program on the screen.

Self-check

1 You want to save the program you have written in the previous activity, and then delete the program from the internal memory. Write down the commands needed.
2 You now wish to get the program from disc and replace line 40 by a new line which causes the computer to GOTO line 80 when any negative number (not just −1) is keyed in. Write down the commands needed.
3 Finally, you want to delete the old program from the disc and save the new program. Write down the commands needed.

If you have a computer, try out what you have written down. (Note that the commands for your particular computer may differ somewhat from those given here.)

ANSWER

1

  NAME MEAN
  SAVE
  SCRATCH

2

  GET MEAN (or LOAD MEAN)
  LIST (this command is necessary only if you want to check the program)
  40   IF $X < 0$ GOTO 80

3

  KILL MEAN
  SAVE

> ## *Optional activity*
>
> By familiarising yourself with a few more BASIC programming commands you could write quite advanced programs. There are a large number of books available on programming in BASIC, and I suggest you get hold of one of these and look up the following commands:
>
> REM
> TAB
> ;
> $
> " "
> DIM
> FOR . . . NEXT
> READ . . . DATA

Part of assignment **3**, if you do it, requires you to use these commands (see pages 230–1).

> ## *Activity*
>
> Produce a brief dictionary of the system commands and program commands you have encountered in this book, as well as the commands you looked up in the above activity. Add to your list other commands that you may have met while using a computer. (Five minutes.)

6 | Systems analysis and design

Introduction

Having found out all he can about data processing, computers, and the business applications of computing, Mike must now set about computerising his business. The remaining three chapters of this book describe what this will involve:

- *Analysing the systems*: analysing the data processing requirements of the various subsystems of his business and designing both manual and computer-based procedures to meet those requirements.
- *Choosing the equipment*: selecting the most appropriate equipment for those procedures.
- *Organising the processing*: organising the day-to-day work of the computer and the data processing personnel.

We begin in this chapter by looking at systems analysis.

> *Self-check*
>
> What is a business 'system'? Remind yourself by jotting down a two- or three-line explanation. For help, revise pages 37–8 and 39.

Systems analysis

Any business – even a small business like Mike's – is a complex thing, and in order to computerise it it is helpful to break it down into its main subsystems. These include the wages system, the sales order processing system, the purchasing system, and the stock control system. A system processes inputs received from its environment (including data contained on documents received from other systems) to produce outputs transmitted to its environment (including action documents sent to other systems). You learned about system inputs, outputs, and processing in Chapter 2.

Systems analysis is concerned with the following tasks:

1 Identifying what the information outputs of a system should be – i.e. what action documents it should produce.
2 Deciding what data inputs are needed by the system to produce these outputs – i.e. what source documents it needs.
3 Deciding how the data inputs should be converted to the required information outputs – i.e. how the processing should be done.

In Chapter 3 you learned that a system has to be controlled, which means that whoever is in charge of the system must ensure that it achieves its planned outputs. Systems analysis is concerned with this also, for it must decide what management reports are needed by the person in charge in order to control the system. This is a fourth task:

4 Deciding what reports are needed on the system, and how these reports are to be produced.

Systems analysis is almost always carried out with the idea of computerising the procedures, and an important part of the work is finding out whether in fact this is going to be worthwhile. This is a fifth task:

5 Comparing the benefits that will come from computerising the data processing with the costs of computerisation.

We are going to look at all of these aspects of systems analysis in this chapter.

Systems analysts

In large organisations *systems analysts* are employed to do this type of work, and part of this chapter is devoted to a description of their work. Small businesses, which are much less complex than large businesses, will normally adopt a more do-it-yourself attitude, and they will tend to rely on the help and advice of the computer supplier.

I begin in the next section by describing what tasks (1) to (4) above involve. If Mike works through the steps described in this section he should be able to decide for himself what he wants from a computer system and what benefits he hopes to gain from it, and he should be able to draw up a statement of requirements to assist him in selecting suitable hardware and software (see Chapter 7).

Self-check

Write down four systems within Mike's business. One system is the wages system – write down the outputs that this system must produce and the inputs it needs.

ANSWER

You can check your answer with figure 16, which indicates a number of systems. The first three decisions listed there, for example, indicate three systems: stock control, purchasing, and paying. The inputs and outputs of each (including wages) are given in the figure.

Look-ahead

Before beginning your study of this chapter, I suggest you look ahead to the section on pages 220–24 describing how a computerised system operates. At this stage don't carry out any of the exercises given in that section, just read it through quickly. It will indicate to you what the systems analysis is heading towards.

The systems approach: the main steps

Before any of the above five tasks can be carried out Mike must identify and write down the systems in his business. To do this properly he should carry out the first two steps described below.

Step 1: Identify the objectives of the business

To utilise a computer effectively it is often necessary to make dramatic changes in the way in which a business is run. To make the most of the opportunities for change that this presents, the management of a company or the owner of a small business should ideally begin by identifying as precisely as possible what the objectives of the business should be.

To illustrate this, here's the true story of a menswear shop that opened in Chippenham a few years back selling mainly cut-price pullovers, jeans, and the like, both over the counter and by mail order. About a year after opening the owner sat back and took stock of his business. He had found that most customers were not buying clothes for themselves, but for other people. He came to the conclusion that he was not in the clothes business, but the gift business. So he started gift-wrapping his sales, he stocked greetings cards and other similar merchandise, and his business boomed! His business objectives had changed from attempting to penetrate the menswear market to attempting to penetrate the gift market.

Self-check

Mike should begin by reviewing his business objectives. He might have thought that he was in the business of selling papered walls and painted wood. Can you think what business he is really in? How might his objectives change? (Look back to the description of Mike's business on page 15.)

ANSWER

Your answer should not limit Mike to conventional decorating. He is, after all, selling home comforts, which can include home extensions, renovations, central heating systems, and fitted kitchens. His objectives might change from seeking to establish himself in the decorating market to establishing himself as a builder, or being in the fitted kitchen market.

Step 2: Identify the business operations needed to achieve these objectives, and the decisions implied by these operations

Having decided that he was in the gift business the shopkeeper in Chippenham had to identify the tasks or operations he needed to carry out on the sales side and on the purchasing side of his business. On the sales side there was the task of making the public aware of the gift nature of the business through advertising and other forms of sales promotion, as well as the tasks of receiving customers' orders, processing orders, etc. On the purchasing side he had to identify the lines of merchandise that were likely to sell, choose suitable suppliers, place orders, and receive and store goods.

He had to include in these operations both his 'office' tasks, such as recording the sales and purchases transactions, and his 'production' tasks, such as dispatching mail order goods and selling to customers in the shop.

In this way he arrived at quite a long list of operations entailed in the running of his business.

Next, he had to write down the decisions he had to make during the course of carrying out these operations.

Self-check

Look at the sentence above which lists the operations on the purchasing side of his business. What major decisions will he be making when carrying out these operations? Turn to figure 16 for help.

My answer to this self-check is:

1 *What should I buy?* (i.e. identifying the lines that he will be able to sell)
2 *Whom should I buy from?* (i.e. selecting suitable suppliers)
3 *When and how much should I buy?* (i.e. deciding, from his stock balances and rate of usage, the timings and quantities of orders)

As you learned in Chapter 2, to make these decisions the

Chippenham shopkeeper needs data inputs, and as a result of making them he will produce information outputs. For example, decision (2) (*Whom should I buy from?*) requires data on the various suppliers (their prices, etc.), and it results in purchase orders being produced. It is these decisions, in fact, which indicate the various subsystems of the business and their inputs and outputs:

1 Decision (1) above is to do with the merchandising system.
2 Decision (2) is to do with the purchasing system.
3 Decision (3) is to do with the stock control and selling systems.

So by writing down all the decisions he has to make in the course of running his business, the Chippenham shopkeeper can identify all his subsystems and their inputs and outputs.

> ### Self-check
>
> Suppose that, after analysing his business objectives, Mike has decided that he is in the business of refurbishing customers' kitchens and that as a result he should, like Pinecrafts, concentrate on the installation of fitted kitchens and the activities associated with this. List four business operations that he will have to carry out in the course of this work, and the business decisions that these imply.

ANSWER

The operations include selling his services, buying in (or making) fitted kitchens and buying in raw materials, installing the kitchens, carrying out the associated decorating work, and so on. The decisions that these imply are shown in figure 16, plus production planning decisions if he is going to make the kitchens himself. (These are deciding when particular items are to be made, in what quantities, and by whom.)

Step 3: List the outputs and inputs implied by each of these decisions

We have covered this step in Chapter 2. The technique is to list the outputs first, and then the inputs required to produce these outputs.

Self-check

What outputs will result from Mike's (or Pinecrafts') decision *What raw materials and parts should I purchase this week?* What inputs does this decision require?

ANSWER

Outputs include purchase orders sent to suppliers. Inputs are data from stock records on items that are running out, and requisitions from production planning on items needed during the next production period. Purchase orders are action documents. Other outputs will be reports; for example, an analysis of purchases by type of item, or by supplier.

Figure 32 shows the result of step (3) in diagrammatic form. It gives some of the subsystems of a manufacturing business linked by inputs and outputs. For completeness it includes prime inputs and outputs (see pages 21–2). This figure is explained in the subsection 'The systems approach to business' on pages 37–8. Read this subsection again now.

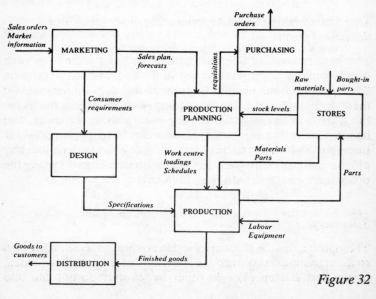

Figure 32

Step 4: Decide how the data inputs to each system should be processed to produce the required outputs

It is at this point that Mike or his adviser (or the systems analyst in the case of a larger business) must compare possible data processing methods. He must investigate manual and electronic alternatives, the object being to arrive at the most cost-effective solution to each system's data processing needs and to the overall data processing needs of the organisation.

He must calculate:

1 The cost of changing over to the new methods, including the cost of any equipment that has to be bought;
2 The value to the organisation of the benefits that will result from the new methods, including the value of any savings in clerical labour and the value of improved management reports.

The best solution is the method for which (2) exceeds (1) by the greatest amount. This calculation is called 'cost/benefit analysis'.

Step 5: Determine the data processing procedures and document them

The data processing alternatives that he has selected for each system must now be worked out in detail. He must determine the DP operations needed to convert the data inputs, and he must document these. He must compile procedure manuals for those parts of the task that are to be carried out manually, and he must bring in a computer programmer to write programs for those parts which are to be computerised. He may decide to buy off-the-shelf software packages, in which case he must make the procedures conform to the requirements of the packages.

Summary

These, then, are the steps involved in systems analysis. Although some organisations go through the whole of the above sequence, many start at step (3) – in other words they do not call into question the objectives of the business. Also, the task of writing the computer programs will not generally be done by the analyst, as step (5) indicates, but by specialist programmers.

We can now move on to describe the work of the systems analyst in more detail.

> ### Review
>
> 1 What is systems analysis? Write a two-line definition.
> 2 Identify the main subsystems of Pinecrafts (see the Appendix) and the main inputs and outputs of each. Draw a diagram like figure 32 showing these systems linked by the inputs and outputs.
>
> (Fifteen minutes.)

The systems analyst

> ### Self-check
>
> You have learned what systems analysis involves. Try to write down in two or three lines a simple definition of the role of the systems analyst.

His role

The systems analyst's role is to analyse and design an organisation's systems, which means to:

- Identify computer applications (and also manual DP applications);
- Define procedures; and
- Specify appropriate equipment.

All organisations have data processing procedures producing action documents and reports, but these procedures do not always work very well. The systems analyst's job is to investigate them and to make recommendations for improvements.

His position

Systems analysis is part of a whole family of management techniques. Organisation and methods (O&M) and work study belong to the same family. They all follow the same broad approach, outlined on page 201:

- Identify the outputs required.
- Determine the inputs that are needed to produce these outputs.
- Decide the best method for converting the inputs to outputs.

O&M is generally concerned with manual office work, and it tends to tackle isolated areas of an organisation rather than adopting an overall approach. Nevertheless, its approach is very similar to the systems approach, and in some organisations the O&M analysts carry out systems analysis.

Work study is mainly concerned with the factory rather than the office, and it concentrates on working methods, staffing levels, and fixing output targets.

Some organisations have a management services department in which systems analysts, O&M analysts, work study officers, and operational researchers work side by side. In other organisations the systems analysts belong to the data processing department and work under the data processing manager.

The systems analyst (or team of analysts) will spend a great deal of time in other departments, investigating their systems. He does not have the authority to decide which departments to study. Only the senior management can decide this, though obviously he will be consulted. And, importantly, the managers of any departments that are to be affected should agree to the study being done before the analyst sets foot in their departments.

The analyst does not have the authority to implement any recommendations that he may make. It is up to the senior management to decide whether and how to implement, and managers of affected departments will obviously have a major involvement. The analyst will of course be closely involved in the implementation, but in a consultative capacity.

His approach

The systems analyst is an agent of change. And change is what people at work fear most. If he is to gain the cooperation of staff in the department in which he is working he must strive to allay this fear. It is important that staff fully understand the reasons for and the potential benefits of the study, and that they do not feel that their jobs are threatened.

To this end members of the senior management and the systems analyst must meet with affected staff before the study takes place to explain the purpose of the study, to emphasise its benefits, and if possible to give no-redundancy guarantees. During the study itself the analyst must be careful not to antagonise staff, and as far as possible he should try to give them a sense of involvement in the study, so that they have a measure of commitment to it.

His work

Unlike the other management techniques referred to earlier in this section, systems analysis is almost always concerned with computerisation. An important part of the analyst's job is to advise management on whether in fact computerisation is worthwhile. He must therefore begin any major project for computerising a business's systems by deciding whether a computer-based solution is feasible and cost-effective. This first phase of the project is called a *feasibility study*, and it is covered by steps (3) and (4) on pages 205 and 207.

Assuming that a computer-based solution is feasible, he must look at the business's subsystems in turn and design computerised procedures for each (step (5) on page 207). As you have learned, to attempt to computerise the whole of a large business in one go is an impossible task.

Finally, he must draw the individually computerised subsystems together so that they form an integrated whole.

We can therefore divide a systems project into three phases:

1 The feasibility study.

2 Designing computerised procedures for individual subsystems.

3 Integrating these subsystems, so that common files and inter-related procedures are used throughout the organisation.

In the remainder of this chapter we'll be taking an in-depth look at these three phases.

How does this apply to Mike?

In a small business like Mike's a full-blown systems project is quite inappropriate. Mike will certainly have to carry out some sort of feasibility study to decide whether he should buy a computer, and he will have to decide what outputs (action documents and reports) a computer system should produce for him. But he will not employ the services of a systems analyst, nor will he use much, if any, specially written software. Instead, he will take his list of output requirements to a computer supplier, and use his services. You will be learning about this in the next chapter.

Review

The management of Pinecrafts has called you in as a systems consultant to advise them on the feasibility of installing a computer and to design computer-based procedures. Explain how you would approach your task, and outline the steps you would take in carrying out the project. (Ten minutes.)

OUTLINE ANSWER

Consult with all staff affected, explain to them the reasons for and benefits expected from the study. Carry out the feasibility study. If management accepts the feasibility of computerisation then design procedures for each system in turn. If management accepts your recommended procedures then assist in the implementation.

The feasibility study

This is the first phase of a systems project, and it covers steps (3) and (4) on pages 205 and 207. It will normally be carried out by a team consisting of staff representing the various parts of the organisation plus the systems analyst. At this stage the analyst may not be an employee of the organisation, but an outside consultant.

The team will look at the organisation as a whole and identify possible areas of computerisation, and it will carry out a cost/benefit analysis to determine whether computerisation is worthwhile.

Self-check

Explain in a couple of lines the meaning of 'cost/benefit analysis'. For help revise page 207.

In carrying out this analysis the team will attempt to quantify (i.e. express in monetary terms) the overall costs of computerisation and the overall benefits to the organisation. It is unlikely that the benefits expected from a single application will justify the use of a computer, but the benefits from a range of applications probably will. Possible benefits are listed on page 72; they include savings on manpower and the provision of better management information.

The team will present the results of this feasibility study (including the expected costs and benefits) in a report. This is used by management to decide whether or not to go ahead with computerisation. Assuming management decides in favour of computerisation, it will need to employ one and possibly several analysts to analyse the possible applications and to design computerised procedures.

The team will also state what document production, reporting, and inquiry capabilities are needed, and it will recommend suitable equipment (computers, VDUs, printers, etc.). After accepting the report the management may sign a contract with the supplier and preparations for installing the equipment may begin.

We shall leave the major topic of purchasing and installing a computer to the next chapter. Instead, we move straight on with a look at what's involved in computerising the individual subsystems of the business.

> *Activity*
>
> Write down the information the management of Pinecrafts needs in order to determine whether computerisation of the business is feasible. Don't carry out any calculations, just list the items of information needed. (Five to ten minutes.)

OUTLINE ANSWER

A list of applications, together with a cost/benefit analysis covering each application, is needed. Your answer should expand on this, and should list items such as the present cost of clerical labour and the cost of purchasing a microcomputer system.

Computerising the subsystems

Computerising the individual subsystems is the second phase of the systems project. It consists of a number of studies, carried out consecutively, each one covering a subsystem of the business. The stages in each study are:

1 The terms of reference.
2 The investigation.
3 The analysis.
4 The design.
5 The implementation.

Let's see what each of these involves.

The terms of reference

Before a study can begin it is necessary to lay down its *terms of reference*. These identify the subsystem which is to be investigated, and thus fix the boundaries of the analyst's investigation. He will need to investigate the way in which the subsystem impinges on other subsystems in the business, but he cannot, during the current study, make recommendations for changing those subsystems.

The senior management must draw up the terms of reference in consultation with the analyst. The terms should include:

1 An identification of the section of the organisation to be studied, and a statement listing in general terms the benefits that are expected to result from the study.
2 An estimate of the expected duration of the study, and the number of staff to be allocated to it. Depending on the size of the study, this will range from a single analyst to a team of several analysts.

Activity

The management of Pinecrafts decides to computerise the business in stages, beginning with the wages system. Try drawing up terms of reference for a study of this part of the business. Your answer should not exceed fifty words. Omit item (2) above.

The subsystem feasibility study

The next two stages of the study are the investigation and the analysis. Together these form the feasibility study of the subsystem. (Don't confuse this with the overall feasibility study carried out earlier.)

Self-check

State in a sentence or two what you think the purpose of this feasibility study is.

The purpose of this study is to identify the ways in which the various procedures within the subsystem might be improved, and to quantify the expected costs and benefits. The cost of running the present system must be compared with the cost of running the proposed system, the cost of changeover must be worked out, and the value of any improvements in management information, customer service, and so on, must be quantified as accurately as possible.

I'm now going to describe the two parts of the feasibility study in more detail.

The investigation

This involves gathering as much relevant information as possible about the system, by interviewing managers and staff (or possibly using questionnaire forms instead of interviews), and by tracing the flow of data through the system. As a result of this the analyst can determine:

- the procedures that are used;
- the action documents and reports that are produced;
- the volumes of work, i.e. how many documents of each type are produced each week, and how frequently the management reports are produced.

Activity

List the items of information that must be collected on Pinecrafts' wages system during the initial investigation. (Five minutes.)

OUTLINE ANSWER

Information required on: number of employees, frequency of payment, method of payment, procedure for calculating wages, information on rates of pay and on deductions, documents produced, reports produced for costing and other purposes.

The analysis

The analyst is now in a position to examine critically the existing procedures and outputs of the subsystem. He will attempt to answer the following questions:

- *Are the managers receiving the information they need at the right frequency?*
- *Are the action-documents suitable – are some unnecessary, or should others be introduced, or should they contain more, or less, or different information?*
- *How can the procedures be made more efficient?*

More discussions with managers and staff are needed at this stage. From these the analyst will be able to tell what outputs (documents and reports) the subsystem ought to produce, and how the procedures can be improved. He will consider not only what the system ought to produce now, but what it might be required to produce in the future. It will be clear at this stage whether a computer is a possible solution, or whether improved manual procedures might be a better option.

The analyst must at this point investigate costs and try to quantify anticipated benefits. It may not be cost-effective to provide all the information needed by managers, and a compromise may have to be worked out. He will eventually arrive at a set of recommendations that he will present to management in a feasibility report. In this he will suggest in outline form the structure of the proposed system, and what reports and action-documents should be produced. He will quantify the benefits of the system and compare them with the costs.

In most instances the management will accept his report, with perhaps some amendments to his suggestions.

The design

Once management has accepted the feasibility report the analyst can set to work on the design stage of the study. In the case of procedures which are not to be computerised this involves:

- revising the manual ways of doing the work;
- redesigning forms;
- producing procedure manuals.

In almost every case, however, some procedures will be computerised, and for these the analyst will need to:

- design the computer files;
- design the computer procedures and the forms required;
- produce a report, called a *system definition*, which describes the proposed system.

Self-check

Jot down briefly what you think is involved in designing

computer files, computer procedures, and the associated forms. (Less than five minutes.)

I gave details on these matters in Chapters 3 and 4. File design involves deciding whether sequential or random access should be used, as well as determining what fields are needed in the file's records. For the computer procedures the analyst must define how the data is to be input, and how the output is to be produced. He must also specify the control procedures. For details on form design for computers see page 100.

In the system definition he will give details of every aspect of the proposed system, from specifying how data is to be input to examples of the reports and documents that are to be produced. It will also state and describe the programs needed and it will include flowcharts showing what the programs must do. These program descriptions and flowcharts are used by the programmers as guidelines for writing the programs needed for the system.

The analyst will also determine the staffing requirements for the proposed system.

Activity

Try your hand at designing a computer-based wages system for Pinecrafts.

This is a major activity, and it will take you about an hour. It will provide you with a useful opportunity to revise important material in Chapters 3 and 4, as well as fixing in your mind the sort of tasks that a systems analyst has to do. You will be using your answer when you come to do the assignment at the end of this chapter.

You must first state the files that will be needed (see your answer to the self-check on page 114). Then state for each file whether it must be random access or whether it can be sequential access (see your answer to the self-check on page 120). Write down the records that must be held on the files (self-check on page 114), and specify the field lengths for these records (page 111) and the coding systems that are to be applied (see page 92). You will find figures 21 and

22 helpful for this part of the activity.

Now deal with the input of data from the clock cards (assume that these are used in Pinecrafts). These cards should be batched, and appropriate controls applied (pages 101 ff.).

You should also specify the output. List the documents that the system must produce, and the data that is to appear on these documents. Don't forget the management reports. For help, refer to the documents produced in your own firm, and refer to your (or a friend's) payslip.

Then decide whether batch processing or real-time processing should be used (page 121), and finally give a brief description of what the wages package must do.

OUTLINE ANSWER

The first part of the answer is given in the answers to the activities and self-checks referred to above. Three fields on the employee records might be:

Works number: two numeric digits (allowing up to ninety-nine employees).
Name: thirty alphabetic characters.
Wage rate: three numeric digits (allowing rates up to 999 (pence) per hour).

Your answer should include a number of other fields (see the answer to the review on page 118).

The controls that are to be applied might include:

- Batch total checks – two totals are the sum of the works numbers, and the sum of the hours worked.
- Other checks – the operator might check that she has keyed in the works number correctly by reading the name displayed by the computer on the screen and comparing with the name on the clock card; also the computer might apply a range check to the hours worked (should be less than sixty).

The documents that are to be produced include the payroll, payslips, paycheques (if paying by cheque), note and coin analysis (if paying by cash), direct debit instructions to bank if paying by direct debit. Other documents are national insurance schedules and tax returns (to tax office). One report will be the analysis of wages by department or section.

Data on the payroll will include the works number, name, wage rate (for standard and for overtime hours), hours worked (standard and overtime), gross pay, tax code, tax payable, other deductions, net pay, and cumulative totals.

The package should, for each clock card, indicate on the screen display the data that the operator has to key in: the works number and the hours worked. It should store this data on the transaction file, and then, in a batch processing run, read the reference data on the master file, perform the wages calculations, and print the transaction data, the reference data, and the results of the calculations in the permitted areas of the payroll and the payslips. It should also update the master data (i.e. the cumulative totals), and print the results on the payroll and payslips.

The package should also produce the other documents and reports required, and it should provide facilities for printing out the audit trail and for maintaining the reference data.

For more detail on the running of packages, see the next section, 'Example of a computerised system'.

Implementation

The implementation of the proposed system must be fully planned by the systems analyst, and these plans should be included in his system definition. In outline, implementation involves the following steps:

- Retraining the staff, in particular the clerical staff who are to operate the new procedures and equipment.
- Creating the master files, by suitably coding the data currently held on manual files and keying it into the system.
- Ordering the computer stationery.
- Testing the new system. Although the individual programs will have been tested by the programmers, there may be errors in the system as a whole. This is best checked by using the computer to process data that has recently been processed by the existing manual system, and comparing the results.

Any discrepancies must be investigated, and errors that come to light in the computer system must be rectified.
● Running the new system in parallel with the existing system for several weeks and investigating any further discrepancies.

The systems analyst will necessarily be closely involved in implementing the system he has designed, and he may in fact supervise the implementation.

Do not confuse the implementation of a subsystem (such as Pinecrafts' wage subsystem) with the installation and implementation of the computer itself. In the case of a large business the computer will be installed and perhaps at the same time one or two subsystems implemented, but most subsystems will be designed and implemented at a later date. In the case of a tiny business (such as Mike's), however, both the installation of the computer and the implementation of the subsystems will be carried out at the same time.

The steps involved in the purchase and implementation of a computer are described in Chapter 7. Whereas much of this present chapter applies to large organisations only, that chapter applies equally to both large and small businesses. Therefore, included in that chapter are details on creating the master files and other implementation matters that are dealt with here in outline only.

Self-check

List the items that will appear in your system definition for Pinecrafts' wages system. (You will find the answer in the last two subsections.)

Example of a computerised system

Before looking at the final phase of a systems project (the integration of the subsystems), let's pause to examine the way in which a (sub)system operates once it is computerised. We'll suppose that you have installed a computer in your small business, and we'll look at the sales order processing system.

This system will include invoicing and the sales ledger. Also, since sales affect stocks of goods, it may also include stock control. (In a larger business, however, stock control may be treated as a separate system.)

> ### Self-check
>
> List the outputs that you think you will want from this subsystem, the data you will have to input to get these outputs, and the files that you will need to store this data. You will find part of the answer in the case study on page 161 and in figure 24. (Five minutes.)

The outputs

The outputs that you will require from the sales order processing system include the following action documents and reports:

Documents *Sales documentation* (i.e. invoices plus copies – see pages 98 and 169); *credit notes* (sent to customers if e.g. goods have been returned); *statements*.

Reports *Aged debtors' lists* (for chasing late payers); *customer activity reports*; *stock reports*; *representatives' sales reports* (if applicable).

A record of transactions will also be needed for audit purposes. This will show sales ledger detail, namely lists of invoices sent to and payments received from customers, together with the current balance for each customer's account.

The inputs

The data that you will have to input to the system to produce these outputs is: *customer orders* (i.e. customer code number, stock code number, quantity); *goods returned* (similar detail on stock returned by customer); *cash received* (customer code number and amount); *goods inwards* (stock code number of quantities of goods received from suppliers).

The files

You will need the following files on magnetic disc: *sales transaction file* containing details of all sales transactions; *sales ledger* (i.e. *customer file*) containing customers' names and addresses, delivery details, terms, credit details, and account balances; *stock file* containing product code numbers and descriptions, VAT codes, price details, discount details, and stock levels.

Operating the system

To operate the system you must begin by switching the computer on and inserting the disc containing the sales order processing programs into a disc drive. By keying in a command (as instructed in the manual of operating instructions) you will cause the computer to copy the programs into its internal memory. This task may take perhaps ten seconds, and when finished the computer displays on the screen a 'menu' listing the procedures that the programs are able to carry out. These will include:

1 Invoicing.
2 Sales ledger entries.
3 Receipts and transfers of stock.
4 Stock control.
5 Amendment of master data.
6 Close down routine.

You can now remove the program disc from the disc drive and insert a disc containing a file that you are going to use, e.g. the sales transaction file. Business microcomputer systems usually incorporate at least two disc drives, enabling you to access at least two files at the same time. Let's suppose you want to do invoicing, then you will put the customer file (i.e. the sales ledger file) in the second disc drive.

Next, you select the procedure you require by keying in the number shown against that procedure on the menu. In this case you will key in '1', telling the computer that you want to carry out invoicing.

Self-check

1 List the operations that the computer must perform to produce invoices from sales orders received by your firm. For help, refer back to the section on procedures on page 53.
2 Using the information contained in the case study on page 161, briefly describe what will take place during each of these operations.

(Ten minutes.)

Operation 1: Inputting the data

The computer will now display on the screen a series of questions which leads you through the sequence of steps for keying in the data and producing the invoices. It will begin by asking you to key in the customer code number and the order data (i.e. the product code number and quantity). You will repeat this for each sales order in your current batch.

Operation 2: Storing the data

The computer will automatically store the data on the sales transaction file. This will be used later for printing out the record of transactions. It will also store the order data (product code numbers and quantities) under the appropriate customer numbers on the customer file.

Operation 3: Retrieving the data, calculating the invoice, printing the invoice

I have grouped these together, as the computer will carry them out at the same time. Before printing the invoices it is of course necessary to set up the invoice stationery in the printer. Also, the customer file and the stock file should be inserted in the disc drives.

The programs will tell the computer to carry out the following steps:

- Read the first customer code number on the sales transaction file. (The clerk will have to key this number in again if a disc drive is not available for that file.) Then look up the name and address stored under that number in the customer file, and print both in the designated area of the invoice form set up in the printer.
- Read the first product code number and quantity for that customer on the customer file, and read the product details and the unit price stored under that number in the stock file. Multiply the unit price by the quantity to obtain the total price for those goods, and print the quantity, description, unit price, and total price in the designated area of the invoice form.
- Repeat this last step for all product code numbers recorded for the first customer, and when the last entry for that customer has been processed, sum the total prices, calculate the VAT, and print the sum, the VAT, and the VAT-inclusive price on the invoice.
- At the same time update the amount owed by that customer on the customer file, and update the stock balance on the stock file.
- Feed the next invoice form into the printer, and repeat the above sequence of steps for the next customer code number. The procedure is repeated until the list of customer numbers in the batch of sales orders is exhausted.

Other procedures

You can carry out other parts of the sales order processing and stock control procedures by returning to the menu and keying in other numbers (see page 222). To exit these procedures you need to key in '6' and follow the brief 'close down routine' that the computer will take you through.

Integrating the subsystems

Let's now return to our study of a systems project. We have looked at the first two phases of a project: the feasibility study and the computerisation of the individual subsystems. In this section you are going to learn about the third and final phase, namely, the integration of the subsystems.

What is integrated DP?

In the last section you read about the operation of a microcomputer system. In such a system there may be quite a lot of duplication of effort and data storage:

1 It may not be possible to update every file from a single data entry. For example, data on goods received from suppliers will be entered on to the stock file as part of the sales order processing/stock control subsystem (see the third procedure of the 'menu' listing on page 222), and it will be entered a second time on to the supplier file as part of the paying subsystem.
2 By the same token an item of data may be held on the files of one subsystem and at the same time held on the files of a second subsystem. One example is the data on goods received, mentioned in (1) above.

In larger computer systems it is possible to avoid this duplication by integrating the subsystems. The idea behind this is that any subsystem has access to any file, and the computer system will automatically update all relevant files from a single data entry.

Self-check

List the benefits to the organisation that will arise from integrating its data processing.

ANSWER

Your list might include: less keying in of data, less possibility of error in data entry, smaller volumes of data held in the computer's store, greater degree of automation in data processing, a department can access any file (according to its needs).

Setting up an integrated data processing system

To do this it is necessary to computerise the individual subsystems first, and then integrate these gradually into a single unified data processing system using common files and coding systems. The steps in setting up an integrated system are as follows:

- Identify the information needed by each decision-maker in the organisation, and identify the various action documents that have to be produced.
- Establish uniform coding systems (part codes, supplier codes, etc.) to replace the variety of coding systems that may have developed over the years in the various departments of the organisation. For example, part numbers in the catalogues produced by the sales department may not match those used in the stores department – this sort of inconsistency must be eliminated. (What may happen in practice is that departments retain their long-established coding systems alongside the new central coding system, communication between departmental and central systems being achieved by a coding translator in the computer.)
- Computerise the individual subsystems in turn over a number of years (as described on pages 213 ff.), setting up computer files as required.
- Design procedures to permit one subsystem to draw upon data held in the files of another. Data can then be entered into the system just once, and any subsystem can access it.

Example For an example of integrated data processing reread the description of the purchasing, goods inwards, and paying procedures in a large company on page 155.

Review

Write a brief account explaining how integrated data processing works in this example. (Five minutes.)

ANSWER

Data on items to be purchased is copied from the stock file on to the buyer's VDU, together with details of suppliers from the purchase record file. From this the buyer makes his purchasing decisions, and data on the orders placed is stored on the purchase record file. Data on goods received is keyed in at the goods inwards department and recorded on the stock file and noted on the purchase record file. Data on the purchase invoices is keyed in in the accounts department, and the computer compares this with the details of goods ordered and received on the purchase record file and so reconciles the invoices.

Security

The systems analyst must build into the systems he designs a number of security procedures. The purpose of these is to protect the programs and files from:

- loss through fire or other accidents;
- theft;
- unauthorised alterations.

A fire would destroy not just the hardware (which is insured and can be fairly easily replaced), but the programs and all the organisation's records – ledgers, personnel files, asset details, etc. – and these may be irreplaceable. Theft may result in competitors getting hold of secret information about the organisation's operations. Unauthorised tampering with the programs could result in the company or its employees being defrauded of large sums of money. In one example of defrauding, each employee's pay is rounded down by a tiny amount, and these amounts are transferred to an unauthorised account. Over a period of time a few pence from the pay of each employee in a workforce numbering many thousands can amount to a considerable sum.

Prevention of loss

To prevent loss through fire or other accident the analyst needs to devise a system for keeping back-up copies of programs and files on magnetic tape or disc in a building removed from the computer installation. These are called security copies.

Self-check

Devise security procedures for protecting the organisation's programs and data, bearing in mind that the data

|| stored on any back-up tapes will quickly become out of
|| date. (Three minutes.)

Programs need to be copied once or twice and the copies secured
in safe locations. Any subsequent amendments to the programs
must also be stored.

Copies of data files will normally be taken at the end of each
day and stored in a safe place. This enables the organisation to
recreate the current files fairly easily in the event of an accident,
simply by keying in again the day's data on to the previous day's
security copies.

The security tape or disc of today's files is called the 'father'
copy, and the live files that remain in the computer system and
which are updated by the system during the next day are called
the 'son'. At the end of the next day a further security copy is
made, which becomes the father, the previous father now becoming the 'grandfather'.

Obviously the father and grandfather copies will be stored
separately from the son, so that a fire or accident will not result
in the destruction of every copy.

At the end of the following day the grandfather copy is erased
and the tape or disc is used to create that day's father, the
previous day's father now becoming the grandfather. This son-
father-grandfather cycle continues indefinitely.

Prevention of theft

Theft may involve the physical removal of files on magnetic discs
or tape, or it may involve unauthorised accessing and copying of
data via a terminal.

The former risk can be guarded against by restricting access to
the computer room and to the disc and tape library, and by
carefully controlling the movements of discs and tapes between
the library and the computer system (see page 282).

The risk of unauthorised personnel gaining access to data via
a terminal is guarded against by the use of passwords. The user
can gain access to the system only by use of the appropriate
password, and the password will only allow him access to those
files that are directly relevant to his work.

Prevention of tampering

Unauthorised tampering with programs or files is a more difficult problem. Every company is required to have its accounts audited to check for accidental mistakes or fraudulent practices, but in the case of computer systems special difficulties arise.

In manual systems the auditors follow an audit trail, which means that they trace items of data through the system from their initial entry to their final use. The purpose of this is to ensure that no errors are being made and that money or goods have not been misappropriated.

In a computerised system, however, there are few documents that can be checked, for the accounts and other records are held electronically. Furthermore, in a small business system any data which is no longer useful is deleted. For example, when debtor's payments are entered in the sales ledger, the balance will be updated but the previous entries may be erased.

To overcome these difficulties the systems analyst may be asked to incorporate programs in the system which produce special print-outs of the day's transactions to enable the auditors to follow items of data through the system. These print-outs are called 'audit trails', and I have referred to them already (e.g. page 122).

In another auditing method the auditor concentrates his attention on the inputs and the outputs rather than on tracing items of data through the processing stages. For example, he may use a test program which inputs both valid and invalid data into the system. By checking the output he can determine whether the valid data has been processed correctly and whether error reports on the invalid data have been produced.

Another audit program he may use checks the contents of files, producing totals and analyses. In this way he can check one file against another and pick up any inconsistencies. Still other programs may be used for checking the processing at random points in the system.

Review

List and briefly describe the security procedures that Pinecrafts should adopt once it has installed a computer system. (Ten minutes.)

Pinecrafts assignment 3

a You have been asked by the management of Pinecrafts to advise on the feasibility of computerising the data processing procedures of the business. Write a feasibility report, in which you should include:

  i A list and brief account of the possible applications of a computer in the business. Include in your account a statement of the expected benefits of computerisation for each application.

  ii An estimate of the costs of buying and implementing a suitable microcomputer system.

  iii An estimate of the volume of reports and documents of different types that the system must produce (invoices, purchase orders, etc.).

  iv A comparison of the cost of running a manual system and the cost of running a computerised system for the business.

  v An estimate of the total value (in £s) of all the benefits given in (i).

  vi A recommendation to the management on the feasibility of a computer.

  Your report should run to about 1,000 words.

b The management decides to purchase a small business computer system. You are asked to computerise the applications listed in your feasibility study, beginning with the wages subsystem. Write a report of around 500 words stating:

  i What outputs the wages subsystem must produce.

  ii What master files will be needed, and what reference data and what master data will be held on these files.

  iii What transaction data will be needed, and how it will be collected

  iv How the system will operate (i.e. how and when the

transaction data should be input, what the programs should do, etc.).

Include in your report a flowchart showing the data processing operations that must be performed on the input to produce the outputs listed in (i).

c The management accepts your report and asks you to write and test the wages program. Do this. Your program should include appropriate validation checks, and the output must be suitably formatted. For simplicity do not create any files, but write the reference data into the program.

HINT

This is the biggest assignment in the book, and you will need to spend several hours on it. You will find your answers to earlier activities in this chapter helpful in answering it. The data in the Pinecrafts case study will enable you to work out the volumes of documents in (a) (iii). The leaflets on small business computer systems that you already have will also be useful. Some of your answers will have to be 'guesstimates', though you may be able to get some help from data processing or systems people in your own organisation or elsewhere.

Now for part (c). In order to store the reference data within the program you must use a DATA statement, and to tell the computer to look for the data within the program when the program is run you must use a READ statement (this is in place of the INPUT statement you have used in previous programs). To write the program you will need to use the commands listed in the optional activity on page 199.

The first part of your program might look like this:

```
5     DIM A$(33), B$(33), C(33), D(33), E(33), F(33), G(33)
10    FOR Z = 1 TO 33
20    READ A$(Z), B$(Z), C(Z), D(Z), E(Z), F(Z), G(Z)
30    NEXT Z
40    DATA "J. SMITH", "01", 120, 3.00, 40, 5.00, 1.20
```

The variables used here are as follows: A$ = name, B$ = works number, C = tax code, D = hourly rate, E = standard hours, F = overtime rate, G = fixed deductions.

7 | Buying and installing a computer

Introduction

Mike's decision to buy a computer arises out of the feasibility study outlined in steps (3) and (4) on pages 205 and 207 and described in more detail on page 212. In this chapter you are going to learn about the tasks involved in selecting and buying a computer system.

> *Self-check*
>
> Explain in a sentence or two what a feasibility study is, and outline its purpose.

The purpose of a feasibility study is to decide whether a computer is a worthwhile acquisition, and, if so, which procedures should be computerised. It is carried out by calculating the benefits that will be obtained by computerising these procedures, and comparing these with the costs involved in buying and installing the system.

The feasibility study will also indicate what the business wants from the computer, i.e. what document production, reporting, and inquiry capabilities it requires for each subsystem. These capabilities are called *facilities*.

The next step

Knowing what he wants from his computer, Mike can now set about buying a system and installing it. This will involve him in the following tasks:

- *Statement of requirements* He (or an adviser) must write down the facilities he requires from his computer system in a 'statement of requirements'.

- *Evaluation* He must evaluate a number of rival systems against this statement.
- *Selection* He must select the most suitable system.
- *Agreement* He must enter into an agreement with the supplier for the acquisition and maintenance of the system.
- *Installation* He must prepare his business for the installation of the system.

In this chapter you will be learning about each of these tasks.

The statement of requirements

Mike analysed his data processing requirements in the first part of Chapter 6. The statement of requirements is a written summary of that analysis. It is a shopping list covering his requirements for:

- Software.
- Hardware.
- Supplier support.

In addition, it should state the expected benefits and the expected costs. Let's see what Mike (or his adviser) should write down under each of these headings.

Software

Standard packages provide a much cheaper and more effective solution to the small businessman's data processing needs than paying an analyst/programmer to write special programs. Mike will therefore almost certainly buy all of the software he requires from a computer supplier. (It may pay a large business, however, to produce its own software rather than conform to the requirements of off-the-shelf packages.)

In order to make a sensible buying decision Mike should list in his statement of requirements the applications that he expects the computer to cope with: wages, purchases ledger, sales ledger, general accounting, and so on. Importantly, for each application he must write down what software facilities are essential for his business.

Self-check

Revise the meaning of the term 'facilities' (see previous section), and list the facilities that Pinecrafts might require for its sales order processing system.

ANSWER

These might include facilities to:

1 Print out invoices.
2 Calculate alternative prices for orders (to allow for different types of customers).
3 Apply discounts to orders over a certain value.

Mike should also write down any non-essential but desirable facilities. These might include, in the case of Pinecrafts' sales order processing, the facility for printing a standard sales message on invoices.

The computer system must also provide safeguards against misappropriation of money or materials. Mike must therefore include the need for periodic audits of the transactions processed by the system (for details see page 229).

Activity

Consider the wages subsystem and write down:

1 The essential facilities that Pinecrafts would need.
2 Any non-essential but desirable facilities that the firm might want.

(Three minutes.)

ANSWER

Don't worry if your list isn't as long as mine. Unless you work in a wages office, you will probably think of only a few facilities.
Essential facilities include:

a Wages should be handled on the basis that a standard working week is assumed for each employee unless otherwise stated.
b Taxation for each employee should be calculated automatically and cumulative totals worked out.

c The facility to pay employees either weekly or monthly.
d The facility to print paycheques should be available.
e A payroll summary should be available for management which should include an analysis by department for costing purposes and an analysis of overtime.
f An audit trail should be produced.

Desirable facilities might include:

g The ability to print tax certificates at the end of the financial year.
h The ability to apply automatically a cost of living increase to wages.

Hardware

Mike's analysis in Chapter 6 will have indicated his requirements for computer hardware. He should be able to write down in his statement of requirements how many VDUs and how many printers he needs. In his case it will be a single microcomputer incorporating a keyboard, screen, and printer; larger systems, of course, will include a number of these devices linked to a central mini or mainframe computer.

Mike does not need to work out how much internal memory his system needs, nor the size of the disc store. This is a technical calculation that is best carried out by the supplier.

Activity

List the hardware that Pinecrafts will require.

ANSWER

Like Mike, Pinecrafts will probably be able to manage with a microcomputer system, which includes:

1 The microcomputer and keyboard (probably in a single unit).
2 A screen (probably separate, possibly housed in the same unit as (1)).
3 Two disc drives.
4 A printer.

However, for £10,000 or so it is possible to buy a minicomputer system (including software) which would be able to support a number of VDUs. This would be useful for production control and stock control, as it would have the capacity needed for production planning, and it would allow terminals to be located in the stores and in the production planning areas.

Supplier support

Mike must also write down what support he requires from the computer supplier in terms of:

- Repair and maintenance of the system once it is running.
- Training for any members of his staff who are to handle the equipment.
- Documentation (i.e. manuals) describing how to work the system.

Let's see what he needs to write under each of these headings.

Repair and maintenance The level of supplier support he needs under this heading depends upon the applications he listed previously in the statement of requirements. A business that must provide invoices on demand to customers, or one which needs facilities for fast inquiries to deal with customer queries as they arise over the phone, requires a very fast repair service, so that if the system fails it can be up and running again in a few hours. Mike is not in such a critical situation, and he will therefore write down that he needs a rather slower (but cheaper) service.

Training This must include not only the training of the computer operators in the actual running of programs and the entry of data, but training of more senior staff on the facilities that the computer can provide, on how to maintain the master files (see page 124), on security procedures (see page 114), and so on. Mike will probably require training for himself (as the senior member) and training for the clerk who is to operate the computer.

Step	Message	Possible responses	Next step
1	CUSTOMER NUMBER?	Key in the number of the customer who is placing this order and press the SEND key. A four-digit number is expected.	2
		Press END key to end the program.	—
2	PRODUCT NUMBER?	Key in the identity number of the first stock item for this order. An alphanumeric code of up to ten characters in length is expected. The description of this product and its price will be displayed.	3
		If the last product number has been keyed, press the first control key to end the order.	END
		To cancel the order, press the second control key.	END
3	QUANTITY?	Key in the quantity of this item and press the SEND key. This line will be priced and stored on file.	2
		Press the backspace key to re-enter the product number. The previous product number will be ignored.	2

Figure 33. A page from an operating manual – operator instructions for the order processing system

Documentation Four types of documentation are needed:

- The *systems overview*, which outlines for the benefit of senior management what the system will do.
- The *systems manual*, which explains in more detail the facilities that are available and what each package can or cannot do.
- The *operating manual*, which should contain a list of all possible questions that might be asked by the computer when running each program, together with an explanation of the questions, the range of acceptable operator responses, and the processing step that will follow each response. Figure 33 shows a page from such a manual.
- The *error manual*, which may be incorporated in the operating manual. This should list all possible error messages that might be produced by the system, and the appropriate operator response for each. Figure 34 gives some examples.

Message	*Response*
STOCK TRANSACTION FILE FULL	There is no room in the stock transaction file to store further details of stock receipts and issues. Run the program which prints the audit trail of stock receipts and issues (the program name will be given here). This will allow further transactions to be keyed.
CUSTOMER NUMBER NOT FOUND	The customer number which has been keyed is not held on the customer file. Rekey the number or use the customer program which adds new customers to the file to create customer details for this number.
DISC ERROR	System error. Call the computer supplier.

Figure 34. Examples of error messages

Activity

If your company or department has a computer system, find out and write down what support the supplier provides, using the headings 'repair and maintenance', 'training' and 'documentation'.

Costs and benefits

You read about the cost/benefit analysis carried out by Mike in Chapter 6.

Self-check

Explain in one or two sentences what 'cost/benefit analysis' means.

Mike quantified (i.e. expressed in monetary terms) the likely benefits to his business of computerisation, and he arrived at an estimate of the costs. He compared the two estimates and so decided whether a computer was feasible for his business.

He must include the results of this analysis in his statement of requirements. If further investigation of possible systems shows that the costs will be above his original estimate, he should be able to determine from what he has written whether the increased expenditure is justified, or whether he should seek some other solution to his data processing problems.

The tender

Mike's statement of requirements is, as I have already stated, a 'shopping list' itemising his requirements. He may find it helpful to write up this list in a formal way for presenting to suppliers. It then becomes a tender document, and its advantage is that it avoids the need for extensive interviews with each supplier to get the facts straight.

Whether Mike's statement of requirements takes the form of a tender document, or whether it remains simply a shopping list, the discipline of producing it will greatly clarify his thinking as to what his needs really are, and it will therefore enable him to make a sensible purchase.

Activity

Write a statement of requirements for Pinecrafts. It should take the form of a shopping list rather than a formal tender, and you should draw upon your answers to previous activities in this section as well as your answer to assignment **3** (pages 230–31). To keep this activity to a manageable length, write down just one facility for each application. (Five minutes.)

OUTLINE ANSWER

Software is needed for sales order processing, stock control, purchasing, wages, and general accounting. Facilities needed for sales order processing and wages have been covered earlier in this section. Facilities needed for stock control include automatic notification of reorder requirements. For purchasing they include supplier comparison, and for general accounting they include automatic updating of accounts from sales and purchase ledgers.

Pinecrafts' hardware requirements and supplier support requirements will probably not differ from Mike's, and we have outlined his in the text above. You have worked out the costs and benefits in assignment **3**.

Review

1 List the items that should appear in Mike's statement of requirements, and state why Mike will benefit from spending time drawing up this statement.
2 State in a sentence or two why the choice of software is crucial to the success or failure of Mike's project.

(Five minutes.)

ANSWER TO Q**2**

If the software is unsuitable the system will not do what Mike wants of it. It will not produce all of the documents and reports that he needs.

The evaluation

Mike's next step is to investigate a number of computer systems. He must evaluate each against his statement of requirements and select the one that most closely fits the bill.

He should first evaluate the software, then the hardware, and then the supplier. He must also check that the overall costs are within the ceilings indicated by his cost/benefit analysis.

Let's now consider what is involved in the evaluation of just one computer system. The steps described here must be repeated for each system that Mike looks at.

Evaluating the software

Mike must begin by asking whether the system has all the essential facilities listed in his statement of requirements. If it has, he must ask whether it offers additional features which meet any of his non-essential but desirable facility requirements.

Mike will obviously reject a system which cannot meet the majority of his requirements. On the other hand, he is unlikely to find a system which meets every one of his requirements, and he will probably have to tailor his needs slightly to match the capabilities of whichever system he finally selects.

Next, Mike must inquire about the degree of flexibility allowed by the software. Can it cope with possible future changes in his business? If it needs to be altered, what will this involve, and what will it cost?

Then he must ask a number of additional important questions:

- Is the software available now, and can it be demonstrated? Many companies, small and large, sell systems for which full software facilities are not currently available. Mike will, of course, want to see a demonstration of both the software and the hardware (see below).
- If the software needs modifying to fit his requirements, how long will this take and how much will it cost?
- Does the software provide sufficient audit trails (see page 229)? As a general rule, a record should be kept for audit purposes of every transaction that results in a file update.

These audit trails should be printed out (normally at the end of each day), and should enable the auditor to trace every transaction through the system.
- Is the system well documented? The manufacturer should provide each of the manuals listed in the previous section.

> *Activity*
>
> Look through the microcomputer leaflets you collected in a previous activity and select the three or four most detailed. As you work through the next few pages, evaluate each of the systems described in these leaflets against the statement of requirements you drew up for Pinecrafts in the last activity. You should do this by placing the systems in rank order under each of the four major headings in the statement of requirements. You will thus arrive at four sets of rankings (see next section on page 248). (Unless you are able to talk to the suppliers of the equipment your rankings under some headings will inevitably be something of a guess.)

Evaluating the hardware

Mike must next consider the computer hardware. He must satisfy himself that the system will run the software he requires and can cope with the sort of work he has in mind. The supplier should be able to demonstrate the system working with the number of VDUs and printers in operation that the business needs under the sort of conditions that are going to occur in practice. Thus the supplier should demonstrate the system operating with something like the type and volume of data that the business will actually be processing, and the purchaser will want to satisfy himself that the system can cope in this situation and deal with inquiries and file updates sufficiently rapidly.

Mike will also want to satisfy himself that the hardware can cope with the possible future expansion of his business. Is it possible to upgrade the system simply by adding additional VDUs and printers, or will another processor also be needed? What is the likely cost of such an upgrade?

Evaluating the supplier

Next, Mike will want to establish that the supplier will give the support he needs after he has bought the system. He must ask the following questions.

- What support will the supplier give if the software develops a fault or needs modification? He will want to find out how quickly the supplier will come to his aid, and what the cost is likely to be. Will the supplier:
  - (a) charge for time spent dealing with problems over the phone as well as for time spent on the customer's site?
  - (b) provide free advice over the phone but charge for call-outs?
  - (c) provide free advice over the phone and free call-outs?
- What support will the supplier give in the event of a hardware fault? Will he:
  - (a) respond within half a day to a call for assistance?
  - (b) replace the faulty unit if he cannot get it working within a set period of time?
- What support will the supplier give in the event of a break-down outside normal working hours, e.g. in the evening, when audit trails might be printed or master files updated?
- Will the supplier give the training needed for Mike's staff to operate the system, and will they provide further future training for new staff?

To answer these questions properly Mike will need to visit one or two *reference sites*, i.e. other customers of the supplier who have similar operations and who use the same hardware and software. Mike can get addresses from the supplier. He will want to get their reactions to the computer system and to the support they get from the supplier.

As a final question Mike should ask himself whether the supplier is likely to be around in three or four years' time. No one wants to buy from a supplier only to find a few months later that they have folded and can no longer give support. A large well-established company is probably a safe bet; however, a small young company trying to gain a foothold in the market is likely to offer good support on favourable terms.

Costs

Mike must also find out the costs of each system. Any which cost more than the cost ceilings indicated by his cost/benefit analysis should be rejected outright. The costs that he writes down should of course include all the hardware costs, the software, and the supplier support costs.

He should at this point study the terms of the contract offered by the supplier (see page 252), as this will contain a number of clauses dealing with costs. He should pay particular attention to any clauses dealing with price changes. This is especially important if he is agreeing to buy a system to be supplied at some future date. He should find out if price increases (caused by e.g. changes in import duty or exchange rates) will be passed on to him, and whether he will benefit from price decreases.

He should also study the clauses dealing with the software costs. The operating system and other systems software are normally included in the purchase price of the hardware, though a small licence fee may be payable at regular intervals to cover the cost of software upgrades. These upgrades are produced from time to time and are sent by the supplier to the customer.

He must also look at clauses dealing with the costs of applications packages. These will be supplied on either of the following terms:

- an initial purchase charge only – in which case the customer is not entitled to any future upgrades;
- a regular rental fee – in which case the customer will receive any upgrades.

Note that the purchase price of the computer system will not include media (i.e. discs and computer stationery), nor will it include items such as printer ribbons, bursters (for trimming the holes from the edge of the computer stationery), or decollators (for separating the copies of multipart stationery after printing).

Activity

Write a brief report (less than one A4 page) on one of the

‖ systems you evaluated in the previous activity. State how it
‖ measures up under each of the four headings in this section.

The selection

Mike should work through the above evaluation procedure for
three or four rival systems, and then look at how each has fared
and select the most suitable. He must compare the rival systems
using the four headings given in the statement of requirements:
software, hardware, supplier support, and costs. Let's see what
he must do in each case.

Software

Any system that does not provide the majority of his essential
software facilities will have been rejected at the evaluation stage.
He must place those systems that do provide the facilities he
needs into rank order.

‖ ### *Self-check*

‖ Write down the questions that Mike will be asking under
‖ this heading. Refer back to the previous sections for help.

PART-ANSWER

- Which offers the most desirable but non-essential facilities?
- Which needs the least modification to meet his essential
  requirements?
- Which is the most flexible and able to adapt most easily to
  future changes in his business?

He also needs to consider ease of use. Which is the easiest to use
and understand?

Hardware

Mike must also compare the hardware, and he should rank again
the systems on their suitability on this score. He should weigh up

for each system the extent to which they incorporate recent technological advances. Although the latest models are likely to shine in this respect, they may not be fully proven in use, and Mike will want to satisfy himself that an advanced machine will actually work properly in his business.

Self-check

Technological excellence is not the only, or even the most important, consideration. Write down the other questions that Mike will ask under the 'hardware' heading (for help, see previous sections).

ANSWER

- Which system will cope best with his demands?
- Which system has the best response time (i.e. deals most rapidly with inquiries and file updates)?
- Which system can be most easily expanded to meet his possible future requirements?

Supplier support

Mike must also compare the support that alternative suppliers offer, and again he should place the systems in rank order. To carry out this comparison it is most important that he visit reference sites to get reactions from other similar customers of these suppliers.

Self-check

Write down the questions that Mike will ask under this heading. For help, revise the subsections on 'supplier support' on pages 236 and 243.

OUTLINE ANSWER

- Which supplier offers the most favourable repair and maintenance support?
- Which offers the best training?
- Which provides the best documentation?

- Do any of the suppliers seem in financial difficulties and likely to fold?

Costs

Costs are obviously an important consideration when choosing between systems. If the price of one system is significantly less than the others, Mike should find out why. It may be because a lower level of support is offered, in which case Mike should assess the value to his business of the additional support levels offered by the more expensive suppliers, and compare this with the difference in cost.

Conversely, if the price of one system is significantly above the rest, why is this? Perhaps a higher level of support is offered, in which case Mike should assess the value of this benefit. A system so highly priced that it lies outside the cost limits stated in his statement of requirements will already have been rejected (see previous section).

There may be many reasons why rival systems differ in price. Mike must look at the total package offered by each supplier – of which price is just one element – and select the one which overall suits him best. Let's now see how he should make his 'best buy' decision.

The decision

Mike should exclude any systems which do not meet his essential requirements (as stated in his statement of requirements), or which cannot be made to meet those requirements without extensive modifications. He will also reject those which are too highly priced. In making his selection from those systems which remain, Mike must consider the rankings that each has achieved under every one of the four headings (software, hardware, supplier support, and costs). If one system is at or near the top of the list in each case, then the choice is easy. Conversely, if a system ranks poorly under every heading, then he can quickly reject it.

Usually, however, the decision is not so clear cut, and then a method of choice based upon *weighted rankings* could be used. One way of doing this is as follows. First, give each system a score under each heading, higher rankings gaining higher scores. If you are considering three systems, then give the highest ranking a score of 3, the next a score of 2, and so on. Next, consider the relative importance of the four headings. The general consensus amongst computer users is that software is the most important, supplier support the next, cost the next, and hardware last. A simple weighting system would be as follows:

Heading	Weighting
Software	4
Supplier support	3
Cost	2
Hardware	1

Multiply each system's score under each heading by the weighting of that heading and add the results to get its overall score.

For example, suppose a system ranks second for software, first for supplier support, third for cost, and third for hardware, then you work out its overall score as follows:

Heading	Ranking	Score	Weight	Weight × Score
Software	Second	2	4	8
Supplier support	First	3	3	9
Cost	Third	1	2	2
Hardware	Third	1	1	1
			Overall score:	20

Carry out this calculation for each of the three systems. The one with the highest overall score is the winner.

Activity

Carry out this calculation for the systems you have ranked in the previous activity (see page 242), and select the one which has the highest score.

Review

Take a fresh sheet of paper and draw up on it a table with the following headings across the top: 'Statement of requirements', 'Evaluation', 'Selection'; and the following down the left-hand side: 'Software', 'Hardware', 'Supplier', 'Cost'. In each of the resulting twelve boxes in this table enter the points to be considered under these headings. (Ten minutes.)

HINT

To answer this question you must revise all of the material covered so far in this chapter. For example, for the box headed 'Statement of requirements' and 'Software' look up the section at the start of this chapter called 'Statement of requirements', and revise the subsection called 'Software'. You will see from this that the points to be considered are: essential facilities, non-essential but desirable facilities, and audit trails. Enter these points in the box, as shown in figure 35.

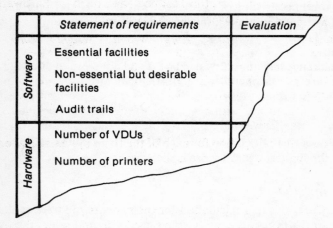

Figure 35

Case study: what went wrong?

Introduction

The following case study illustrates the results of failing to work through the steps outlined so far in this chapter. It describes what actually happened to an organisation which bought a computer system without first working out exactly what it wanted to get out of it. At the end of the case study I'm going to ask you to list the wrong moves made by the management of the organisation.

The organisation was a charity employing fifteen staff. About half of the staff were social workers, the rest administrative. The charity wished to computerise some of its administrative work (the accounts and the payroll) in order to reduce labour costs.

The purchase

The charity purchased, fairly inexpensively, a second-hand minicomputer consisting of a processor with a VDU and a printer. It was a reputable make offering the possibility of future expansion. The charity also signed a maintenance agreement for the hardware.

It did not buy any software, and it had not worked out what its software requirements were. Instead, it hired an analyst/programmer to analyse its requirements and to produce the software. Its contract with the analyst/programmer specified the hourly rate that would be paid for the job, but it did not lay down the facilities that were required, and it did not put a time limit on the job.

The installation

The hardware was successfully installed, and the analyst/programmer began work on the software. Within a few weeks he had produced a subsystem of the payroll system (which carried out the wages calculations but did not produce the cheques and other documentation), and this was found to be usable, although needing minor alterations. The analyst/programmer had other jobs in the pipeline which he had to attend to, but he promised to begin work on the rest of the system in the near future.

Eighteen months later

The hardware had proved very reliable, although it had not been heavily used. On the software side, however, the analyst/programmer had done scarcely any work, for he had other more profitable projects which occupied his time. As a result the charity found the computer system to be something of a white elephant, and the staff regarded it with derision. Even those parts of its procedures that were computerised had to be checked manually owing to minor programming errors.

The management found itself in an increasingly uncomfortable position. It had backed the project, and it had insisted on the computer being used, but it had made the grave mistake of not making adequate software arrangements. Furthermore, due to the high cost of writing programs, the money that it had spent on the small amount of software that was so far working was excessive. Buying commercial packages would have proved much cheaper, faster, and more effective.

Self-check

Analyse the case study and list the wrong moves made by the management. Note down in each case the moves it should have made. (Five minutes.)

ANSWER

It failed to carry out a cost/benefit analysis or to draw up a statement of requirements. It should have done both of these.

It purchased the hardware and then thought about the software. It should have considered the software first.

It opted for specially written software instead of buying commercial packages.

It failed to draw up a proper contract with the analyst/programmer, with properly laid-down targets and penalty clauses requiring compensation if the targets were not achieved.

The agreement

Let's assume that Mike has worked through the statement of requirements, evaluation, and selection tasks that I have described so far, and that he has finally chosen his system. He must now sign two documents:

- An agreement with the supplier for the purchase of the system – this is called the *contract*.
- An agreement with the supplier for after-sales maintenance of the system – this is called the *maintenance agreement*.

The contract

The supplier will have a standard contract that he presents to all customers who purchase his computer systems, and it is unlikely that Mike will be able to persuade him to change any of its terms. Even so, Mike should study its contents carefully to get clear in his mind exactly what are his responsibilities and what are the supplier's responsibilities. If he has any doubts about the practical implications of any of the contract's clauses he should obtain advice from the supplier's reference sites.

> ### Activity
>
> List as many items as you can that should be included in the contract. If possible look at the contract that your firm (if you have one) has entered into. For help, turn to the subsection on costs on page 244.

OUTLINE ANSWER

Price, equipment, terms of delivery and installation, responsibilities of supplier, responsibilities of customer.

The maintenance agreement

Like the contract, this will be a standard agreement presented by the supplier to the customer. It spells out the supplier's responsibilities for the after-sale repair and maintenance of the computer system as well as the fees that will be incurred by the customer.

The maintenance agreement should specify the supplier's call-out time (i.e. the delay between receiving a call for help and arriving on site to fix the fault) and whether the supplier will replace faulty units if they cannot be fixed within a set time. It should also state the level of service that will be offered in the evening or at weekends (when batch jobs such as audit trails, updating of master files, and production of statements are normally done).

Mike should check that this agreement commits the supplier to the level of service he quoted during the system evaluation stage (see previous section), and he should determine what penalties the supplier will incur if he fails to arrive on site within the quoted call-out time. He should also, of course, check on his own commitments and the amount he will be charged (see page 244).

Review

Write a memo (one A4 page) advising the management of Pinecrafts of the questions they should raise before signing the contract and the maintenance agreement for their chosen system. You will find the information needed for this exercise in the subsection on costs on page 244 and in the above section.

Installation

The installation of a computer can be a very traumatic time for a business. Jobs and responsibilities change, friction and resentment can be created, and the changeover from manual to electronic methods involves a great deal of extra work. To minimise these problems, and to take maximum advantage of the benefits that the computer offers, Mike should make sure that his business is properly prepared for the computer.

The computer link man

Mike should make someone within his business responsible for the installation of the computer. His business is so small that he may well take this responsibility upon himself; in a larger business, however, someone below the man at the top will be in charge of installation. It may be someone from within the organisation who has an interest in and knowledge of data processing and computers, or it may be someone brought in from outside the firm (see the case study at the end of this chapter, page 259).

The individual with responsibility for the computer will be the link man between the organisation and the computer supplier. In a large organisation the management should make sure that his identity is known to everyone in the organisation who will be affected by the computer, and that everyone knows that management is firmly behind him and committed to the task that he has to carry out. (A small business does not have the communications problems that exist in a large organisation, and everyone will know the link man.)

The link man will have the job of checking the terms of the contract and the maintenance agreement, agreeing the installation timetable with the supplier, and attending any training courses run by the supplier. He must also prepare and train the clerks who are to operate the equipment, as well as preparing one or two people appointed as deputies to share the responsibilities he will have once the computer is installed. These deputies should also attend any training courses run by the supplier.

Once the computer is up and running, the link man will have overall responsibility for the operation of the computer. This responsibility will cover the computer start-up procedures before the day begins, the normal working hours operation of the computer, and the security procedures, audit trial print-outs, and other activities that take place after the day ends. You can see why deputies must be appointed to share his responsibilities, and also to cover for him if he is sick, on holiday, or leaves the company.

Assuming the computer link man remains with the company, he will become the data processing manager. His duties are described in Chapter 8.

Self-check

The computer link man will have to carry out a number of major tasks before the installation of the computer. Write down as many of these as you can think of.

ANSWER

Some of these tasks have been mentioned above: checking the contract and maintenance agreement, agreeing the installation timetable, attending any training courses, and preparing staff within the firm. There are other tasks, however, that directly concern the computer itself. You are going to learn about these in the subsections below. They are:

- Ensuring that the business's data is put into a suitable form for keying into the computer.
- Designing and ordering the computer stationery.
- Drawing up contingency plans to enable the business to switch to manual procedures in the event of a computer breakdown or power failure.
- Setting up security procedures.

Here's what each of these entails.

Preparing the data

The first of these tasks is ensuring that the business's data is suitably prepared for entry to the computer system. As an example of what needs to be done, consider the stock records.

The computer link man must begin by finding from the supplier:

- the order in which the stock information is to be keyed in, and
- the number of characters in each stock record field and the type of characters allowed (alphabetic, alphanumeric, or numeric).

Then he must check that the existing stock records are suitably coded and that each stock item has a unique code number. If this is not the case, he must design a suitable coding system (see page 90). He must also ensure that in each case the description of the stock item is meaningful, and that the supplier, the reorder level, and other details to be keyed in to the system are clearly stated.

At the same time he should design the source document on to which all this data is to be copied, ensuring that the entries on this document are in the same sequence as the order in which they are to be keyed into the computer. The source document should normally incorporate the questions that will be displayed on the VDU screen when the operator keys in the data. It should also have boxes into which the data can be copied, each box marked out with the number of character positions allowed in that field.

He must arrange for the printing of the required number of copies of this document, and then for the manual copying of the stock data on to it in preparation for the creation of the computer stock file.

Note that this source document will include only reference data, not master data. The reason is that master data is changing frequently, and it will therefore be keyed into the computer immediately before the system goes live. In the above stock example, the master data is the stock balances. The procedure is to do a stock-take over the weekend immediately before going live, the balances being entered into the computer system at that time.

Activity

Design the source document for putting the reference data for Pinecrafts' wages system on to the computer. To keep the task simple, include only the employee's number, the name, the address, and the date of birth.

ANSWER

Figure 36 gives the answer.

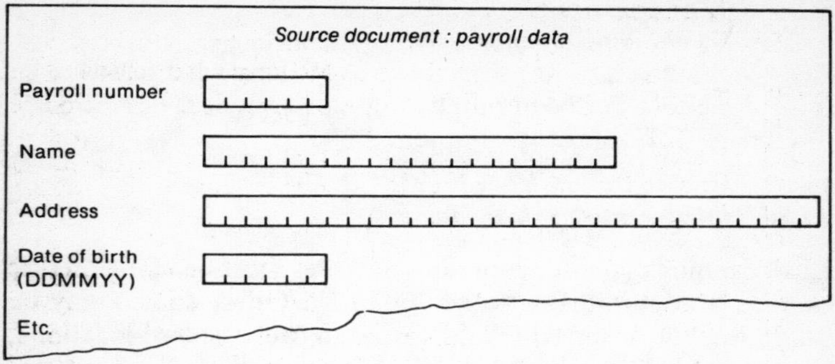

Source document : payroll data

Payroll number

Name

Address

Date of birth
(DDMMYY)

Etc.

Figure 36

Ordering the stationery

The computer link man will also have to liaise with the supplier over the design of the computer pre-printed stationery (invoices, remittance advice notes, payslips, etc.). He will have to do this job, and order the stationery, several weeks before the system goes live. He will also have to order blank computer stationery for management reports.

Drawing up manual contingency plans

If there is an extended equipment or power failure after the equipment has been installed, then the company will have to revert to manual processing. The computer link man must draw up contingency plans in consultation with the supplier, and together they must decide upon the manual procedures that are to be used. It is obviously essential that these procedures are feasible and produce all necessary output documents.

He should also find out from the supplier what are the implications for the computer system of a power failure, and what is the procedure for starting up the computer again. Will the data be lost and have to be keyed in again? Is it feasible to provide a battery back-up unit for maintaining the computer memory during a power failure?

> ### Self-check
>
> Write down two or three lines explaining what needs to be
> done to secure computer programs and files. For help see
> page 227, 'Prevention of loss'.

Establishing security procedures

Each evening copies of programs and files must be made on disc
or tape and stored in another building. Other copies may be
made weekly or monthly and stored in more secure locations,
such as a bank. The computer link man must think about and
design these procedures, in consultation with the supplier, before the computer goes live.

Going live

There are two stages to the task of actually installing the computer system and getting it up and running:

- Setting up the hardware on site and making sure that it is
  working properly.
- Implementing the various applications, such as the wages
  system, the stock control system, and so on.

The first of these is the responsibility of the supplier, though
obviously the customer must make ready a suitable site.
Although in the case of large systems this will involve preparing
a special air-conditioned room, in the case of a small system it is
sufficient to provide space in an ordinary office. Small systems,
in fact, are very easy to install.

The second of these tasks is much more time-consuming, for it
involves creating the files by keying in first the reference data
and then the master data, and then it involves running the
existing manual system and the computer system in parallel for
several weeks to make sure that there are no bugs in the latter.

As I have explained earlier on, it is quite impractical to
computerise the whole of the business in one go. It is necessary
to computerise it subsystem by subsystem, usually over a period
of several months or years.

It is probably best to start by picking a single subsystem of the business, such as payroll, and computerising it in isolation from the rest of the organisation. Payroll is a particularly popular choice, as it does not impinge much on other subsystems, and any difficulties experienced with it will not have repercussions on the rest of the business. By gaining experience of computerisation in this isolated subsystem, the organisation is better prepared for the computerisation of the business as a whole, in particular for the computerisation of those subsystems which are more crucial because they affect many business activities.

Case study: what went right?

Introduction

This factual case study describes the experience of two jointly owned companies – a ladies clothing wholesaler and a light engineering company – in carrying out the steps outlined in this chapter. They were looking for a system that would computerise their sales and accounts procedures, namely order processing, sales ledger, purchases ledger, general ledger, stock control, and sales analysis.

Their main objectives were:

- To enable the businesses to grow without increasing administrative staff numbers.
- To provide management with better information for improved decision-making.
- To provide a better customer service.

General requirements

The companies produced the following list of minimal requirements that they were looking for in a computer system.

- In order to ease the problems of installation they wished to purchase fully tested hardware and software from a single supplier.

- The software had to be sufficiently flexible to cope with the needs of both organisations with minimal modification.
- The cost of the system had to be within specified limits.
- The installation had to be completed within a specified time.

They also included in their list a statement of required software facilities.

The selection

Three alternative systems were evaluated, and a supplier was selected who could offer software and hardware meeting all the above requirements (although his offering lay at the top of the price range). Additionally, the software provided facilities over and above those listed in the statement of requirements. Other factors influencing their choice were:

- The software required no modifications.
- The supplier was able to refer management to a number of reference sites, each of which spoke favourably of both the hardware and the software.
- The supplier offered in his contract a certain number of man-days for installation and training.

The installation

No employee of either company had previously worked with computers, and so an accountant with considerable computer experience joined the management team for a few months. Management gave him responsibility and backing for training the staff in the use of the new system, and he had overall control of running the system. This greatly eased the problem of changing over from manual to computerised procedures.

The order processing, sales ledger, stock control, and sales analysis subsystems were implemented first. Then, after two months of successful running, the purchases ledger was implemented, and finally, two months after that, the general ledger. Management maintained a direct interest and involvement with the computer system throughout the implementation period.

One year later

Both the hardware and the software were running smoothly and reliably. The companies had made such a good choice of software that they were able to process the accounts of another branch without needing to modify the software in any way. The staff themselves had fully accepted the computer and complained if it was ever unavailable (e.g. as when maintenance was being done).

Self-check

Write down why you think this computer system was successfully installed. (Aim to suggest at least five reasons.)

ANSWER

(provided by the supplier's analyst responsible for this project)

1 Management understood the importance of selecting suitable software as well as suitable hardware.
2 In evaluating rival systems, most time was spent comparing software facilities rather than the technical specifications of the hardware.
3 Management maintained a direct interest and involvement in the computer and its implementation. This helped the staff to realise that the computer was there to stay and that the companies were committed to its success.
4 An implementation schedule was agreed from the beginning, and it was adhered to by both parties.
5 The short-term involvement of an independent person with appropriate experience was a wise move in view of the lack of computer knowledge among existing staff. This person was able to make the management aware of its responsibilities, and he was able to prepare the companies for computerisation. At the same time he ensured that the supplier was fulfilling his obligations.
6 The companies were not afraid to choose one of the more expensive solutions, knowing that they would receive a consistently high level of support from the supplier in return.

Review

Write brief notes (less than one A4 page) advising the
management of Pinecrafts of the steps it must take to
prepare for the computer. Refer back to the section on
installation as well as to the case study above for the
information you need. The case study on page 250 will also
help.

8 | DP organisation and staffing

Introduction

To computerise his business Mike (or his adviser) has to:

- analyse its systems;
- choose the equipment;
- organise the processing.

In Chapter 6 you learned about systems analysis and design, and in Chapter 7 you learned about choosing the equipment. This chapter deals with organising the processing.

What does this involve?

First of all, data processing must be organised so that users obtain an efficient and cost-effective service. You will be learning about this in the first section of the chapter, 'DP organisation'.

Secondly, the data processing staff must be organised and their work planned so that the day-to-day DP tasks are carried out on time and accurately. You will be learning about this in the second section of the chapter, 'DP staff'.

Thirdly, the jobs of the DP staff should be designed so that their work is stimulating and provides them with a sense of achievement. The final section of the chapter, 'DP job design', deals with this.

DP organisation

We begin this chapter by looking at the ways in which data

processing is organised in businesses. Let's start off by reviewing what you learned about this in Chapter 4.

> ## *Self-check*
>
> Write down briefly what you understand by the following terms:
>
> Real-time processing.
> Batch processing.
> On-line equipment.
> Off-line equipment.

ANSWER

Real-time processing: items of data are processed individually as they arise. This has the advantage that the master files are always up to date, but it leads to heavy demands on the computer during peak periods.

Batch processing: data is processed in batches rather than as individual items. The processing of batched data can be done at times when the computer is not busy, which leads to a more efficient use of the computer, but owing to the delay between the receipt of the data and its processing the master files will normally be slightly out of date.

On-line equipment: equipment which is connected to the computer, and which is therefore able to send data to it or receive data from it. A VDU is an example of an on-line device.

Off-line equipment: equipment which is not connected to the computer, such as a keypunch.

I shall be referring to these terms frequently in this section.

Ways of organising DP

As you will learn in the following subsections, data processing can be organised in a number of ways. Firstly with regard to *where* it is processed:

- It can be processed centrally, in a data processing department. I shall refer to this as centralised data processing.

- It can be processed throughout the organisation, in the departments that are using the data. I shall refer to this as decentralised data processing.
- It can be processed outside the organisation, by firms which specialise in processing data on behalf of clients. I shall call this external data processing.

Secondly, with regard to *how* it is processed:

- It can be processed manually.
- It can be processed electronically.

Let's begin by looking at what was historically the earliest form of data processing.

Decentralised DP, using manual methods

This is the type of data processing that is done in the traditional office. Examples are clerks in the wages office carrying out the wages calculations by calculator and producing the payroll manually, clerks in the sales office producing the sales and dispatch documentation by manual methods, and so on.

Self-check

Write down what you think are the advantages and disadvantages of this way of processing data. For help on the manual aspects of this question, see page 70.

Although old-fashioned, this way of organising DP has a number of advantages:

- Users can process data in their own way and at their own times, instead of having to conform to the requirements of a central facility. So urgent matters or inquiries can be dealt with promptly.
- The user can enter data directly into the system instead of filling in and sending a source document to the DP department for entry.
- Since the processing facilities are decentralised it is less likely

that a machine breakdown or a strike by a handful of people will disrupt the entire organisation.

The disadvantages are mainly that it is a slow, labour-intensive way of processing data, and its accuracy is inferior to that achieved by other methods.

Centralised DP, using electronic methods

Nowadays we always associate data processing departments with computers. In fact, centralised DP began fifty years before computers, when punched card equipment was introduced. This equipment made it possible to automate data processing, so that it could be done faster, with less labour, and more accurately than by manual methods. However, the equipment was large and expensive, and it was impractical to supply it to every department of an organisation. So the idea of a central data processing department emerged, equipped with large and expensive machinery, and manned by specialist DP personnel.

Nowadays, of course, punched card equipment has largely disappeared, having been superseded by smaller, cheaper, faster, and more reliable electronic computers, but centralised data processing remains.

With the centralisation of DP came batch processing. Punched card equipment was designed to process cards in large batches, and the earliest computers could be operated economically only in this way. Additionally, these computers were designed for use with punched card data entry equipment. The data was keyed in on an off-line keypunch, and subsequently read into the system in batches via high-speed on-line card readers. This minimised the use made of expensive computer time.

So in the 1960s and 1970s, when computers began to spread throughout business, computerised data processing required a central facility employing batch processing techniques with data being entered via off-line devices.

Activity

If you work for a company with a large computer, write down three applications for which it is used. Write down against each one whether it is carried out centrally in the DP department or whether it is decentralised. Try to find out the reasons for these ways of organising the processing.

Decentralised DP, using electronic methods

Further developments in computers are now causing a reversal of this trend towards centralised DP. The emphasis is now once again on decentralised data processing, with data entry being carried out on on-line terminals in user departments, and with the processing also under the control of those departments. Real-time rather than batch processing methods are favoured in most applications, so that each item of transaction data and each inquiry is dealt with via the terminals as it arises, and with up-to-date information being always available.

The reasons for the re-emergence of decentralised data processing are as follows:

● VDUs and even small computers are now so cheap that it is economically feasible to place them in user departments.
● Applications programs are steadily becoming more 'user friendly', meaning that they can be understood and run by staff in user departments who are not DP experts.
● Computers are now so powerful that the arguments in favour of reducing the data processing load during peak periods by centrally processing the data in batches hardly apply.

Let's pause at this point in our survey of the ways of organising DP to look at the implications of decentralised electronic data processing. We'll look first at the implications for the large central computer which must support all the terminals in user departments, and second at the implications for the departments themselves.

Multiprogramming

Decentralised data processing involves a number of on-line terminals in user departments each making simultaneous use of the computer system. Users in the sales department will be keying in customer orders and dealing with inquiries at the same time that users in the purchasing department are keying in purchasing decisions and calling up purchase records. In order to carry out these tasks simultaneously the computer must have what are called *multiprogramming* capabilities.

These capabilities are provided by a sophisticated operating system (see page 179) which switches from one terminal and program to another at lightning speed. This enables the computer to handle each terminal's next processing step in turn, the speed of execution and switching being so fast that each user is not normally aware of any delay between one processing step and the next.

Multiprogramming also increases the efficiency of the computer in batch processing applications. With single-program execution one part of the system may be idle while another part is carrying out its stage of the processing, while at other times in the program run the situation is reversed and the previously idle part is now busy while other parts are now idle. Multiprogramming avoids this. It also enables the computer to handle batch processing and real-time processing applications simultaneously.

Activity

Before reading the next subsection revise the first part of the case study on sales order processing (pages 161–7).

The implications for user departments

For many applications data processing can be organised in either a centralised or a decentralised way. Sales order processing is one example. As you read in the case study in the last activity, this can be carried out in a centralised batch processing manner, with the data being keyed in in batches by the DP department. It can also, however, be carried out in a decentralised real-time manner, with on-line terminals in the sales office connected by cable to the central computer.

Self-check

What are the advantages of this method for (a) the customer and (b) the sales staff?

It allows the sales staff to key in orders immediately they are received. If a customer is phoning his order in, then the sales clerk can give an immediate response: in the space of a fraction of a second the computer looks up its stock file and displays on the terminal screen the quantity of stock available, and it looks up its customer file and gives the credit status of the customer.

The convenience of this sort of system is obvious:

- Data is entered directly into the system instead of being first passed to the DP department.
- The data is processed more quickly.
- The master files are always up to date.
- The speedy response will improve customer satisfaction.
- The sales office staff have more responsible and interesting jobs.

If there are no problems with the customer's order the computer then carries out the remainder of the processing: it validates the input data, updates the master files, and prints the sales documentation.

In most organisations using computers both ways of organising DP can be found. Typically, the production of management reports and audit trails and file maintenance are carried out centrally (in the DP department) in a batch processing manner, whereas transaction processing, document production, and inquiries are carried out in a decentralised way, using real-time processing.

Self-check

In the above section I have described how the first part of the sales order processing procedure described in the case study in Chapter 5 would be carried out if processing were decentralised. Now read the rest of the case study (pages 169–72) and write down in a few sentences how you think

‖ the remainder of the procedure described there would be
‖ carried out with decentralised processing.

OUTLINE ANSWER

A printer would be located in the warehouse to print picking
lists. A VDU would also be placed there for confirming on the
order file that orders have been filled, for updating the stock file,
and for amending invoice details.

The electronic office

The so-called *electronic office* takes decentralised processing one
stage further. Each terminal in this case is a microcomputer
capable not only of communicating with the central computer
(and in fact with other similar terminals) but also of carrying out
limited data processing on its own. Such terminals are referred
to as *electronic workstations*, and they are revolutionising office
work.

Up to the mid-1970s computerisation directly affected only
one part of the work of the office, namely clerical activities
involving the routine handling of large volumes of data to
produce action documents and management reports. It did not
directly affect the jobs of secretaries and managers. Their work
is highly variable and not readily amenable to computer
processing.

However, computers are becoming so powerful and so cheap
that it is now cost-effective to use them for many low-volume
variable tasks, such as some secretarial and managerial tasks.
The most common type of electronic workstation is the word
processor used by secretaries. You can find a brief description of
this on page 77.

Electronic workstations for managers are also appearing on
the market, and these enable the manager to get instant up-to-
the-minute reports from the computer system, displayed on his
screen. It also enables him to communicate electronically with
other people in the organisation with electronic workstations,
using a local area network (page 149). Many word processors
can also communicate in this way, and where this occurs the
need for the conventional office memo or internal form is greatly

reduced. In some organisations the 'paperless office' already exists, with electronic workstations on many desks, each able to communicate with any other workstation in the organisation.

External processing

So far we've looked at ways of organising DP within the business. Let's turn now to the final way of organising DP, namely external processing by an outside agency. There are two ways of doing this:

- By using firms which specialise in processing other people's data. These are called *computer bureaux*.
- By using communications networks which incorporate data processing facilities. These are called *value-added networks (VANs)*.

Self-check

Write down two advantages and two disadvantages to the business of using a bureau to process its data.

Computer bureaux There are around 300 bureaux in this country offering data processing facilities based upon mainframe or mini computers. The bureau provides the computer hardware and software, the client firm has to send in the data. In one arrangement the source documents are sent through the post, and the bureau enters it, processes it, and sends back the output. In another arrangement the client keys in the data himself on a terminal somewhere in his premises, and it is sent via the telephone network to the bureau's computer. Batch processing will often be used, as this minimises both the telephone line time and the computer time.

A similar service is offered to small business users by some chartered accountants. In this case a microcomputer is used. An operator plus microcomputer visits each client by car once a week, spending anything from an hour or two to half a day dealing with the week's accumulated data processing work. In an alternative arrangement the client's source documents are taken to the accountant's office for processing.

The advantages to the client of using a bureau are:

- He does not face the problems of buying and maintaining computer hardware and software.
- It provides him with useful experience of computer processing, so that he is better able to make a sensible choice of computer hardware and software if he does eventually purchase his own system.

The disadvantages to the client are:

- The data is processed in a batch way, so that he cannot make use of real-time processing (unless he is prepared to pay much more for telephone line time and computer time).
- If he is a heavy user of the bureau he will face high charges.
- He will have to adapt his procedures to conform with the requirements of the bureau's standard applications packages, though if necessary the bureau will write tailor-made programs for the user (who must obviously bear the programming cost).

Value-added networks VANs are communications networks set up by commercial or public institutions which incorporate computing power. Users can not only transmit their data over these networks, they can also use them in the same way that they might use bureaux, i.e. to process their data. The data that is input is converted to useful information by this processing, hence the name 'value-added'. For a fee, anyone with a suitable terminal can use these networks.

British Telecom's System X, which will become operational in the mid-1980s, will provide services of this sort. It will give the individual business user access to enormous computing power for minimal capital expenditure (i.e. the cost of a terminal).

The advantages and disadvantages to the user are the same as those that apply to bureau services.

Review

Imagine yourself in Mike's shoes. Review the DP alternatives you have looked at in this section and note down

|| which of these are relevant to him and the advantages and
disadvantages of each. (Five minutes.)

ANSWER

In a very small business, such as Mike's, there are no clearly
defined departments and so the centralisation/decentralisation
issue does not arise. All data processing and other office work
will be handled by one or two people, and a microcomputer, if
installed, will be placed on a convenient desk in their office.

The issue is therefore whether he should buy his own microcomputer system or use a chartered accountant's microcomputer
service. The latter would provide a useful introduction to computing for him, but the former solution is best, at least in the
long term. As I pointed out on page 160, an important application of a computer to his business is likely to be the production of
estimates, and an accountant will not provide this. Also, the fees
he will have to pay the accountant will, in the long term, exceed
the cost of buying and running his own system.

The advantages and disadvantages of a chartered accountant's
microcomputer service are covered on page 272.

DP staff

The data processing department

Every company with a large computer installation has a data
processing department. It is staffed by systems analysts (who
design the computer-based systems), programmers (who produce and maintain the programs for those systems), and computer operations staff (who enter the data and run the
programs), all under the control of a data processing manager.
A typical organisation chart is shown in figure 37.

In some large companies the analysts and some of the programmers are grouped into project teams, each under a project
team leader. Figure 38 shows this arrangement. Each project
team will be assigned to specific systems projects. Programmers
not assigned to these teams are employed on systems mainte-

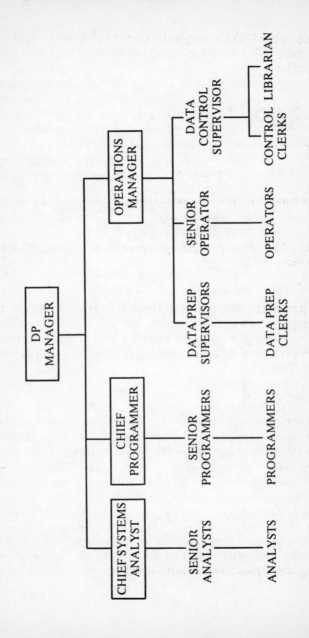

Figure 37. The data processing department

nance (see pages 278–9), under the control of a chief programmer. On page 290 I compare these two ways of organising the DP department.

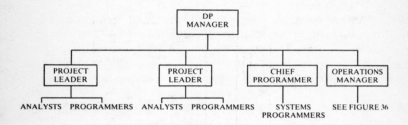

Figure 38. The data processing department – project team arrangement

In this part of the chapter we will look at the role of each of the types of staff shown in these figures, and the personal qualities required by each. We will also examine how computer operations (i.e. preparing data and running programs) are organised and controlled.

Activity

Draw an organisation chart for the DP department of your company (if appropriate). Make sure you are clear whether it is organised along the lines shown in figure 37 or along the lines shown in figure 38.

Data processing manager (DPM)

The DPM has overall responsibility for both the development of new systems and programs and for the day-to-day work of processing the organisation's data. In his former role he advises other managers on possible computer applications in their departments and he provides them with analysts and programmers to design and implement those applications. In his latter role he is responsible for ensuring that the data is input accurately, that processing is organised efficiently, and that the output is passed to the user on time.

In most companies he is directly responsible to the managing director, and he has 'functional' authority over other managers in the DP area. This does not mean that he can tell them how to run their departments, but it does mean that they cannot develop their departmental data processing systems according to their own whims; the DPM must be involved.

With regard to managing his own department the DPM's tasks are, in essence, no different from those of any other manager: he must plan, organise, and control his department so that the business's needs are most effectively met, and he must motivate each member of his staff to give of his best. The DPM is primarily a manager and secondly a DP expert. In selecting a DPM, a company should look for managerial rather than technical excellence, though ideally the person appointed should possess both.

Self-check

You have just been appointed DP manager of your company. Jot down a brief job description (about ten lines), and list the qualities you would need to bring to the job. For help with this and subsequent self-checks in this section talk to the relevant DP staff in your company.

ANSWER

A possible answer is:

1 Job description:

Title Data processing manager
Responsible to Managing director
Responsibilities
(a) Planning, organising, and controlling the DP department so that the data processing needs of the organisation are met.
(b) Overall responsibility for systems development throughout the organisation.

(c) Advising top management on suitable data processing hardware and software.

Immediate subordinates Chief systems analyst, chief programmer, operations manager.

2 Desirable qualities include: managerial ability, ability to master technical matters, openness to new ideas, ability to liaise with other managers.

Systems analysts

We have dealt with the role of the systems analyst in depth in Chapter 6. It is to analyse existing systems and design new ones. In larger organisations the analysis part of the job may be separated from the design part, the latter being carried out by systems designers. In this case the analyst is concerned with investigating and analysing systems and producing the feasibility reports (see page 212), while the designer is concerned with designing the computer procedures and files and with drawing up the system definitions (page 216).

Systems analysts and designers are allocated to projects by the DPM or by the chief systems analyst (if there is one). The DPM is also responsible for ensuring that the analysts' work is properly organised and carried out within a reasonable timescale. He will therefore be involved in drawing up the terms of reference of projects (page 213).

In the past systems analysts (and DPMs) have tended to take a rather narrow view of their role, excluding from projects any procedures that were not amenable to computerisation. Such procedures include, for instance, gathering information on the business environment from government statistical publications, from libraries, from periodicals, and from contacts with customers and suppliers. As a result the typical departmental manager now receives a great deal of information generated by computer-based systems from internal data, but inadequate information from external sources. The split is about 80% to 20%. It is reckoned, however, that external data on the environment is at least as important to the average manager as information generated from internal data (see pages 60–61).

Because systems analysts see themselves, and are seen, as

analysts of high-volume data processing systems, they have also not been involved in the rapidly expanding office automation field (see the section on the electronic office on page 270). However, the dividing line between office equipment (e.g. word processors) and data processing equipment (e.g. microcomputers) is now almost non-existent.

As a result, there have been moves in recent years to extend systems thinking in both the external information and the office automation areas. Some have foreseen the rise of 'office systems analysts' who will extend the traditional role of the systems analyst into the office environment. A number of companies have appointed information specialists charged with the task of finding out the total information requirements of managers and ensuring that data from many sources, inside and outside the organisation, is collected and brought together to satisfy their requirements. One major supplier, in another similar move, is encouraging the users of its equipment to appoint 'information system managers', whose role is to coordinate all electronic office and data processing activities in the firm.

Self-check

Jot down a brief job description for a systems analyst in a medium-sized company, and list the personal qualities needed for the job. For help refer back to Chapter 6.

OUTLINE ANSWER

Job description: to investigate systems, to evaluate ideas about how the systems can be improved, to report on this evaluation to management, to design the new systems, to implement the new systems.

Personal qualities include: ability to get on with people at all levels in the organisation, an analytical mind and problem-solving skills, attention to detail, and an understanding of how business operates and of potential areas of computer application.

Programmers

There are two types of computer programmer:

- Programmers responsible for systems maintenance. Their function is to maintain (i.e. make changes to or correct) the systems software – such as the operating systems and other programs described on page 179.
- Programmers who write the applications programs needed for systems projects. These programmers work closely with systems analysts and designers, possibly as members of a project team.

As you have already found out, it is not difficult to learn to write applications programs in high-level languages. A programmer can be trained in just a few weeks, and he can expect to be reasonably proficient after around six months of programming experience.

Self-check

Write down a brief job description for an applications programmer, and list the personal qualities needed for the job.

OUTLINE ANSWER

Job description: to produce applications programs in accordance with the systems flowcharts produced by systems analysts, to test the programs, and to amalgamate these programs into packages and to test the packages.

Personal qualities include: ability to think logically, problem-solving skills, patience, and attention to detail.

The computer operations staff

If you are to understand the roles of the various members of staff in the computer operations section (shown on the right-hand side of the organisation chart in figure 37) you must first form a picture of the overall purpose of the section. It is helpful to think about what goes on in a small business (such as Mike's business or Pinecrafts) and then to extend this to a large company.

Self-check

Imagine you are employed by Pinecrafts to operate their

small business computer system. One of your jobs each Thursday is the wages run. Using the knowledge you have gained of Pinecrafts' wages system from the exercises you did in Chapter 6, jot down briefly all the tasks you must do, from the receipt of the clock cards to putting the wages slips into the paypackets.

We can split up these tasks under five headings, which will form the basis of our discussion of the computer operations section. These headings are:

Receive, check, and batch the source documents Your first job on the Thursday wages run is to receive all the clock cards, count them to ensure that none are missing, and batch them (i.e. put them into two or three piles and produce batch totals for validation purposes). Exactly the same sort of thing goes on in the computer operations section of a data processing department whenever batch processing is carried out, except that here the task is done by specialist staff known as data control clerks. (See figure 37 and also the description of their work below.)

Get and load the programs and files Your next job is to get the payroll package and the employee file and load them into the computer in readiness for the run. In a DP department a disc and tape librarian is responsible for getting the programs and files from the disc and tape library for the computer run, and for returning them after the run. The task of loading programs and files is carried out by the computer operators.

Key the data Your next step is to work through each batch of clock cards, keying in for each employee his works number, the standard hours worked, and any overtime. You also key in the batch totals for the validation check. In a DP department this task is done by data preparation clerks.

Run the computer Next, you run the computer so that it operates on the data in accordance with the program instructions and produces the payroll, the payslips, and the paycheques. In a DP department this task is carried out by the staff that loaded the program and files, namely the computer operators.

Receive and distribute the output Your final task is to collect the payslips and paycheques from the printer and put them into the paypackets for distribution to the employees. In a DP department the task of receiving and distributing the computer output is handled by the data control clerks (who also carried out the task of receiving and checking the source documents, under the first heading in this list).

If you check with the organisation chart in figure 37 you will see that I have omitted from the above list the post of operations manager. He is in charge of the section, and he has the special responsibility of organising the computer runs so that the equipment is fully utilised. This means arranging the batch processing jobs so that successive runs overlap. The object of this is to utilise the computer's multiprogramming capabilities so that a piece of equipment not needed for one job can be used for another, instead of standing idle. For example, the central processor cannot be working on a job while the discs or tapes containing the programs and files for that job are being loaded, and to prevent idle time it must therefore work on another job.

Having introduced the various personnel in the computer operations section, let's now look at what their jobs involve and the qualities they need.

Activity

If appropriate, talk to the computer operations staff in your organisation. Try to find out, in outline, the duties of each of the posts mentioned above.

Operations Manager (OM) The OM has overall responsibility for the work of the computer operations section. (However, in a small installation, there may be no OM, the DP manager assuming direct responsibility for the work of this section.) He must be a good organiser, able to schedule jobs so that the equipment is utilised efficiently, and so that the work progresses smoothly through the department, from data control, data entry, processing, through to distributing the output. He also has responsibility for incorporating into his schedules new systems produced from time to time by the analysts and programmers.

Data control clerks Their task is to count and check the source documents received from user departments, to batch them, and to produce batch totals. They enter these totals on control slips that accompany the batch through the data entry stage of the process, and which at that point are checked against the batch totals produced by the computer. Then, after the data has been entered and the computer run completed, the data control clerks take charge of the output and distribute it to the users.

Data preparation clerks The task of keying in the data from the batches of source documents is carried out by these clerks. The speed at which an experienced clerk can key data is impressive: it is in excess of 15,000 characters an hour.

In batch processing the whole batch of data must be keyed in, and the batch totals checked, before any processing can begin. In the past the data was keyed on to punched cards for later entry to the system via a high-speed card reader, but nowadays it is normally keyed directly on to a transaction file on magnetic disc or tape.

Librarian The librarian looks after the discs and tapes which hold the installation's programs and files. The duties of this post include identifying and storing the discs and tapes, issuing them for computer runs, and logging their movements. Security is an important aspect of the job, and library material must be issued only when it is needed for a computer run, and then only to authorised staff.

Computer operators These people load the discs and tapes on to the computer in accordance with the operating instructions for each job, and operate the computer so that it processes the data for the job. As mentioned earlier, each job must be scheduled, and the loading and running must be carried out at the times fixed by that schedule.

During a computer run the system may malfunction, perhaps

as a result of faulty data, a programming error, or faulty equipment. When this happens an error message will be printed out, and the run may come to a halt. It is the operator who must interpret the error message and take appropriate action. To do this he does not require much technical knowledge of the computer hardware, but he must be familiar with the operating system of the computer and he must have an understanding of the operating system documentation (see page 238).

Review

What sections might be found in the data processing department of a large company? List the main responsibilities of each. (Five minutes.)

OUTLINE ANSWER

1 Systems analysis – investigating systems, evaluating the feasibility of possible improvements, reporting back to management, designing and implementing new systems.
2 Programming – maintaining the systems software, writing the applications programs needed by the new systems.
3 Computer operations – receiving, checking, and batching source documents, keying the data, loading the programs and files, running the computer, and distributing the output to the users.

DP job design

The production-line approach to jobs

Over the centuries, as business organisations have developed and grown in size, there has been an increasing division of labour. People's jobs have become more and more specialised, covering a narrower range of tasks. The logical conclusion of this trend is the production line, in which tasks are broken down to their smallest elements, each operative being given just a few elements to perform repeatedly. The production line as a whole carries out the total task, but the individual worker does a tiny part only of it. The work of the computer operations section, described above, is organised like this.

There are considerable advantages in organising work in this way:

- Training time is minimised, since each person has to learn only a small part of the job.
- Each person becomes highly practised and skilled at his job.
- Jobs can be accurately timed, and output targets set.
- People do not have to spend time transferring from one job to another.

The whole-task approach to jobs

If you visited a small firm like Pinecrafts you would find that many jobs are organised quite differently. For example, if a microcomputer were installed, then all the computer operations tasks described in the previous pages would be carried out by the one computer operator. Because this person is carrying out such a wide variety of tasks the advantages listed above would not apply. On the other hand, there are advantages to this way of organising work that do not apply to the production-line approach.

> ### Self-check
>
> Write down four advantages that you think might apply to the whole-task approach to work.

This way of organising work is obviously much more interesting and fulfilling for the operator, who:

- has a much more varied job;
- is completely responsible for getting the data into the computer accurately and on time, and for operating the computer;
- can see the result of his or her efforts and can take a pride in it;
- controls his or her own work.

With the 'whole-task' approach to the organisation of work, the worker carries out a complete range of tasks leading to an identifiable end-result.

Job satisfaction

A great deal of research has been done on job design and on what motivates people at work, and the results point clearly to the following.

- Money and good working conditions do not satisfy people at work, nor do they motivate them to work well. However, if the money is poor and the working conditions are poor, then people will be dissatisfied and they will be largely unaffected by the factors that do motivate.
- Satisfaction and motivation at work arise from the job itself. Jobs designed on whole-task principles lead to good levels of satisfaction and motivation (unless, as indicated above, the money or the working conditions are poor), whereas jobs designed on production-line principles lead to poor levels of satisfaction and motivation.

You have probably heard it said that the new technology of the silicon chip will make office work boring and meaningless. You may also have heard it said that the new technology will make it more satisfying and interesting. Which is true? It depends on how the work is organised.

The new technology widens the spectrum of job design possibilities. Varied jobs can become even more varied, and repetitive jobs can become even more repetitive. To show you what I mean, let's consider the work of typing.

Self-check

What are the two ways of organising typing in the traditional office? Which uses the production-line approach, and which uses the whole-task approach?

Typing in the manual office In the manual office the production-line approach is exemplified by the typing pool, the whole-task approach by the personal secretary. In the former system letters are dictated on to magnetic discs or tapes, which are distributed by the typing pool supervisor to the typists, who transcribe the contents on to paper via typewriter keyboards. The task is very repetitive, requiring no skill or judgement other than a narrow range of typing skills.

The personal secretary, on the other hand, carries out a very wide range of tasks. The production of letters is only a part of her duties, and even this requires a wider range of skills: taking dictation in shorthand, minor editing possibly of the text of the letter, as well as the actual typing. Quite a high proportion of her day will be spent on a range of administrative tasks – dealing with incoming mail, diary management, travel arrangements, and giving a general back-up service to her boss.

Between these two extremes is a variant of the typing pool system in which each typist carries out administrative tasks for two or three executives to whom she is assigned, as well as typing their letters in the pool.

Typing in the electronic office Give a personal secretary a word processor, and her job becomes more varied and interesting:

- Much repetitive typing is eliminated, for any rearrangement and correction of text can be done on the screen instead of retyping the whole thing, and also standard paragraphs can be recalled from the machine's memory instead of having to be keyed in each time.
- Her output is increased, so that she can handle the work of two executives instead of perhaps only one.
- She must acquire and use a wider range of keyboarding skills.

Bring the new technology into the typing pool, however, and the work may become more monotonous than before, with each individual carrying out a much narrower range of tasks. A common arrangement is to set up a production line with three stages:

- a pool of typists operating ordinary electric typewriters;
- an optical character reader (see page 133);
- a word processor operator.

What happens is this:

- Authors dictate their material on to audio tapes or discs, which are distributed to the typists (as in the traditional typing pool).
- The typists transcribe the material at the highest possible speed, not correcting any errors.
- The typed material is returned to the authors, who mark any errors and insert alterations with a special pencil.
- The typed material is then scanned by the optical character reader, which converts it to electronic form and deposits it in the memory of a word processor.
- The word processor operator calls up each letter in turn on to the screen, and edits it in accordance with the author's pencilled instructions.
- The operator then presses the 'print' key, which causes the printer to print out the corrected material.

Activity

Consider the work of your office, or one with which you are familiar. At which end of the job design spectrum does it lie, or does it lie in the middle? How else might the work be organised?

The implications for DP

Data processing work can also be organised according to the production-line approach or the whole-task approach. Think about how work is organised on the sales side of a business, for example. (Assume for the moment that manual procedures are used.) One clerk (or group of clerks) deals with inquiries, another processes the order, another deals with credit control, and so on. The paperwork moves, as on a production line, from one to another.

Self-check

How else might the work be organised?

In the whole-task approach each clerk (or section) is assigned to a particular segment of the market – this might be customers in a certain geographical area, or of a certain type – and handles all the work for that group of customers. So the one individual or section deals with inquiries from those customers, order processing, credit control, and any after-sales follow-up.

In some ways this would be technically less efficient than the production-line approach – more training would be needed, and clerks would be switching from one type of work to another during the day. But there are a number of advantages.

> ## Self-check
>
> Think about what these advantages might be, and jot down four.

1 Each clerk would have complete responsibility for a group of customers, would become familiar with the needs of those customers, and would take an active interest in ensuring that the orders for those customers were filled on time.
2 Each clerk would have a much more varied and interesting job, and would have a greater sense of responsibility and commitment.
3 Each clerk would be doing a whole task leading to an identifiable end-result (the orders for their customers being filled).
4 The clerks would get feedback from their customers (e.g. if orders are delayed), enabling them to control their own work and thus reduce the burden that falls on their supervisor.
5 The additional responsibility and knowledge required for the job would better equip them for promotion.

Clerical work and data processing are obviously a fruitful area for the application of whole-task principles. Let's see how these might be applied to the DP tasks described earlier in this chapter.

> ## Self-check
>
> Think again about the sales office, but assume now that computerised procedures are used. Write down the two

ways in which the work might be organised, and note against each whether it corresponds to the production-line approach or the whole-task approach. For help see page 268.

Data processing could be centralised, in which case the source documents (the customer orders in this case) are passed to the DP department for entry and processing. On the other hand it could be decentralised, in which case the sales staff carry out all the entry and processing via terminals in the sales office.

One of the disadvantages of centralised data processing is the fact that DP tasks are broken down in a production-line way, some being done in the user departments and some being done in the DP department. In decentralised data processing the user departments do almost all the tasks, which means that a clerk in such a department is more likely to have a whole job, with greater interest, variety, and responsibility than is the case with centralised DP. So you can see that the trend towards decentralised, real-time DP will improve the quality of much office work.

In the DP department itself the production-line approach is adopted in the computer operations section, the total task being broken down and split amongst data control clerks, data prep clerks, librarian, and computer operators. The whole-task approach would seek an arrangement which allows a clerk (or group of clerks) to take a job of work through the whole process, from receiving and batching the source documents, through entering the data into the system, getting the required discs or tapes, and running the job on the computer.

There are very good technical reasons why this system cannot be fully implemented. Large computers run several jobs simultaneously, and utter confusion would result if more than one section became involved in this part of the work. However, some enlargement of tasks is sometimes possible, leading to greater variety of work. For example, data control and data preparation could be combined, each clerk receiving, checking, batching, and then keying the data for specific jobs, and then receiving and distributing the output from those jobs.

Self-check

Now think about the work of the applications programmers. How might their work be organised on (a) a production-line basis, (b) a whole-task basis?

Figure 37 gives the production-line approach, figure 38 the whole-task approach. In the latter, the applications programmers are assigned to specific projects and remain with those projects for their entire duration, working closely with other members of the project team and under the control of the project team leader. The whole approach is task-based, and their primary loyalty is to the task.

In the former approach their primary loyalty is to the programming section, and they will tend to identify with their particular programming part of a project rather than with the project itself.

You can see that the new technology does not necessarily imply that jobs will become boring and meaningless. Work can be organised so that they become more interesting and meaningful. Efforts are being made in many countries to devise ways of improving the quality of working life in this age of the silicon chip, and a lot of free advice is available. In this country the main agency for research and advice is the Work Research Unit of the Department of Employment, Steel House, Tothill Street, London SW1H 9NF.

Review

1 Why is the production-line approach to work so successful and so widely adopted? What are its disadvantages?
2 Outline the principles of the whole-task approach to work. What benefits result from applying these principles to data processing and office work?

(Ten minutes.)

OUTLINE ANSWER

1 The production-line approach is successful because it is very efficient. It reduces the amount of training needed, people

become highly specialised and therefore highly skilled at their jobs, it eliminates lost time arising from changing from one task to another, and it permits the accurate setting of output targets. However, it reduces job interest and satisfaction, and it does not lead to motivation at work. Also, people learn a narrower range of skills and are less able to transfer from one job to another.

2 People should carry out whole tasks leading to identifiable end-results in which they can take a pride. They should control their own work (rather than be controlled by a production line), and be able to decide for themselves how best to achieve their targets. The benefits are improved motivation at work and a happier workforce; also people are more able to transfer from one job to another as a result of their wider range of skills and experience.

Pinecrafts assignment 4

The management of Pinecrafts is ready to computerise its data processing procedures (see assignment 3). Write a report of around 1,500 words outlining what it needs to do to implement a small business computer system. Your report should explain:

a the factors to consider in buying a system;
b how to prepare the organisation's data for transfer to computer files;
c how to prepare the organisation's staff for computerisation.

Include in a an account of the systems compared in the activities in Chapter 7 and your recommended choice.

Appendix

Pinecrafts: a case study and assignment programme based upon the proposed expansion of a small business making pinewood kitchen furniture

The case study describes an actual business, namely the Pine Workshop, Great Missenden, Bucks. You can obtain two supporting video programmes on the business and its proposed expansion from the Chiltern Consortium, Wall Hall, Aldenham, Watford WD2 8AT. The programmes each last twenty-three minutes, and they are entitled *In Business: Starting Up* (quote C309) and *In Business: Moving On* (quote C310).

The assignments based on the case study are located at the ends of Chapters 2, 4, 6, and 8. They are suitable for students taking any of the BTEC modules listed at the start of this book (see page 9). An additional assignment for students taking the BTEC Award in Computer Studies Module 'Information in Organisations' is given at the end of the case study. Each assignment is split into three parts so that students attending classes can, if desired, work on them in small groups.

This case study, together with a somewhat extended version of the assignment programme, was a winning entry for the 1980 Case Study of the Year Competition run by the Case Clearing House of Great Britain and sponsored by Unilever Ltd. Model answers to the original assignment programme are available from bookshops – ask for *Model Answers to Business Administration Assignments* by Roger Carter, published by Heinemann. These answers are relevant to most of the assignments in this text.

The case study

Introduction

The idea of forming a partnership to make pinewood furniture was first discussed by Mick, Paul, and John in January 1979. Mick was a skilled woodworker employed by a large furniture company making prototypes from original designs; Paul was a technical sales rep for a machinery manufacturer, able to bring into the partnership his technical knowledge; and John was an accountant with both administrative experience and a flair for carpentry.

The three men gave up their jobs in the summer of 1979 and set up business in a small workshop in Great Missenden in Buckinghamshire, trading under the name Pinecrafts. They managed to acquire all the equipment they needed second-hand for a little over £2,000 (the new price would have been many times that figure). It comprised:

1 Dominion Universal machine (for planing, thicknessing, through-sawing, and morticing) for £450;
1 bandsaw (for sawing) for £400;
1 spindle-moulder and tenoner (for rebating, moulding, and tenoning) for £400;
1 double-drawn sander (for sanding large surfaces) for £420;
1 lathe (for turning and drilling) for £350;
1 bobbin-sander (for shaping work) for £10;

and Mick already owned his own handtools (new value £1,000).

The business was an immediate success. The three partners started by making small articles such as wall-racks and small wall-cupboards, which they displayed at local craft shows. Here they got orders for larger cupboards, wooden fireplaces, and a complete fitted kitchen (i.e. sink unit, cupboards, working surfaces, etc.), and from these beginnings their business has steadily grown. Although their market is limited to the South Bucks area, they have found that there is a big demand for fitted pinewood kitchens, which they currently produce at the rate of about fifteen per year. Kitchens comprise about 70% of their business, the remaining 30% being smaller items.

The work is divided among the three men in the following way:

- Mick machines parts (panels, legs, etc.) and assembles the parts into units of furniture. He also visits potential customers to discuss their requirements and works out quotations.
- Paul also machines and assembles, and in addition he maintains the machinery.

- John spends about half his time on finishing the assembled product (polyurethaning, polishing, etc.) and preparing it for dispatch, and the rest on general administrative duties, including buying in raw materials (mainly wood) and parts (such as screws).

There are a number of other jobs that are shared out on an informal basis among the partners. The complete list of tasks, and the percentage of time spent on each, are as follows:

Machining	28%
Assembling	28%
Finishing	10%
Inspection and dispatch	2%
Maintenance	1%
Delivery to customers	3%
Installing	10%
Marketing, design, quotations, and liaison with customers	6%
Purchasing	2%
Accounts, invoicing, and credit control	4%
Miscellaneous (costing and other management information, writing letters, etc.)	6%

They design the fitted kitchens themselves, in consultation with their customers. At the time of writing the price charged for a typical kitchen is £1,400. They reckon they could charge about £400 more, but they are keeping their prices low to establish a reputation and to build up business as a basis for future expansion.

The materials for a kitchen cost about £600, leaving £800 gross profit. From this they pay their overheads of £120 per month (£100 for rent and rates, £20 for electricity and sundries), their transport costs of £30 per month (they hire a van for one day a fortnight for deliveries), and their wages, and also put money aside for future growth.

Expansion

The great success of the firm and the large market for pinewood kitchens have prompted the three partners to think seriously about embarking upon a substantial expansion of the business in the near future. John has recently inherited £50,000 which he will put into the business. The plan is to make only kitchens, producing them at the rate of one per working day. They intend to charge £1,800 for the typical kitchen, and they estimate that the material costs will decrease to £450 (because it will be possible to bulk-buy timber in large uncut sections). 80% of the material costs will be wood, the remainder will be screws, glue, polyurethane, laminate, etc.

To produce kitchens at this rate they estimate that they will need to employ the following staff:

3 foremen, earning £150 per week each;
22 woodworkers, earning £120 per week;
4 driver/installers, earning £120 per week;
4 (experienced) office staff, earning £120 per week.

The woodworkers will supply their own handtools, but a substantial investment will have to be made in woodworking machines. The existing machines will be inadequate for the greatly increased volume of work and will be sold (Paul reckons for about 20% less than the price they paid). The following machines will have to be purchased, probably new:

1 tenoner	£5,000	1 dimension saw	£1,500
1 morticer	£5,000	1 borer	£1,000
1 thicknesser	£3,000	1 dovetailer	£2,000
1 overhead planer	£2,000	1 straightline edger	£5,000
1 router	£4,000	1 dust-extraction unit	£2,500
1 bandsaw	£3,000	spray guns and booth	2,000

The partners estimate that it will cost £1,500 to install the machines. Additionally, they estimate that £10,000 will be required to equip and furnish the office area. A large van will be required by the driver/installers to deliver the completed kitchens and this will cost £7,000, its running costs amounting to £2,600 per annum. Premises of about 8,000 sq ft will be needed to house the business, the expected rental being £4 per sq ft per annum. Electricity and other overheads are expected to amount to £2,600 per annum.

Organisation

It is planned to split the enlarged business into three departments: sales, production, and the general office (which will include purchasing). Paul will be the sales manager, Mick the production manager, and John will be the general manager, having overall control of the business as well as looking after the general office. The sales department will incorporate a small showroom.

Production will be split into three sections, each under a foreman: machining, assembly, and finishing (including inspection and dispatch). The machines listed above will be used by the machining section, with the exception of the spray guns and booth, which will be used by the finishing section. Timber will be held in the raw materials store, which will be attached to the machine shop and under the control of the machine shop foreman. The parts produced by the machining section and the bought-in parts (screws, hinges, etc.) will be held in the parts store, which will be under the control of the assembly foreman. Finished kitchen units will be stored under the control of the foreman of the finishing section.

Production and storage

The main steps in the production of a fitted kitchen are:

1 Designing the kitchen in consultation with the customer and calculating the price. Once the enlarged business is set up it is anticipated that most customers will purchase standard units, as displayed in the showroom or advertised in a catalogue.
2 Purchasing and storing the raw materials and the bought-in parts.
3 Machining and storing the made-in parts (door panels, shelves, legs, etc.).
4 Assembling the parts to make the kitchen units.
5 Finishing the kitchen units (polyurethaning, polishing, etc.) and dispatching (packing).
6 Delivering and installing the finished kitchen.

Raw materials and bought-in parts (2 above) are bought on a bulk basis. Once the enlarged business is set up it is reckoned that the amount purchased of each item (the reorder quantity) will be equivalent to ten weeks' usage of that item, and that an item will be reordered when the amount in stock falls to the equivalent of six weeks usage (the reorder level). This will give an adequate leeway for delivery delays (the average time between placing an order and receiving delivery being three weeks).

Made-in parts (3 above) are produced in bulk, so that long production runs and therefore greater output is achieved. It is intended that the reorder level in this case will be two weeks' usage, and that the reorder quantity will be six weeks' usage.

It is estimated that the raw materials store will contain some forty different sizes of timber; and that there will be 300 different types of bought-in parts and 1,000 different types of made-in parts in the finished parts store. There will be about ten orders per day placed for raw materials and bought-in parts.

Administrative procedures

At the moment very little paperwork is required to plan the work, coordinate activities, and progress customers' orders. Once the enlarged business is set up, however, formal administrative procedures will have to be installed. It is anticipated that, in outline, these will be as follows:

1 Some fitted kitchens will be produced on a made-to-measure basis, and in response to an enquiry for one of these the sales manager will visit the house to discuss the design and take measurements. Back at the office he will draw up a *quotation* for the kitchen (if necessary in consultation with the production manager), and send it to the inquirer. Many kitchens, however, will consist of standard units, selected by customers in the showroom or by post from the catalogue, and only if special parts are required will a quotation be necessary.

2 Following the acceptance of a quotation by the customer, or the placement of an order for standard units from the showroom or catalogue, the sales department will produce a *sales order*, listing the standard parts required plus a description of any special parts that need to be made.

3 Since kitchens will be installed at the rate of one per working day, the delivery and installation date of a kitchen can be booked by the sales department by means of a simple *diary system* and confirmed with the customer at the time the order is placed. The booked date will be noted on the sales order, one copy of which will be handed or sent to the customer, another copy being passed to the production department. (This copy will form the *works order* and subsequently the *receipt note*.)

4 *Stock records* must be kept for the raw materials store to record materials received from suppliers, materials issued to the machining section, and the balance left in the store. Similar records will be kept for the parts store, to show receipts from suppliers and from the machining section, issues to the assembly section, and the balance.

5 The foremen in charge of the stores will be responsible for maintaining the stock records and for noting any items which fall to the reorder level, together with the standard reorder quantities, on a *reorder suggestions list*. These lists will be sent to the production manager every week, and as a general rule he will authorise the ordering of the standard reorder quantities from outside suppliers or from the machining section, as appropriate. Sometimes, how-

ever, he may decide not to order the standard quantities – if, for example, a part is to be phased out, or stock levels are to be reduced to ease a cash flow problem.

6 The production manager will notify the purchasing clerk of orders to be placed. This clerk will decide which supplier to use, referring to records of previous purchases kept on *purchase record cards*, and will make out a *purchase order*.

7 On the basis of the copies of the sales orders received from the sales department and the reorder suggestions lists received from the parts store, the production manager will plan the work of his department.

It is the job of the machining section to produce the made-in parts required by the parts store, as indicated on the reorder suggestions lists. The production manager must ensure that each machine is correctly *loaded*, so that the work is fairly distributed, or balanced, between the machines (to avoid bottlenecks caused by a build-up of jobs each requiring the same machine); and he must ensure that the work is properly *scheduled*, i.e. the various jobs must be programmed through the machine shop so that the required parts are produced prior to the assembly date. The workers must be given *job cards* for each part to be made, specifying the operations that have to be carried out.

It is the job of the assembly and finishing shops to assemble the required kitchen units from the parts stored in the parts store, and to polyurethane, polish, or otherwise finish the units in accordance with the customers' requirements. The work of these shops will be programmed in fortnightly batches: a fitted kitchen involves one full day's work in each shop, and so ten fitted kitchens can be assembled and finished in a fortnight. Prior to the assembly fortnight the production manager will send the works order for the ten kitchens to be built in that fortnight (and which are therefore due for delivery and installation in the following fortnight) to the assembly foreman, who will informally schedule the work through his section in batches, e.g. 10 sink units, followed by ten cupboards, and so on. The foreman of the finishing shop will do no scheduling – he will deal with the work in the order in which it leaves the assembly shop.

8 The foreman in each shop will be responsible for the detailed allocation of jobs to the workers. For each worker he will make out a *time sheet*, on which he will enter the jobs to be done and the standard times of the jobs.

9 The installers' programme of work will be shown in the diary system kept in the sales department. They will collect the appropriate kitchen units from the store adjoining the finishing shop, together with the works order/receipt note, load them on to the van, deliver to the customer's house, and install. The customer will sign the works order/receipt note to confirm receipt and installation.

10 The final step is to send an *invoice* to the customer requesting payment.

Additional assignment: organisation and coordination

1 The case study gives the departments into which the enlarged company is to be divided, the number of posts, and the proportions of time currently spent on the various tasks. Using this information construct an organisation chart (assume that the proportions hold for the enlarged business).

2 Produce job descriptions for the general manager, the sales manager, and the production manager, and write down the main tasks that each of the four office workers will undertake.

3 The orders received by the sales department will determine the jobs to be done by the production department, which in turn will determine the raw materials and bought-in parts to be bought by the purchasing function in the general office. In other ways too the work of the three departments must be closely coordinated. Using the lists of responsibilities and tasks drawn up in your answer to (2) above, carry out the following exercise:

For each department write down five tasks for which coordination is required with either or both of the other departments, and state the results of non-coordination. In each case suggest how coordination might be achieved (e.g. by a documentation system, or by a meeting, or by a verbal message or memo).

Index